# THE KINGDOM OF SAUDI ARABIA

Architecturally, the University of Petroleum and Minerals at Dhahran, the world's largest university of oil technology, triumphantly exemplifies the Arab features of low closed masses and one vertical element (the water tower).

TRANSWORLD ARABIAN LIBRARY

STACEY INTERNATIONAL   LONDON

# Principal contributors

**Editorial Direction and Research**
Hugo de Klee
Anna Dowson
Robin Dunipace
Rhona Hanbury
Anthony Lejeune
Rosamund McDougall
Angela Milburn
Charlotte Odgers
Jane Rawlinson
T. C. G. Stacey
Hilary Wilton-Steer

**Art Direction**
Anthony Nelthorpe MSIAD
Keith Savage

**Arabic usages**
E. F. Haddad
Ahmed Mostafa
Greg Shapland
Samir Shishakli

**Indexers**
Michèle Clarke
Gertrude Mittelmann

**Editorial Adviser, Revised Edition**
Nigel Harvey

The Kingdom of Saudi Arabia
Stacey International
128 Kensington Church Street, London W8 4BH
Telex: 298768 Stacey G

© 1977 Stacey International
© *Second edition* 1978
© *Third edition* 1978
© *Fourth edition* 1979
© *Fifth edition* 1980
© *Sixth edition* (revised) 1983

ISBN 0 905743 28 8

Maps and diagrams specially prepared by
Arka Cartographics Limited, London
*Designer* Le Roy-Chen
*Cartographers* Peter Arnold, Roger Bourne,
Bob Brett, Lee Brooks, Kevin Diaper,
Paul Draper, Allan Rees

At the time of going to press certain boundaries
between Saudi Arabia and her neighbours were
under negotiation.

Set in Monophoto Century by
Tradespools Limited, Frome and
SX Composing Limited, Essex, England
Colour origination by
Culver Graphics, High Wycombe, England
Printed and bound in Japan by
Dai Nippon Printing Company Limited, Tokyo

Contributors were attached to the organizations listed at the time of writing.

**Professor Sir Norman Anderson**
*Institute of Advanced Legal Studies,*
*University of London*
**H. St. John Armitage, O.B.E.**
**Dr. Randall Baker**
*University of East Anglia*
**Jeremy Barnett and John Ewart**
*British Council, Riyadh*
**Dr. Richard A. Chapman**
*University of Durham*
**Hajj D. Cowan**
*School of Oriental and African Studies,*
*University of London*
**Peter Duncan**
*Stanford Research Institute, Riyadh*
**Dr. Abdullah S. El-Banyan**
*Ministry of Labour and Social Affairs, Riyadh*
**Professor William Fisher**
*University of Durham*
**Dr. Hassan H. Hajrah**
*King Abdul Aziz University, Jiddah*
**G. R. Hawting**
*School of Oriental and African Studies,*
*University of London*
**Dr. Abbas Khalidar**
*School of Oriental and African Studies,*
*University of London*

**Professor T. M. Johnstone**
*School of Oriental and African Studies,*
*University of London*
**Dr. Fadil K. Kabbani**
*Deputy Minister for Mineral Resources,*
*Saudi Arabia*
**Dr. Geoffrey King**
*School of Oriental and African Studies,*
*University of London*
**James P. Mandaville**
*Arabian American Oil Company, Dhahran*
**Elizabeth Monroe, C.M.G.**
*St. Antony's College, University of Oxford*
**Dr. Theodore Prochazka**
*University of Riyadh*
**Dr. Fazlur Rahman**
*University of Chicago*
**Dr. George Rentz**
*Hoover Institution, Stanford, California*
**Cécile Rouchdy**
*Dar el-Hanan School, Jiddah*
**Dr. Mahmoud Esma'il Sieny**
*The Arabic Language Institute,*
*University of Riyadh*
**Dr. Ibrahim Zaid**
*General Organization for Social Insurance,*
*Saudi Arabia*

**Principal photographer:** Peter Carmichael
All photographs by Peter Carmichael except the following:
S. Al-Ghamdi, Aramco 20(2), 28, 156; Al-Khalifa, Aramco 36, 89, 97, 99(3), 102, 105, 106(4), 117, 159, 176–7, 182, 192, 197, 210–11, 213, 221(2), 222–3, 233, 234; Al-Yousif, Aramco 42–3, 85; S. Amin, Aramco 13, 86, 87, 100, 107(2), 147(2), 158, 175, 177, 179, 180, 212, 221; Aramco 12–13, 13, 28, 34, 68, 80–1, 85, 105, 144, 147(3), 166(2), 167(3), 174(3), 183, 186, 188–9, 198, 233, 236; Central Press 28, 31, 33, 101, 130–1(4), 135, 137, 140, 152, 153(2), 163, 241; M. Clarke (MEPhA) 157; G. Duncan 157, 163; M. Evans 33(2), 140, 147, 156, 163, 164, 242; Cliff Foster 148–9(4), 161(2); A. Greenway, (John Topham Picture Library) 163, 165; D. Hadley 24 (2), 40; Dr. D. Harrison 20, 21(2), 22; A. Hutt (MEPhA) 162; S. Kay (JTPL) 35; Keystone Press Agency Ltd. 87, 131; T. Kiillsgaard 24 (2); Dr. G. King 36(4); C. Kutschera 56, 63, 65, 68, 85, 96, 114–5, 154, 214; J. Mandaville 20(4), 21, 22; K. Constable-Maxwell 215; MEPhA 65, 70(2), 94–96, 108, 109, 148, 160, 187, 221, 225, 245; Ministry of Information, Riyadh 10, 11, 70, 71, 91, 96(2), 147(2), 188(3); B. H. Moo Moody, Aramco 69(2), 84(2), 132–3, 143, 174–5, 176, 204–5, 209; S. Naamani 96, 103, 105, 106, 107(2), 109; A. Nelthorpe 31, 167; M. Oppersdorf 13, 36–7, 49, 58–9, 63; C. Osborne (JTPL) 164; Dr. A. Pesce (Ministry of Information, Riyadh) 50–1; W. Pridgeon 22(2); R. Roberts 24; H. Ross 117, 235(2); M. Routh (MEPhA) 30; Royal Geographical Society 78(6); P. Ryan (MEPhA) 96, 123, 136, 160(2), 161, 162, 238; Saudia 13, 19, 20(5), 33, 121, 144–5, 159, 167; D. Shirreff (MEPhA) 138, 153, 157; S. Pendleton 30, 53, 54(2), 55(2), 83; S. Tart 32.

The publishers gratefully acknowledge help from the following organizations and individuals:

Fuad al-Angawi; Abdul Rahman al-Ansari; Mohammed El Aqeel, Ministry of Communications, Riyadh; Aramco World Magazine, Beirut; Aramco Public Relations Photography Unit, Dhahran, and Burnett Moody; H. St. J. Armitage, O.B.E.; Tarif Asad; Majid El-Ass; Salem Azzam, C.V.O.; British Council, Riyadh; British Embassy, Jiddah; British Library, London; British Museum (Natural History); Ministry of Planning; Riccardo Cesati, Milan; Cusdin, Burden and Howitt, Chartered Architects, London; Ghaleb Abdul-Faraj; H. E. Dr. Fouad Al-Farsy; Mohammed Said Farsi, Jiddah; Fauna Preservation Society, London; Nassir Haidary; Dr. David Harrison; Osman Himut; David Howard, Robert Matthew & Co.; Hassan Husseini, University of Petroleum and Minerals, Dhahran; Robert Irving; Abdul Karim Jamal; Major E. R. L. Jones; Mohammed Khayyat; Stuart Laing; Colonel Brian Lees, OBE; Ministry of Information, Riyadh, and H. E. Dr. Abdul Aziz M. Khoja; National Geographic Society, Washington, D.C.; Ismail Nawab; Reda Nazer; Bob Nordberg, Aramco; E. D. O'Brien, Organization; Dr. Dunstan Perera, Central Statistics Office; Dr. Angelo Pesce, Naples; Abdul Aziz Al-Quraishi, SAMA; Fuad al-Rayis; Michael Rice & Co. Limited; Alan Rothnie, C.M.G.; Royal Geographical Society, London; Royal Institute of International Affairs, London; Saudia, Jiddah: Public Affairs Division; Saudi Credit Fund; Saudi Arabian Embassy, London; Saudi Arabian Monetary Agency; St. Anthony's College, Oxford; S.O.A.S. University of London; H.E. Sheikh Fahd K. al-Sedayri; H.E. Turki bin Ahmad al-Seydayri; Said Sieny; H.E. Dr. Abdul Aziz al-Sowayegh; Stanford Research Institute; University of Durham; Dr. Abdullah al-Wohaibi; World Wildlife Fund, London; H. E. Dr. Mohammed Abdu Yamani.

# Maps    Diagrams

Charts, diagrams and maps are based on the latest facts available at the time of their preparation, but subsequent developments may have superseded information contained therein.

# Contents

*NOTE: The Publishers and Contributors crave the indulgence of the reader who finds that the latest developments have overtaken the facts and figures recorded in this work. Saudi Arabia is a Kingdom on the move, and fine books are not made in a day. But the mere difficulty of leaping astride a galloping horse is no reason for allowing Saudi Arabia's achievements to go unrecorded in durable print.*

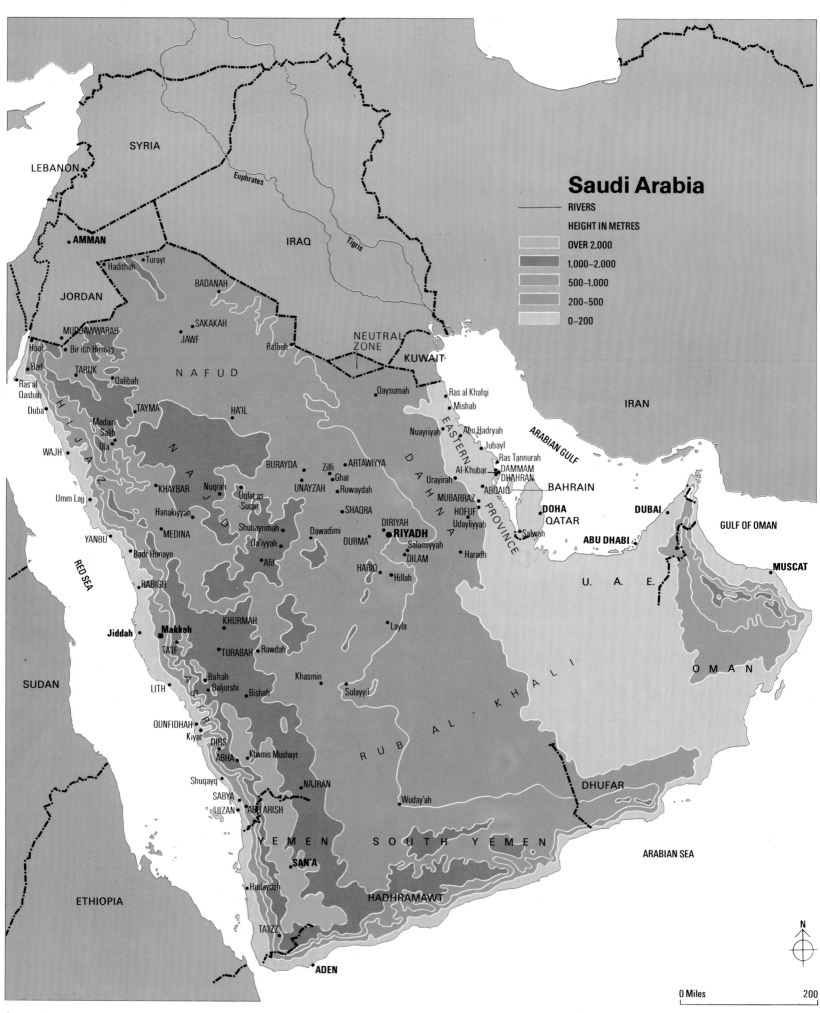

## Saudi Arabia

RIVERS

HEIGHT IN METRES

OVER 2,000
1,000–2,000
500–1,000
200–500
0–200

SYRIA

LEBANON

AMMAN

Euphrates

IRAQ

Tigris

JORDAN

Hadithah    • Turayt

BADANAH

SAKAKAH

JAWF

MUDAWWARAH

Rafhah

NEUTRAL
ZONE

KUWAIT

Haql    Bir ibn Hirmas

Bad

TABUK    Qalibah

Ras al
Qasbah

Duba

TAYMA

HA'IL

NAFUD

Qaysumah

Ras al Khafqi

Mishab

Madain
Salih

Ula

WAJH

N
A
J
D

Nuayriyah    Abu Hadryah

Jubayl

Ras Tannurah

Umm Lajj

BURAYDA    Zilfi    ARTAWIYYA

Ghat

KHAYBAR    Nugrah    Uglat as
Sugar    UNAYZAH    Ruwaydah

Urayirah

Al-Khubar    DAMMAM
DHAHRAN

EASTERN

Hanakiyyah    SHAQRA

MUBARRAZ    ABQAIQ

BAHRAIN

Shubayrimah    Dawadimi

DIRIYAH

HOFUF

DOHA

DUBAI

MEDINA

Qa'iyyah

DURMA    RIYADH

Udayliyyah

QATAR

GULF OF OMAN

YANBU

Afif

Salwah

Badr Hunayn

HARIQ    Salamiyyah

ABU DHABI

RED
SEA

RABIGH

DILAM

Haradh

DAHNA

PROVINCE

MUSCAT

Hillah

Makkah

KHURMAH

Layla

U. A. E.

Jiddah

TA'IF

TURABAH    Rawdah

Bahah

Khasmin

Baljurshi    Bishah

O
M
A
N

LITH

Sulayyil

QUNFIDHAH

Kiyat

DIRS

Khamis Mushayt

R
U
B

A
L

K
H
A
L
I

ABHA

Shuqayq

SABYA    NAJRAN

Wuday'ah

DHUFAR

JIZAN    ABU ARISH

YEMEN    SOUTH    YEMEN

ARABIAN SEA

SAN'A

Hudaydah

HADHRAMAWT

ETHIOPIA

SUDAN

TA'IZZ

ADEN

IRAN

ARABIAN GULF

HIJAZ

ASIR

N

0 Miles    200

# The Islamic calendar

## Comparative Tables of AH and CE Dates

The Islamic era is based on the Hijrah, the migration of the Prophet Muhammad from Makkah to Medina, which took place on 16 July 622 CE. The Islamic year is lunar, and has 354 days. There are approximately 103 Hijri years to a Gregorian century; AH stands for Anno Hegirae (hegira being the Latinized form of Hijrah), and CE for Christian Era. The Hijri year begins on the day of the month indicated.

**THE HIJRAH MONTHS**

- Muharram
- Safar
- Rabi al Awwal
- Rabi al Thani
- Jumada'l Awwal
- Jumada'l Thani
- Rajab
- Shaban
- Ramadan
- Shawwal
- Dhu'l-Qadah
- Dhu'l-Hijjah

| AH | CE | | AH | CE | | AH | CE | | AH | CE | |
|---|---|---|---|---|---|---|---|---|---|---|---|
| 1 | 622 | 16 July | 600 | 1203 | 10 September | 1160 | 1747 | 13 January | 1362 | 1943 | 8 January |
| 10 | 631 | 9 April | 610 | 1213 | 23 May | 1170 | 1756 | 26 September | 1363 | 1943 | 28 December |
| 20 | 640 | 21 December | 620 | 1223 | 4 February | 1180 | 1766 | 9 June | 1364 | 1944 | 17 December |
| 30 | 650 | 4 September | 630 | 1232 | 18 October | 1190 | 1776 | 21 February | 1365 | 1945 | 6 December |
| 40 | 660 | 17 May | 640 | 1242 | 1 July | 1200 | 1785 | 4 November | 1366 | 1946 | 25 November |
| 50 | 670 | 29 January | 650 | 1252 | 14 March | 1210 | 1795 | 18 July | 1367 | 1947 | 15 November |
| 60 | 679 | 13 October | 660 | 1261 | 26 November | 1220 | 1805 | 1 April | 1368 | 1948 | 3 November |
| 70 | 689 | 25 June | 670 | 1271 | 9 August | 1230 | 1814 | 14 December | 1369 | 1949 | 24 October |
| 80 | 699 | 9 March | 680 | 1281 | 22 April | 1240 | 1824 | 26 August | 1370 | 1950 | 13 October |
| 90 | 708 | 20 November | 690 | 1291 | 4 January | 1250 | 1834 | 10 May | 1371 | 1951 | 2 October |
| 100 | 718 | 3 August | 700 | 1300 | 16 September | 1260 | 1844 | 22 January | 1372 | 1952 | 21 September |
| 110 | 728 | 16 April | 710 | 1310 | 31 May | 1270 | 1853 | 4 October | 1373 | 1953 | 10 September |
| 120 | 737 | 29 December | 720 | 1320 | 12 February | 1280 | 1863 | 18 June | 1374 | 1954 | 30 August |
| 130 | 747 | 11 September | 730 | 1329 | 25 October | 1290 | 1873 | 1 March | 1375 | 1955 | 20 August |
| 140 | 757 | 25 May | 740 | 1339 | 9 July | 1300 | 1882 | 12 November | 1376 | 1956 | 8 August |
| 150 | 767 | 6 February | 750 | 1349 | 22 March | 1310 | 1892 | 26 July | 1377 | 1957 | 29 July |
| 160 | 776 | 19 October | 760 | 1358 | 3 December | 1318 | 1900 | 1 May | 1378 | 1958 | 18 July |
| 170 | 786 | 3 July | 770 | 1368 | 16 August | 1319 | 1901 | 20 April | 1379 | 1959 | 7 July |
| 180 | 796 | 16 March | 780 | 1378 | 30 April | 1320 | 1902 | 10 April | 1380 | 1960 | 26 June |
| 190 | 805 | 27 November | 790 | 1388 | 11 January | 1321 | 1903 | 30 March | 1381 | 1961 | 15 June |
| 200 | 815 | 11 August | 800 | 1397 | 24 September | 1322 | 1904 | 18 March | 1382 | 1962 | 4 June |
| 210 | 825 | 24 April | 810 | 1407 | 8 June | 1323 | 1905 | 8 March | 1383 | 1963 | 25 May |
| 220 | 835 | 5 January | 820 | 1417 | 18 February | 1324 | 1906 | 25 February | 1384 | 1964 | 13 May |
| 230 | 844 | 18 September | 830 | 1426 | 2 November | 1325 | 1907 | 14 February | 1385 | 1965 | 2 May |
| 240 | 854 | 2 June | 840 | 1436 | 16 July | 1326 | 1908 | 4 February | 1386 | 1966 | 22 April |
| 250 | 864 | 13 February | 850 | 1446 | 29 March | 1327 | 1909 | 23 January | 1387 | 1967 | 11 April |
| 260 | 873 | 27 October | 860 | 1455 | 11 December | 1328 | 1910 | 13 January | 1388 | 1968 | 31 March |
| 270 | 883 | 11 July | 870 | 1465 | 24 August | 1329 | 1911 | 2 January | 1389 | 1969 | 20 March |
| 280 | 893 | 23 March | 880 | 1475 | 7 May | 1330 | 1911 | 22 December | 1390 | 1970 | 9 March |
| 290 | 902 | 5 December | 890 | 1485 | 18 January | 1331 | 1912 | 11 December | 1391 | 1971 | 27 February |
| 300 | 912 | 18 August | 900 | 1494 | 2 October | 1332 | 1913 | 30 November | 1392 | 1972 | 16 February |
| 310 | 922 | 1 May | 910 | 1504 | 14 June | 1333 | 1914 | 19 November | 1393 | 1973 | 4 February |
| 320 | 932 | 13 January | 920 | 1514 | 26 February | 1334 | 1915 | 9 November | 1394 | 1974 | 25 January |
| 330 | 941 | 26 September | 930 | 1523 | 10 November | 1335 | 1916 | 28 October | 1395 | 1975 | 14 January |
| 340 | 951 | 9 June | 940 | 1533 | 23 July | 1336 | 1917 | 17 October | 1396 | 1976 | 3 January |
| 350 | 961 | 20 February | 950 | 1543 | 6 April | 1337 | 1918 | 7 October | 1397 | 1976 | 23 December |
| 360 | 970 | 4 November | 960 | 1552 | 18 December | 1338 | 1919 | 26 September | 1398 | 1977 | 12 December |
| 370 | 980 | 17 July | 970 | 1562 | 31 August | 1339 | 1920 | 15 September | 1399 | 1978 | 2 December |
| 380 | 990 | 31 March | 980 | 1572 | 14 May | 1340 | 1921 | 4 September | 1400 | 1979 | 21 November |
| 390 | 999 | 13 December | 990 | 1582 | 26 January | 1341 | 1922 | 24 August | 1401 | 1980 | 9 November |
| 400 | 1009 | 25 August | | | | 1342 | 1923 | 14 August | 1402 | 1981 | 30 October |
| 410 | 1019 | 9 May | | *Transfer from Julian to* | | 1343 | 1924 | 2 August | 1403 | 1982 | 19 October |
| 420 | 1029 | 20 January | | *Gregorian calendar* | | 1344 | 1925 | 22 July | 1404 | 1983 | 8 October |
| 430 | 1038 | 3 October | | | | 1345 | 1926 | 12 July | 1405 | 1984 | 27 September |
| 440 | 1048 | 16 June | 1000 | 1591 | 19 October | 1346 | 1927 | 1 July | 1406 | 1985 | 16 September |
| 450 | 1058 | 28 February | 1010 | 1601 | 2 July | 1347 | 1928 | 20 June | 1407 | 1986 | 6 September |
| 460 | 1067 | 11 November | 1020 | 1611 | 16 March | 1348 | 1929 | 9 June | 1408 | 1987 | 26 August |
| 470 | 1077 | 25 July | 1030 | 1620 | 26 November | 1349 | 1930 | 29 May | 1409 | 1988 | 14 August |
| 480 | 1087 | 8 April | 1040 | 1630 | 10 August | 1350 | 1931 | 19 May | 1410 | 1989 | 4 August |
| 490 | 1096 | 19 December | 1050 | 1640 | 23 April | 1351 | 1932 | 7 May | 1411 | 1990 | 24 July |
| 500 | 1106 | 2 September | 1060 | 1650 | 4 January | 1352 | 1933 | 26 April | 1412 | 1991 | 13 July |
| 510 | 1116 | 16 May | 1070 | 1659 | 18 September | 1353 | 1934 | 16 April | 1413 | 1992 | 2 July |
| 520 | 1126 | 27 January | 1080 | 1669 | 1 June | 1354 | 1935 | 5 April | 1414 | 1993 | 21 June |
| 530 | 1135 | 11 October | 1090 | 1679 | 12 February | 1355 | 1936 | 24 March | 1415 | 1994 | 10 June |
| 540 | 1145 | 24 June | 1100 | 1688 | 26 October | 1356 | 1937 | 14 March | 1416 | 1995 | 31 May |
| 550 | 1155 | 7 March | 1110 | 1698 | 10 July | 1357 | 1938 | 3 March | 1417 | 1996 | 19 May |
| 560 | 1164 | 18 November | 1120 | 1708 | 23 March | 1358 | 1939 | 21 February | 1418 | 1997 | 9 May |
| 570 | 1174 | 2 August | 1130 | 1717 | 5 December | 1359 | 1940 | 10 February | 1419 | 1998 | 28 April |
| 580 | 1184 | 14 April | 1140 | 1727 | 19 August | 1360 | 1941 | 29 January | 1420 | 1999 | 17 April |
| 590 | 1193 | 27 December | 1150 | 1737 | 1 May | 1361 | 1942 | 19 January | 1421 | 2000 | 6 April |

# Introduction

*HM King Fahd of Saudi Arabia*

*This comprehensive work is recording a seminal period in the history of Saudi Arabia, as one of the most exceptional countries in the world emerges into modern statehood.*

*As the extent of the bounty of its natural resources became apparent, the ancient land of Arabia, under Saudi leadership, had various options. That it chose firmly to seize its opportunities and accept its full responsibilities both to itself, now and in the future, and in the Islamic, Arab and world communities, is a* measure of the quality of the Saudi Arabian people and the leadership they have enjoyed.

King Khalid died on June 13, 1982, widely mourned – in the words of his brother, King Fahd – as "a father and brother to us all".

King Fahd smoothly assumed the leadership of the nation and the full direction of policy in domestic and foreign affairs in which he had played a central role for several years – policies established under King Faisal (1964–1975 CE) and rooted in the country's commitment to Islam from which, as King Fahd has said, "emanate all our ideals". In the context of Islam the Five Year Plans have evolved, bringing radical improvements in the standard of living of Saudi Arabians, their welfare and social security, their education and personal expectations. In industry and agriculture maximum self-sufficiency had become the goal, securing the future with sound husbandry of today's finite resources.

A similar continuity prevails in foreign policy, rooted in the reign of the late King Abdul Aziz ibn Saud. Put simply, it is one of peace and Islamic solidarity – a policy proven actively to contribute to good sense and stability. By the same token, Saudi Arabia remains a force for stability in the world economy, fully alive to its responsibilities on a global scale.

On becoming King, Fahd bin Abdul Aziz spoke of seeking the glory of Arabs and Muslims. He reaffirmed his determination in the "march of progress and development". All members of Government, he declared, were committed to helping in the realisation of the hopes and ambitions of the people, while adhering to divine teaching and the Prophet's tradition.

HRH Prince Abdullah ibn Abdul Aziz, Crown Prince of Saudi Arabia

HRH Prince Sultan ibn Abdul Aziz, Second Deputy Prime Minister

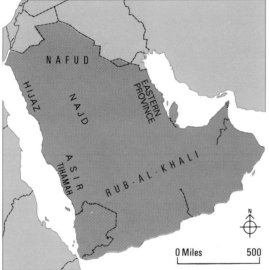

# 1 The Country

*The heat is often forbidding, the face of the landscape often cruelly dry. And yet temperatures and seasons vary greatly, and parts of Saudi Arabia's vast area enjoy dependable rains. Underground water from past geological eras can be tapped to make the rich powdery loess bloom. The great sand deserts alone must always defy the ingenuity of man to make them bring forth. But they too can be made to yield their mineral wealth.*

*In contrast to Saudi Arabia's familiar image, the green uplands of Asir, in the south-west* (far left), *are well watered and have sustained a settled population from ancient times. Given regular water supply, much of the dun landscape of loess scrub desert* (top picture) *would bring forth plentifully. The second picture* (above) *shows the typical sabkhah territory of the Gulf coast and islets. The only regions condemned to barrenness are the great deserts of Nafud in the north, and the Rub al-Khali, or Empty Quarter* (bottom picture), *in the south.*

# Geography and Climate

THE Arabian peninsula, of which the Saudi Arabian state forms by far the largest part, covers well over three million square kilometres (Saudi Arabia itself comprises 2,300,000 square kilometres – nearly 900,000 square miles). The whole area is thought to be a detached fragment of an even larger continental mass which included Africa (*see also* page 20). Large rifts (it is suggested) developed because of thermal currents in the lower mantle of the earth, forcing apart surface masses or "plates". The Arabian plate is held to have drifted northwards, impelled by the opening of the Red Sea and Gulf of Aden, and by subsequent spreading of the sea floors – a movement that may well be continuing.

As it moved, the Arabian plate tilted, with the western side upraised and the eastern side lowered, so that the east became covered by layers of younger, sedimentary rocks. In the west, disturbance associated with the opening of the Red Sea led to much upwelling of magma, which has produced the extensive lava fields (*harrah*) that occur all along the west side of the country, mostly in the Makkah-Jiddah-Medina area. Because of this geographical origin, with ancient resistant rocks in the west, capped here and there with very recent lava, and progressively younger rocks towards the east, Saudi Arabia exhibits in its geography, very broadly speaking, a north-south running "grain". In the extreme west, along the Red Sea, there is a coastal plain (Tihamah), flat and usually very narrow, except in the Jiddah area where it offers a small but useful lowland gap giving access to Makkah and the interior. Then immediately to the east is a formidable succession of high plateaux with steep scarp edges dominating the Tihamah below. Here occur the highest peaks in Saudi Arabia; particularly south of Makkah, where heights of over 8,200 feet are reached. East again of this highland zone is an extensive region of irregular plateaux and upland basins, the largest of which are those of Medina and Rakbah,

*The mountains of the south-west plunge from plateau of 8,000 ft and peaks of 10,000 ft to lowland valleys, where regular crops are grown.*

14

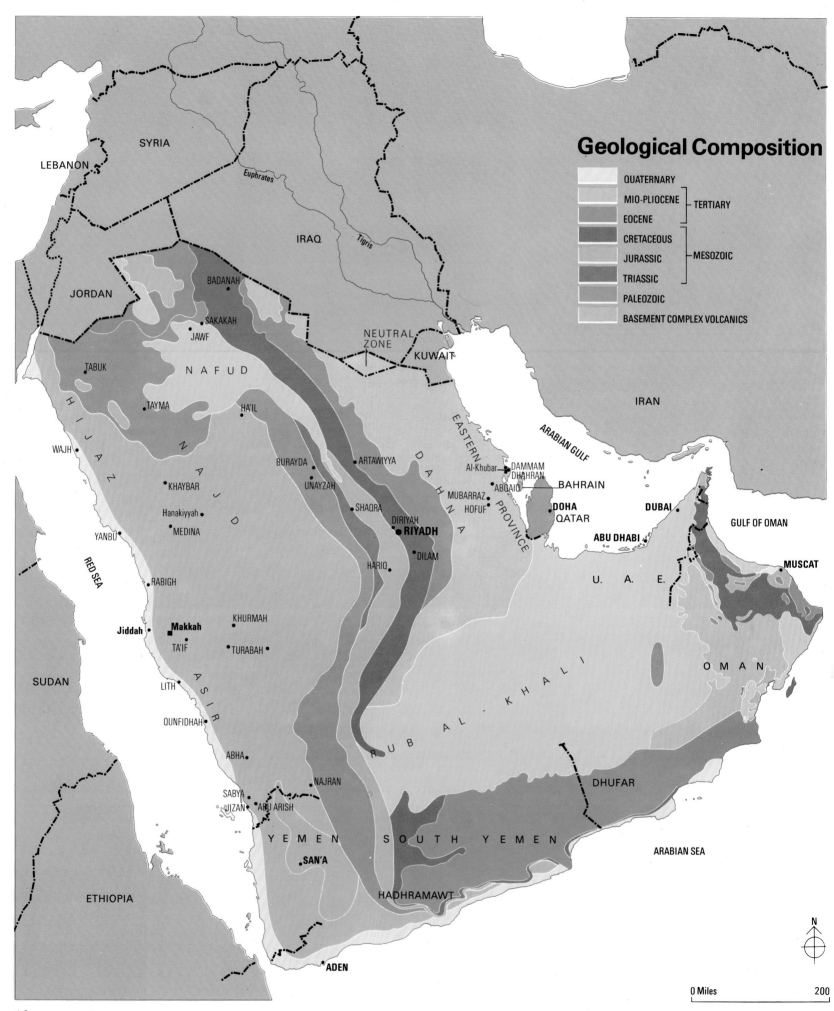

# Geological Composition

- QUATERNARY
- MIO-PLIOCENE ⎤ TERTIARY
- EOCENE ⎦
- CRETACEOUS ⎤
- JURASSIC ⎬ MESOZOIC
- TRIASSIC ⎦
- PALEOZOIC
- BASEMENT COMPLEX VOLCANICS

LEBANON

SYRIA

Euphrates

JORDAN

IRAQ

Tigris

BADANAH

SAKAKAH

JAWF

NEUTRAL ZONE

KUWAIT

TABUK

NAFUD

IRAN

TAYMA

HA'IL

ARABIAN GULF

WAJH

BURAYDA

ARTAWIYYA

EASTERN

Al-Khubar

DAMMAM
DHAHRAN

KHAYBAR

UNAYZAH

SHAQRA

ABQAIQ

BAHRAIN

MUBARRAZ
HOFUF

Hanakiyyah

MEDINA

DIRIYAH

RIYADH

DAHNA

DOHA

QATAR

DUBAI

YANBU

HARIQ

DILAM

PROVINCE

ABU DHABI

GULF OF OMAN

RED SEA

RABIGH

U. A. E.

MUSCAT

KHURMAH

Jiddah

Makkah

TA'IF

TURABAH

O M A N

SUDAN

LITH

R U B    A L - K H A L I

QUNFIDHAH

ABHA

NAJRAN

SABYA

DHUFAR

JIZAN
ABU ARISH

Y E M E N    S O U T H    Y E M E N

ARABIAN SEA

SAN'A

ETHIOPIA

HADHRAMAWT

ADEN

N

0 Miles 200

16

where collection of sub-surface water allows human settlement on a larger scale.

Further east, altitude gradually declines, but then occurs a whole succession of younger, sedimentary rocks – sandstones, limestones and marls. The harder series stand out as scarps or isolated ridges, with lower, flatter valleys formed in the less resistant strata between. The most imposing of these scarps is the Jabal Tuwayq, a limestone ridge that attains 3,200 feet and extends in a sinuous curve north-west and south-west of Riyadh, which lies in a gap breaking through the Jabal. Gradually, altitude diminishes eastwards, until one of the last of these scarps occurs near Hofuf, after which the surface drops to form the low-lying coastal plain of Hasa.

Although some lowland areas or basins consist of bare rock pavement, most tend to be covered in loose rock deposits eroded by wind, by shattering due to temperature contrasts and, in the recent geological past, by water action. Near hill or plateau bases are stony areas of larger rock fragments; further away are outwash gravels, while in areas of low relief sand predominates, with silts in valley bottoms. Sand covers large areas. In the north, the Great Nafud is an expanse of sand dunes (*uruq*), often reddish in colour, interspersed with areas of bare rock pavement. A narrower zone of sand, ad Dahma, links the Nafud to an even larger expanse of sand, indeed the largest sand desert in the world – the Rub al-Khali (Abode of Emptiness), which occupies much of the south of Saudi Arabia. In the extreme west the Rub al-Khali is a "sand sea" (Bahr es Safi) surrounded by gravel plains: in the east, there are massive dunes with salt basins (*sabkhah*). The whole area was for long an extreme barrier to human movement, but oil prospecting and the discovery of artesian water have reduced its difficulty.

Of all the sizeable countries on earth, Saudi Arabia is probably the driest. It derives its weather mainly from the north and west: climatically it is linked to the eastern Mediterranean and adjacent lands, in that it has a long, hot and almost totally dry summer, with a short cool winter season during which a little rain occurs. This is because air masses reaching Arabia have been largely exhausted of their moisture. Although Arabia is surrounded on three sides by sea, aridity is the dominant feature.

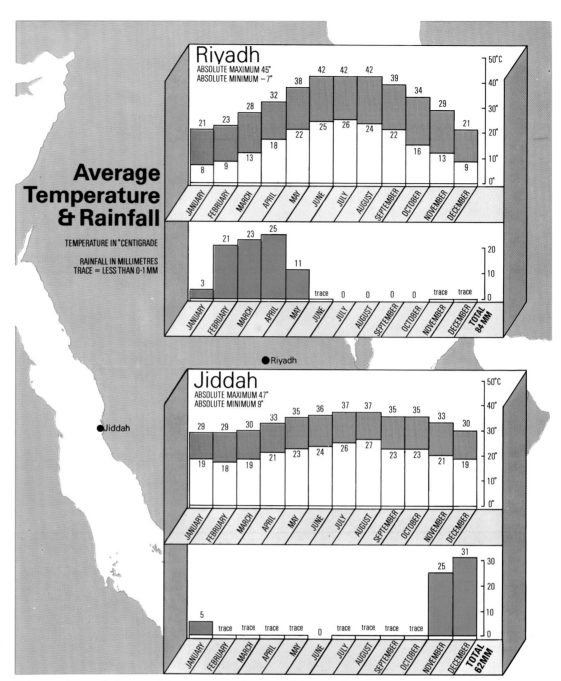

*The surface of the Arabian peninsula is slightly on the tilt – higher in the west, and dropping gently from the geologically very ancient Western Plateau towards the Gulf.*

*The sea keeps temperatures fairly constant in the coastal regions; in the interior day/night and summer/winter temperatures vary sharply. Rain, though scarce, can cause flooding.*

With the sole exception of Asir in the extreme south-west, any influences from the southern tropical zones are excluded by the highland rim that runs from Oman through the Hadhramawt to the Yemens.

Because of the dryness of the air reaching Saudi Arabia, and the consequent lack of cloud, insolation is considerable, producing very high summer temperatures – up to 45 or 50°C, and sometimes even more in the southern deserts. But the cloudlessness also allows heat to escape from the surface at night, especially in winter; so temperatures

drop quite markedly between day and night, and between summer and winter. The night coolness, with a 10 to 22°C drop at both seasons, is a boon in summer but leads to sporadic frost in the interior of the centre and north during winter; −7°C has been recorded at Riyadh.

Rainfall is scanty, irregular and unreliable, occurring mostly during the months from October to April. Except along the Red Sea coast, and inland over the mountains of Asir, summers are practically rainless, and in the interior several years may elapse without rain. The extreme south of Saudi Arabia, the

*While Saudi Arabia has no permanent rivers reaching the sea, a dependable flow of water nourishes the deep wadis of the south-west in winter months.*

virtually uninhabited Rub al-Khali, is almost entirely without rain – one of the driest areas on earth; but over the rest of the country (Asir excepted) annual totals amount to about 100 mm, though 150 mm have been known to fall locally within twenty-four hours. Because of temperature contrasts, winds can be strong, even violent, raising dust storms from time to time. On the coasts relative humidity is high, due to sea breezes that bring in moisture; this effect is, however, local, and most of the interior is extremely dry. The mean figures given on page 17 for Jiddah and Riyadh illustrate the principal features of the Saudi Arabian climate, as well as the contrasts between coast and interior. The hills of Asir, however, do participate in the marked summer rainfall which benefits the Yemen plateau.

Until recently the difficulty of the terrain, its aridity and the consequent scarcity of good soil sharply controlled the ways of life within Saudi Arabia. Apart from a few fishermen and traders, Saudi Arabia was able to support only a small population, estimated at 1.5 to 2 million in the 1930s. Possibly half of this could be regarded as "rural settled" – cultivators, village craftsmen and shepherds moving locally over short distances with their animals. At least a quarter of the population was wholly nomadic, following a regular pattern of rough grazing of sheep, goats and camels, which involved considerable annual movement. Both ways of life depended upon the use of wells which tapped water-tables at moderate or shallow depth; for there is no perennial river.

In some cases, catchment of water is local, from rapid percolation of rainfall, but over many parts of Saudi Arabia there is a much larger series of water-tables that allow "creep" of water underground from the better watered south-west through to the east coast. Some of the wells which tap this kind of water-table are large; Makkah and Medina have a number, and others occur, for example, at Mudawwara, Tabuk and Ula. Some of this underground water is from wetter climatic phases of an earlier geological time, and is not replaced by present-day rainfall when drawn off.

Today, with the advent of planned irrigation and exploitation of underground water resources, four or five times the former population is supported, and major cities have rapidly evolved at Riyadh, Jiddah and Makkah.

*The giant groundsels and bearded lichen on evergreen trees* (seen on the right) *characterize the sub-tropical Alpine vegetation of highland Asir.*

*The remarkable variety of Saudi Arabia's flora is due to the country's range of climate and soils. In some areas a sudden rainfall will make an apparent desert bloom in a matter of hours. Many other "garden" species only survive if regularly watered.*

*The yellow cassia*

*A young pomegranate*

*The spiny echinops*

*A flowering hibiscus*

*Centaurea sinaica (thistle)*

*Acacia ehrenbergiana*

*Anthemis deserti*

*Rumex vesicarius*

*Cistanche Tubulosa*

*Echinops*

*Opuntia*

*The Tamarisk survives the fiercest droughts.*

*Calatropis Procera*

# Flora and Fauna

MAPS and geography books make Arabia a part of Asia, but plant and animal life clearly bear out the theory that it is really an extension of Africa. The desert steppes which now link the peninsula with Asia are the bottom of an ancient sea which once divided the continents. The Red Sea is a rift through a single mass of igneous rock, the Arabian-African Shield.

Saudi Arabia's wildlife is thus a complex of evolving and mingling species: the tropical African, the oriental from the Asian mainland, the Palaearctic from Europe, North Africa and northern Asia, and a few species endemic to the peninsula.

The animals and plants of northern and north-eastern Saudi Arabia are generally closely related to or identical with Saharan species. To the south and the west, wildlife assumes its older, tropical African character. Only in the Oman mountains, known to be geologically related to the highlands across the Gulf, do we find strong Asiatic elements.

**Plant Life**

Except in parts of the Asir highlands, where the juniper, the wild olive, and some other larger trees grow together over large areas, there are no forests in Saudi Arabia. In some parts, scattered small acacia trees are common. Further east and north the vegetation is typical of arid steppes – hundreds of square kilometres of small, drought-adapted shrubs, a metre or less high. Often one species, such as the *rimth* saltbush or the yellow-flowered *arfaj* shrublet, dominates the landscape. The ground between these shrublets is green for only two to three months of the year, when winter rains bring forth a host of herbs. Among these annuals, known collectively as *usht* by the Beduin, are the desert *Anthemis* or camomile, many species of the mustard family, and a striking iris.

Only the salt-impregnated bottoms of *sabkhahs*, small areas of rock-floored desert, and a few fields of actively moving dunes do not support any plants. Even most parts of the Rub al-Khali have scattered shrublets of the prickly *hadh* saltbush, a *Tribulus*, or the scarlet-fruited *abal*.

## Mammals

The largest wild mammal of Saudi Arabia is the Arabian oryx. This one hundred-kilogram antelope with long, straight horns, which was known in this area in Biblical times became extinct in the wild in the early 1960s, but a herd has been successfully bred in Arizona from captured specimens, and the oryx has now been re-introduced into its natural habitat in Oman. With the effective new hunting laws and game parks it may not be long before the oryx returns to Saudi Arabia.

Graceful gazelles were once common throughout most of Arabia, but their numbers are now much diminished, due to overhunting in the 1930s and 40s. The lovely Rheem is known to survive on the edge of the Rub al-Khali; the Idhmi still inhabits the mountains and foothills of the south and west; the Afri is extant but rarely encountered, while its endemic sub-species, the Dorcas, which used to range the south-east of the country, is alas probably extinct. Like the oryx, the gazelles of Arabia have adapted to desert life, obtaining much of their water needs from the scanty vegetation.

The ibex was also once widespread, but it is now rarely to be encountered except in the mountains of the north-west, and possibly the Hijaz and south-west.

The cheetah was seen sometimes on the broad plains of the far north and south, but now may well be extinct. The caracal probably still exists in the north, while the leopard has been reported from the highlands of Asir and the rare Arabian sand cat, amazingly like a domestic cat in appearance, in barren sand country.

The Arabian wolf, *canis lupus arabicus*, jackals, foxes, and the striped hyena are found in Arabia, as are the hedgehog, the porcupine and the ratel, or honey badger. More common rodents are the small Arabian hare and the jerboa, or kangaroo rat. The rat-like jerd and mouse-sized gerbil burrow beneath desert shrubs, while the shy, brown hyrax lives amongst rocks. Baboons are not unusual in the central Hijaz and Asir highlands, where they raid terraced croplands.

## Birds

Thousands of millions of birds, including flamingoes, storks, swallows, wagtails, warblers and many more, pass through Arabia on their spring and autumn migrations. Many end their journeys in Saudi Arabia to winter there. The bird-life of the country is consequently rich and varied and includes African, oriental and northern species.

Among the true desert residents are six species of sandgrouse and several larks, including the sweet-voiced hoopoe lark, known to the desert Arab as *Umm Salim*, "Salim's mother".

Game birds in Saudi Arabia include the *hubara* bustard, the Quail, partridges, doves, the stone curlew, and the courser. Among the birds of prey are harriers, buzzards, several species of eagle, and falcons which are often trained to catch hares and *hubara*. Water birds, such as ibises, herons, egrets, gulls and pelicans inhabit the rich tropical coastal areas.

The ostrich, which has figured in Arabic poetry since pre-Islamic times, is now extinct. One of the last sightings was in 1938.

## Reptiles

The water-conserving body structure of reptiles makes them well adapted for life in arid lands, but many cannot endure extremes of heat and must lead nocturnal or subterranean lives. Thus, although some fourteen species of snake have been reported from Saudi Arabia, few are seen. One of these might be the small, thick-bodied sand viper, a venomous but seldom lethal creature that moves like the sidewinder of the American South-West. More dangerous, but fortunately very rare, are the Arabian hooded cobra, found in well-vegetated areas of the mountainous west, and the all-black hoodless cobra in the central and north-eastern deserts. Harmless snakes are more common, among them the *malpolon*, which spreads its neck into a hood when cornered and is often mistaken for a cobra. Potentially dangerous, but shy, sea snakes are found in the Arabian Gulf.

There are no poisonous lizards in Arabia, although two species are imposingly large: the sixty-centimetre long, plant-eating *dabb*, and the even longer, whip-tailed *waral*, or monitor lizard. Skinks, agamids, geckoes and lacertids are other kinds of lizard frequently encountered in Arabia.

## Marine Life

Brilliantly coloured and exotically shaped tropical fish such as Butterflyfish, Angelfish and Parrotfish, fill the seas and reefs of Arabia – unparalleled under-

*Arabia's famous hunting dog, the saluki.*

*A kitten of Arabia's rare sand cat.*

*The oryx – saved from extinction.*

*The spiny hedgehog is well defended.*

*Many species of reptiles are found in Saudi Arabia – most remarkable of the lizards being, perhaps, the* dabb *(right), which can absorb its moisture by breathing (the only animal in the world to do so), allowing it to live in a waterless desert.*

*Both the Red Sea and the Gulf abound in garish marine life, of which the banded Bluefish, the red speckled Angelfish and the furry sea spiders are typical examples. Brilliantly coloured fish haunt the coral reefs along Saudi Arabia's Red Sea coast.*

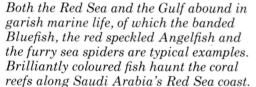

water paradises for the naturalist, diver, and photographer. Extraordinary coral structures provide homes not just for the spectacular fish, but also for a wealth of urchins, anemones, starfish, squid and crustaceans. Here also lurk some of the more dangerous inhabitants of the deep: the Moray eel, the Stonefish and Scorpionfish, both of which use their camouflaging abilities to avoid detection by unsuspecting prey.

Sharks are common in the Gulf, but they are not a threat to bathers. The deeper waters of the Red Sea are better shark territory. Sea mammals include the porpoise, the dugong and the occasional whale. Several species of turtle still breed on offshore islands.

### Insects

Saudi Arabia is remarkably free of insect pests. Mosquitoes and malaria have been wiped out by Government campaigns in most districts.

Among the more common desert insects are the dark-hued ground beetle and the scarab beetle. Not strictly insects, but arachnids, are the scorpion, the large, non-venomous camel spider, and the crimson velvet mite.

A wide variety of butterflies and moths can be seen in Arabia, including the beautiful Painted Lady, the African Lime Swallowtail and the Oleander Hawkmoth.

### Conservation

The Saudi Arabian Government, realizing that many of Arabia's animals are near extinction, has now outlawed hunting except under strict conditions; a few years ago "Operation Oryx" was launched by the Fauna Preservation Society, the World Wildlife Fund, and various other international organizations for nature conservation, and two males and a female were taken to the United States of America. Here, in Arizona, they were settled and bred successfully; a group of selected animals from this herd was re-introduced into Arabia in 1980.

The Saudi Arabian Government contributed to this brave rescue; the next step is to be the restocking of animals in their former natural ranges and the development of such herds to ecologically balanced sizes; King Khalid's interest in conservation is well known. The gazelle may yet roam the central and northern plains again; the ostrich and cheetah resume their ancient habitat.

*Arabia's larger mammals now protected by conservation policies include (left to right, from the top): the Arabian ibex, believed to be the progenitor of the domestic goat; the Arabian gazelle, found in the mountains and foothills of the west and south; the caracal lynx, still to be seen in remoter corners of the country; and the fleet-footed cheetah, whose speed over short distances of semi-desert can reach 60 mph.*

*Today all hunting is banned by law, and a programme for the establishment of National Parks is being implemented. The first, the Asir Park, is already in operation, and studies for parks at Billasmar, Namas and Bilqarn are under way. The Environmental Protection Support Services now have the responsibility of preserving the Kingdom's flora and fauna by the control of pollution and the preservation of natural ecology.*

# Mineral Wealth

*The Kingdom's Pre-Cambrian Arabian Shield is a classic site for mineral wealth, and extensive geological investigation is revealing the deposits to found a mining industry, including gold, silver and copper.*

ANCIENT mineworkings have always hinted at Saudi Arabia's natural non-oil mineral wealth. It is being intensively prospected by geologists from the Deputy Ministry of Mineral Resources with help from the US Geological Survey, the

The top picture *shows complex folding of pre-Cambrian shield rock in the south-west. Nickel gossan, and gossan from pyrite* (above left and left) *of the Arabian shield point to exploitable deposits; copper mining has already begun at Ma'had Dhahab* (above), *Arabia's most historic mine.*

French Bureau de Recherches Géologiques et Minières, and the British based Riofinex mining company. They are determining the geologic and tectonic position of deposits.

Most of the modern discoveries have been in central and western Saudi Arabia in rocks of the Precambrian Arabian Shield, although some finds have also been made in the much younger rocks along the Red Sea coast. Palaeozoic rocks which overlap the Shield in the north and east are also being investigated.

The Precambrian metallic mineral deposits fall into four major types: stratiform iron-nickel deposits; massive polymetallic base-metal deposits; gold-silver deposits; and disseminated molybdenum-tungsten deposits. Other metal deposits occur on the Red Sea coastal plain, and in hot brines and sediments of the deeps

in the axial trough of the Red Sea.

Known occurrences of metal deposits form regional belts of mineralization which relate closely to structural rock formation. Seven principal mineral belts and/or zones have been delineated in the Precambrian rocks of the Arabian Shield. These include the Bidah, Sabya, Nuqrah and Al Amar copper-zinc belts; the Salwah copper-zinc zone; and the Hijaz and Najd gold-silver belts. Recent exploration has also indicated several massive sulphide deposits, although the main economic metal is copper, with lesser amounts of zinc, gold and silver.

Many of the reported gold-silver deposits in the Shield appear to form belts that parallel the dominant northwest trend of the Najd fault system or trends of related subsidiary shears. Hundreds of ancient gold-silver prospects have been located and examined, and current exploration suggests that these mines have future potential.

Important iron deposits, large massive and disseminated strata-bound pyrite deposits and massive stratiform nickel-bearing sulphide deposits discovered in the Arabian Shield approach economic size, grade and access requirements.

Of the economically significant non-metallic mineral resources to be found, phosphate, magnesite, glass sand, gypsum, salt, and structural and cement materials are all being mined in increasing quantities.

Structural materials including clays, shales and perlite are being investigated for the production of light weight aggregates. Marble in pleasing colours and patterns is quarried from many localities in the Arabian Shield and three cement plants in Saudi Arabia are utilizing the abundant cement materials indigenous to the country.

So far, all estimates of the size, quality and variety of metallic and non-metallic mineral resources suggest that Saudi Arabia's natural reserves can be relied upon to provide much future wealth.

*Mounded basalt characterizes the surface of part of the Jabal Hashahish Quadrangle* (immediately above).

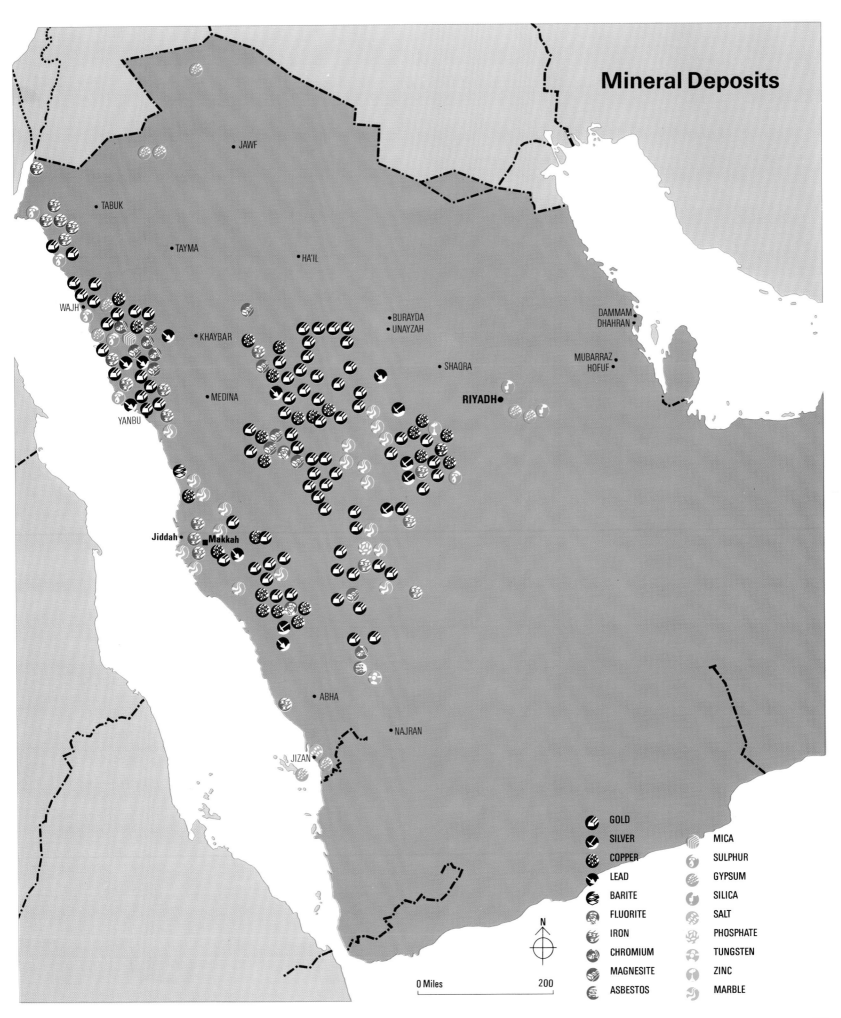

# Mineral Deposits

JAWF

TABUK

TAYMA

HA'IL

WAJH

KHAYBAR

BURAYDA
UNAYZAH

DAMMAM
DHAHRAN

MEDINA

SHAQRA

MUBARRAZ
HOFUF

YANBU

RIYADH

Jiddah • ■Makkah

ABHA

NAJRAN

JIZAN

N

0 Miles          200

| GOLD | |
| SILVER | |
| COPPER | MICA |
| LEAD | SULPHUR |
| BARITE | GYPSUM |
| FLUORITE | SILICA |
| IRON | SALT |
| CHROMIUM | PHOSPHATE |
| MAGNESITE | TUNGSTEN |
| ASBESTOS | ZINC |
| | MARBLE |

25

# 2
# The Cities

*The cities into which people are flocking today may be modern but are seldom new. Settled people have for centuries outnumbered nomadic.*
*Makkah's and Medina's scholastic pre-eminence has at times been rivalled by Jerusalem or Damascus, Baghdad or Cairo, but never their spiritual role.*

*Despite the many massive modern buildings that dominate the skyline of Riyadh, the fastest growing city in the Middle East, the blend of the traditional with the new has been preserved. Certain historic buildings, such as the palace in the foreground, survived for a while the surge of modern development, but most such relics of the era of Abdul Aziz have disappeared. Yet several new Government buildings have kept architectural faith with traditional Arab designs. The map (below) shows the sites of major cities.*

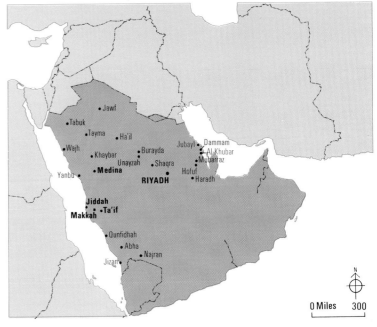

# Cities~an Introduction

SURPRISINGLY – in the light of popular belief – the greater part of the people of Saudi Arabia have lived the settled life, rather than the nomadic one, at least over recent centuries. Many of these, it is true, have lived in villages, whose size would be determined by the quantity of fresh water available. On the other hand, links with and awareness of their major cities have since ancient days belonged deeply to the patterns of thought and life in the Arabian hinterland.

The first city of Saudi Arabia must always be the Holy City of Makkah, spiritual capital of all Islam. Though Makkah's permanent population is much less than that of modern Riyadh or Jiddah (both with populations around the million mark), at the height of the annual pilgrimage of Muslims to Holy Makkah it contains over two million people. Makkah's founding is attributed to the presence of the well opened in the desert by God to save the lives of Hagar and her son, Isma'il, from whom – with his father Abraham – the Arab race traces its descent. Other stories tell of Abraham labouring with his son Isma'il to rebuild the Holy Ka'bah as a stone structure and site of worship. The Ka'bah, of course, remains, though it has been reconstructed from time to time throughout the centuries.

Although Makkah boasts many fine modern buildings, including its splendid Islamic conference centre, determined efforts have been made to preserve its traditional Arabian character. The same is true of Arabia's other Holy City of Medina, the "shining city", which to the delight of the pilgrim or Muslim visitor has remained a small city of some one hundred thousand souls and whose life centres round its magnificent green-domed mosque and famous library and its Islamic University.

By contrast, Riyadh is today very largely a modern city, spaciously laid out, graced with several fine ministerial

*Lively oriental imagination is displayed by the Ministerial building in Ta'if* (below) *and on the approach to Makkah* (bottom).

*The fortified wall of old Jiddah – captured by the forces of Abdul Aziz in 1925 – is still visible* (below) *in an aerial photograph taken in the 1930s. It had already been pulled down by 1950, to allow Jiddah to*

buildings, and growing fast on the basis of imaginative city planning. It was restored by King Abdul Aziz as the site of the Saudi capital. With its plentiful water and its site by the Wadi Hanifah, Riyadh's history is ancient. As the historic city of Hajr it was the oldest capital of the Yamamah region. It is the centre of a relatively fertile area.

Jiddah – the Bride of the Red Sea – founded by Caliph 'Uthman ibn 'Affan in 647 CE, but certainly a fishing settlement before that – is today the largest port on the Red Sea, with a magnificent modern harbour. Much of the picturesque Jiddah of traditional Arab architecture has been pulled down to make way for

modern office blocks, banks, apartment blocks and the like. As the diplomatic capital up to the early 1980s, it was the site of over seventy embassies; these, however, were scheduled to be moved to Riyadh in 1983.

While Saudi Arabians watch the towns of Yanbu and Jubayl expand as major industrial centres, several other cities are developing fast – in every case under town plans which control the use of land for residential, industrial or agricultural purposes, the development of public utilities, population density and road and traffic systems. They include Burayda and Unayzah, in the Qasim area, and Ha'il further north. In

the east, Dammam and its neighbours al-Khubar and Dhahran were beginning to take on the aspect of a single megalopolis, which could in time embrace Saihat, Qatif, Safwa; Tarut Island (linked to the mainland by a causeway), and Ras Tannurah. Eastern oil towns like Abqaiq and Udayliyyah are also growing apace. In the South West, the principal sites of sharp expansion are the region's port Jizan, which is to have a new city as the old one was built on an unsteady salt-dome, Najran, the military town Khamis Mushayt and its neighbouring administrative capital Abha, and Baha. In the North West, Tabuk grows rapidly as a regional centre for defence.

*begin its expansion* (bottom left).
*The spacious planning of today's Jiddah is already just visible in the aerial shot taken in 1968* (below), *showing the first version of the main roundabout, and the edge of the*

*lagoon. But by the mid-seventies* (bottom) *the heart of Jiddah was that of a noisy, gleaming international city. Jiddah's development today is masterminded by a City Planning Office which has sited the*

*airport (circled in red) north of the city centre and has designated open spaces for recreation (green)* (below).

| | |
|---|---|
| خدمات حكومية مدنية | Civic |
| مراكز تجارية | Commercial |
| مكاتب | Offices |
| الميناء - المخازن والصناعات | Port. Warehousing & Industry |
| مستشفى كبير | H Large Hospital |
| الاسكان حسب التقديرات الادنا | Housing. Low Population |
| الاسكان حسب التقديرات العليا | Housing. High Population |
| مناطق الترفيه ومساحات مكشوفة | Recreation & Open Space |
| ممرات مصممة للطرق الرئيسية (التقديرات الادنا) | Primary Road Corridor Low Population |
| ممرات مصممة للطرق الرئيسية (التقديرات العليا) | Primary Road Corridor High Population |
| شبكة عبور سريع | Rapid Transit |
| الجامعة | U University |
| للاغراض التعليمية | E Education |
| مركز استقبال الحجاج | R Hadj Reception |
| منطقة زراعية | Agricultural Area |
| منطقة حكومية خاصة | Special Government Area |
| المطار | R Airport |

N
0 1 2 3 4 5 6 7 8 Km

# Riyadh

NO roads led to Riyadh at the beginning of the century. Indeed, until the early 1950s, it was still a desert city of clay palaces surrounded by a cluster of mud-brick buildings and heavy mud walls. Then came the boom years and this city, the very symbol of Najdi culture and the Islamic puritan reformation, began to alter. Today all roads lead to Riyadh, for a modern capital city has visibly been created.

Riyadh's original reason for settlement was its vast oasis of palm trees and other vegetation – hence its name ar-Riyath, "the Gardens". Situated in the heart of Central Najd, on a sedimentary plateau 600 metres above sea level, at the confluence of Wadi Hanifa and its tributaries Wadi Aysan and Wadi Batha, it has a very dry climate and low rainfall, but a good underground water supply makes it one of the few naturally fertile areas in the Kingdom outside the South-west.

When the name Riyadh was first used by Ibn Bishr in 1636 it referred to the ancient site of Hajr and its gardens. In 422 the little town was deserted by its inhabitants and the tribe of Bani Hanifa moved to it with their chief and took and defended thirty houses. Thus the early city took on the name of Hajr, or "defended".

Once established as a desert city in the middle of the eighteenth century, Riyadh became an object of dispute between forces in the area. After it joined the Wahhabi cause in 1773, it was just one of the many towns in the first Saudi state. But the fall of that state in 1818 at the hands of the invading Turkish armies brought renewed interest in Riyadh as the focal point of efforts to revive the power of the House of Saud. In the early nineteenth century it became the capital of the Najd, but during that century Riyadh saw a succession of Saudi and other rulers, as many elements vied for its control.

The Riyadh of January 1902, which the young Abdul Aziz al Saud so daringly captured was probably not more than a few hundred yards across at its widest. A thick mud wall about seven metres high surrounded it, in which immense north,

*By night the lights of Riyadh give evidence of its vigour and size.*

south, east and west gates were set. Inside it was a maze of twisting alleys, some so narrow that it was difficult for two men to walk abreast.

The only open space was the central market. On one side was a large mosque and on the other the fortress-palace which Ibn Rashid had seized from the House of Saud. Nearby was a tiny market place reserved for women.

All the buildings were made of the same adobe as the walls. Half were single storey buildings while the rest had an upper floor. The outside walls, in the simple tradition of the desert, were blank except for occasional, tiny protruding windows.

Riyadh's subsequent history is closely associated with the resurgence of the purified faith and the rise of the House of Saud. Its recapture by Abdul Aziz was a watershed for the House of Saud; he used it as the base from which he reunified the Najd and the most of the rest of the Peninsula. When the new Saudi state was nearly built, he began building Riyadh as its capital.

The basic character of Riyadh changed as the city – along with the country itself entered a period of very rapid growth. The population quintupled, concrete and

asphalt were introduced and used widely, and the old adobe desert town was engulfed in the large and modern city. First the railhead from Dammam and first airport were built; then it was decided to assemble most of the Ministries in Riyadh.

Today nearly all Riyadh's inhabited dwellings are non-mud structures and all have basic water, electric and sewage facilities. The pace of development accelerated further still from 1974, as the comprehensive new city plan – looking forward three or four decades – began to be realised. By 1980 the population stood at over a million and was increasing yearly.

As the capital city, it became the home of thousands of government officials and fine government buildings multiplied. Riyadh became a centre of commerce and industry; villagers and tribesmen from all over the country were attracted by its opportunities. Arab immigrants and temporary residents from all over the world were admitted to assist in the capital's development and functions. Today in Riyadh as in many another world capital, the majority of the population was not born there.

For short periods the strain of exceptionally swift development told, and in the early 1970s the old and new were jumbled together. The cars and trucks of Batha Street moved in a cacophony of horns, stirring up dust from the broken pavements. Dust coated villas and sickly trees. It was a city seeking a new identity. Down came the old buildings. And down came some of the new to be replaced immediately by the newer and finer edifices.

But vigorous planning and archi-

*Fine government buildings sprang up in the capital* (below).

tectural control told in the end. By the 1980s it was already becoming a modern city with a character of its own – a Najdi desert identity – combining, the stark simplicity of the Musmak fort, (seized by Ibn Saud with his seven companions in 1902, and now preserved as an historic site) with contours and facades of many official buildings and palaces that bear the stamp of traditional Arab or central Arabian architecture.

The interaction between nomadic, sedentary and urban populations cannot be seen more effectively than it is seen in Riyadh today. This and the climate have influenced Riyadh's architecture. During the day in summer the desert burns with fierce heat. There are ferocious glare and occasional sandstorms. The Riyadh home traditionally has an enclosed courtyard, and often a roof-area giving residents access to the sky's coolness at night, though today of course virtually every house and office is air-conditioned.

With its tree-lined boulevards and flyovers, its first-class hotels and dawning golden age of fine twentieth-century architecture influenced by local traditions, Riyadh is coming into its own. It is no longer the "secret city" to which the romantic travellers of the nineteenth century journeyed. It has its own radio and television production complex, large and modern universities, colleges, schools, hospitals and clinics. It has developed into a sophisticated host-capital for the 1980s move of the entire diplomatic corps in stages from Jiddah: between 1983 and 1990 buildings and amenities are expected to expand to accommodate some ninety diplomatic missions and 15,000 people. And, because of expansion and increasing air traffic, a new airport was to open in 1982; it was designed specifically to cater for the forecast fifteen million passengers a year by 2000 AD. These development factors would put paid to Riyadh's traditional isolation and allow it to take on the role which it has sought since the beginning of the early eighteenth century, that of the pivot of the Arabian Peninsula.

In less than a decade, Riyadh has taken its place as one of the most important capitals of the world – as witnessed by an annual stream of Heads of State and public figures from Western, Arab, Islamic and developing countries in search of consultation and co-operation.

# Riyadh Landmarks

*Riyadh's most familiar landmark has become its central water tower.*

*King Abdul Aziz' favourite Palace was the Qasr al-Murabba, built in 1936.*

*The Saudi Arabian Monetary Agency's massive twins opened for business in late 1978, one of which is seen above.*

*A spacious modern Arabian style characterizes the Officer's Club on Airport Road.*

# Jiddah

SITUATED about half-way along the eastern coast of the Red Sea, Jiddah is an Arabian city-port of great age: gateway to Holy Makkah and Western Arabia, this ancient "Bride of the Red Sea" is today one of the most cosmopolitan cities ever. But confined as it was for several centuries by its desert hinterland and an uncertain water supply within massive walls of bleached coral, its core is still traditionally Arab.

Ever since the profitable Red Sea spice trade, Jiddah has been the main port and commercial centre of Arabia. But with the mounting sea power of Europe, Jiddah ceased to be a commercial *entrepôt* of importance, subsiding into its other role as a pilgrim port, and in 1517 the town fell under the sometimes interrupted power of the Ottoman Turks, as part of the domain of the Sharif of Makkah. However, the opening of the Suez Canal in 1869 proved a boon for Jiddah and, by the turn of the century, its merchants were handling a regular volume of commerce with other Arabian ports, India, Egypt, Africa and even Liverpool and Marseilles.

*Beit Nassif* (above) – *one of the finest examples of architecture in Old Jiddah* (right). *Wholly modern skyline of the old city* (bottom).

From this period date the many fine merchant family houses that survive in the old city. The most celebrated of such houses is Beit Nassif, home of the Nassif family for over a century until the house was passed to the care of the Government in the mid-1970's. Designed by a Jiddah master-builder of the day, it is built of coral limestone tied by teak beams, and contains fifty high-ceilinged rooms, including a famous library of 6,000 volumes.

The character of the town had changed little over the years. Pilgrims came, and, if they could afford it, went; ships still edged through the dangerous gateways between the three coral reefs; sweet water remained the perennial problem. The town grew upwards and became compact as a hive. T. E. Lawrence describes the Jiddah of 1916 in *Seven Pillars of Wisdom*:

"It was indeed a remarkable town. The streets were alleys, wood-roofed in the main bazaar, but elsewhere open to the sky in the little gap between the tops of the lofty white walled houses ... housefronts were fretted, pierced and

# Jiddah Landmarks

pargetted till they looked as though cut out of cardboard for a romantic stage setting. Every storey jutted, every window leaned one way or another; often the very walls sloped."

The town surrendered to Abdul Aziz and his Saudis in 1925. But its modern history does not begin until May 1933, when his Finance Minister signed an oil concession with the Standard Oil Company of California; thirty-five thousand pounds in gold sovereigns were counted across a table in Jiddah. Five years later oil began to flow in the Eastern Province and Jiddah's days as a walled city were numbered.

For a hundred years up to 1945 the population had been stable at about twenty-five thousand; by 1980 it had leapt to nearly one million. In the nine years following 1971, the number of cars in the city multiplied about twenty times. Far more serious in the eyes of the Municipality was the haphazard growth to the north and along the Makkah road as prices of land and property spiralled out of control. But the greatest challenge was to be met by Jiddah harbour now obliged to feed the demand for building materials and consumer goods from the whole country. Whereas cargo offloaded in 1946 was a mere 150,000 tons, by 1977 ships were discharging over eight million tons a year.

The Pilgrimage remained a priority and has been managed with increasing skill. At the new King Abdul Aziz International Airport, which covers 40.5 square miles, provision has been made for a million and a half pilgrims (as well as six million other passengers) each year. All this is reflected in the 1980 budget for Jiddah which was about SR 100 million, while its overall share of the Third Five-Year Plan budget is about

*Saudia training centre* (above left); *Youth Affairs Headquarters* (above); *the new King Abdul Aziz international airport* (above right); *the Queen's Building* (right); *the former British Legation* (below right); *and public sculpture* (bottom right).

SR 2,247 million.

What has been accomplished in the past five years in Jiddah would take fifty years in any city growing naturally. Like Venice, Jiddah suffers from a rare contradiction. Architecturally and infrastructurally it is by far the richest Saudi city. But its commercial importance leaves it also at the developer's mercy. Many felt that the glittering shops and apartment blocks had lost their sense of direction, petering out in dusty spaces, and that the new town lacked solidity and permanence. The authorities, in particular, were concerned that the town's appearance did not sufficiently reflect Jiddah's place in Islam or history. It was turning its back on the sea, the source of all its prosperity.

Jiddah's climate, its humidity, will always be harsh, but planning will make it bearable. Until the 1920s, Jiddah – like Brooklyn – boasted but a single tree, still standing under Beit Nassif. Today, with the solving of the water problem, the town has grown green around it. The city has also taken over twenty-six areas of waste ground for parks. Most important, the city has taken over twenty miles of coastline – the Corniche project – solely for the purposes of providing recreation. It is this grand imaginative gesture of road, promenade, parking area, trees and monuments that has brought back the sea decisively into the heart of the city.

# Traditional Architecture

*In Makkah, a determination to preserve the ancient character of the spiritual centre of the world of Islam has dampened tendencies to tear down the glories and intimacies of the past. Only Muslims are allowed to enter holy Makkah, whose foundation dates from God's miraculous provision of a well for Isma'il, son of Abraham, and his mother, Hagar.*

URBAN communities are nothing new in Saudi Arabia; in certain areas they have existed for centuries. Between them is desert inhabited by a now dwindling number of tent-dwelling Beduin. Isolated by great distances and with different social conditions, climates and building materials, these settled areas have evolved distinct regional styles of architecture.

Extant buildings in a traditional style are rarely more than two hundred years old: but until the recent and almost total transformation of Saudi Arabia by determined modernization there was no stimulus to change the indigenous styles, so that buildings erected not long ago adhered completely to the old techniques and designs.

Four main Saudi Arabian architectural styles are characteristic of four regions – eastern Najd, central Hijaz, southern Hijaz and Asir, and the Arabian Gulf coast.

## Eastern Najd

The main building material is unfired mud-brick; the completed wall is made smooth by the application of mud-plaster. These walls are very thick, and provide insulation against the extremities of the local climate. The roofing consists of wooden beams, usually of tamarisk, with palm matting or twigs spread above. This is covered with a layer of mud. Stone is used only as the foundation of a house or in fortifications.

The Najdi mosque consists of a walled enclosure around an open courtyard, with a covered sanctuary built against the *qibla* wall. Cut into this wall is the *mihrab* niche, which projects beyond the back wall of the mosque; an arrangement common in both ancient and modern mosques in Saudi Arabia. The roof of the sanctuary rests on colonnades with keel-arches, the number of colonnades depending on the mosque's size and im-

*The traditional architecture of the Eastern Najd can be seen in the village of al Janub, near Dhahran. Official encouragement is given to the preservation of ancient architectural techniques, with the characteristic thick thick mud-brick walls, to provide insulation against the extremities of the local climate.*

wooden doors, and the windows by wooden shutters. Both shutters and doors are decorated with incised geometric patterns picked out in colour, or by geometrics burned into the pale wooden surface. The only other external decorations are rows of V-shaped mouldings on the walls, and crenellations which vary in design from area to area.

local conformity is attributable to common influences brought about in the area by the *hajj*, by trade and by trading connections further afield, particularly with Egypt.

The buildings common to all these cities are two, three or more storeys high, with level roofs. The entrance is often vaulted by a round-headed or

portance. Some mosques have underground prayer-chambers for use in winter. In Arid and further south, one or two staircases nearly always give access to the roof; in this area the mosques are either without minarets, or have only a diminutive tower over the staircase to the roof. In Sudayr and Qasim, however, minarets are tall and cylindrical.

Najdi houses are often built around a central courtyard, with only a few openings on to the street, thus maintaining the privacy of family life. The buildings have one, two or three storeys depending on their importance. The entrances to the houses are closed by large rectangular

Elaborately shaped mud finials stand at the corners.

The position of the reception rooms varies. In most larger houses the lower rooms are used for storage, and visitors are received upstairs. However, rooms designed to receive guests appear in Sadus and Unayzah on both the ground floor and the upper storey. In a corner of these reception rooms there is usually a small hearth for coffee-making, with shelves above.

**The Central Hijaz and its Coast**
Makkah, Medina, Ta'if and Jiddah all have a similar type of architecture. This

pointed arch, and the wooden doors are decorated with rather stiff and stylized carving. The outer walls are frequently, but not always, whitewashed.

Decoration is concentrated in the elaborate wooden screens which face the upper storeys of the building around windows and balconies, with an effect recalling the *mashrabiyya* screens of Cairo. These screens guard from view people standing at windows or on balconies. They are arranged on the facade of the building in various ways; in some houses they occupy the whole of the upper area, while in others, two very high screens are set to right and left of a

The tremendous impact of the petroleum industry has by no means destroyed the traditional character of all ancient towns of Arabia's eastern region – as witness the view of Qatif (below). Like Hofuf, it was the site of a Turkish fortress until captured by Abdul Aziz in 1913, in the drive for unity. The map indicates architectural areas.

Traditional architectural techniques are illustrated by (from the top) a typical village of the south-east (Ghamid), palaces and houses in Riyadh, Jiddah houses with slatted balconies, and a pavilion-style house in Tarut, eastern Saudi Arabia.
(Drawings are by Geoffrey King)

*The unique charm of Saudi Arabia's Red Sea coast is illustrated by such fishing settlements of Wajh* (below), *where peaceful communities linking Red Sea trade and fishing with the interior have survived for centuries. Offshore, parts of this coast are skirted by coral reefs, breeding grounds of many varieties of brilliantly coloured fish.*

tecture. These have inward-sloping walls, slight crenellations and small apertures, but they vary in height and proportion.

The houses of the Abha area are built of mud or stone or a combination of both. In those buildings constructed of mud, layers are applied successively and each layer is left to dry before another is added. Horizontal rows of protruding stone

Although there is no single local form of building, technical and decorative devices recur in structures otherwise quite different. All of these eastern buildings, however, are distinguished by fine proportions, both in dimensions and decoration.

The wind-towers of Bahrain and Dubai do not appear on the Saudi coast. In-

small central screen. Yet other houses have much smaller screens around the windows alone, occupying a lesser area of the whole façade.

**Southern Hijaz and Asir**

From Bilad Zahran and through Bilad Ghamid, north of Abha, the standard building material is rough-cut stone. These villages are often defensively positioned on hilltops, especially in Bilad Zahran, and the continuous faces presented by the outermost houses give the effect of a fortified wall. Elsewhere, in valleys and plains, the villages are in less defensible positions. In both regions one or two rectangular towers are a constant feature of the village archi-

slabs are placed between each mud-layer to break up the flow of rainwater, which would otherwise dissolve it. The mud areas of the houses are often white-washed, thus emphasizing the horizontal division of these tower-like structures.

**The Arabian Gulf coast**

The eastern towns of Saudi Arabia are situated between the desert and the Gulf. The climate is similar to that of the Red Sea shore, with a high rate of humidity and persistent uncomfortable heat in summer. Also as on the Red Sea coast, the building material is coral aggregate and wood. The walls are made smooth with plaster. The roofing system employs palm thatch and wooden beams.

stead, on the Saudi shore, certain rooms are arranged to benefit from the slightest breeze, while other rooms are better suited to cooler winter conditions. Thus in the centre of Qatif the houses are of several storeys. The lower rooms have small windows, whereas the uppermost storey has large arched openings piercing the walls for ventilation. On the outskirts of the town two-storey kiosk-like buildings once existed, with walls pierced by large arches. They appear to have been summer pavilions.

This eastern architecture bears no significant relationship to buildings inland, but has a marked similarity to those found in Bahrain, Qatar and Dubai and its neighbours.

# 3 The People, their habitat & way of life

*The interplay of the hard, disciplined, wandering life of the desert and the settled life of farmers, craftsmen, merchants and teachers in the scattered towns has for countless centuries formed the character of the people. Today, well tested values stand remarkably firm among the challenges of modern city life.*

*A boy from Diriyah demonstrates his desert heritage no less by his fine clear-cut features than by his characteristic red headdress, the* ghotra. *Fundamentally of Armenoid stock, Saudi Arabians have effortlessly accepted intermingling as a result of fourteen centuries of Muslim pilgrimage and trade. Settlers have arrived from China and Islamic Central Asia, from South-East Asia and South Asia, and from Africa and the Eastern Mediterranean.*

**Arabian Faces**

Variety in apparel and headdress can indicate the influence of locality, profession, or social standing. The red and white check *ghotra* (*as below*) is as a rule worn in winter months, for it is warmer, and the *ghotra* of light white cotton (*top row*) in summer.

Top row, left to right: *Saudis from the south-west, east coast, and Qasim.* Centre: *A coppersmith, and an oilworker.* Below: *While the majority of Saudi Arabia's traditionally nomadic population has now chosen to settle, desert disciplines and the lifestyle that accounts for the dignity and serenity of the Saudi character still prevail among a substantial minority.*

# The Unity of the Saudi Arabian People

IT is the town culture – markedly Islamic – which brings together the various strands in Arabian society, to form a complex but harmonious whole, combining the virtues of Beduin life with merchanting acumen and a high standard of literacy and education.

The ancient records of Arabia show a society simultaneously at many distinct but interdependent stages of development. Beside the high civilization of the ancient South there is mention of Beduin, who do not, however, seem to play a role of any great importance. In early Islamic times, the interrelationship between nomads and townsmen is closer, each depending on the other for essential goods and services.

Although the early towns were organized in quarters corresponding to the tribal origins of their inhabitants, the conditions of settled life produced a culture superior to that of the tribes in the desert. One aspect of the rise of Islam can be seen as a clash between the aspirations of the town and the customs of the desert, where animism had been the principal religion. Many of the most important historical events during the first centuries of Islam must be interpreted to some extent in tribal terms, but there was a strong reaction by those who thought of the Islamic community as a whole.

The old poetry gives a good account of Arab life in pre-Islamic times. It describes a heroic society demanding heroic virtues. The heroes are the symbol, the poets the voice, of their tribes.

It was the task of the poet, and of the invisible being who whispered inspiration into his ear, to act for the tribe in diplomatic negotiations, and to vanquish the opposing poet's familiar spirit. Before a battle he had to create martial ardour in his own people and weakness in the enemy. These incantatory poets verged on sorcery, which is doubtless why they are condemned in the Qur'an.

Some of the customs of early tribal society – such as the habit of exposing unwanted female children – were banned by Islam. Gambling and the drinking of wine were also forbidden, warfare between Muslims was condemned and revenge discouraged.

The old way of life still persisted to some extent, however. The Qur'an complains that the Beduin sometimes put tribal obligations above their duty to Islam. Over the centuries, urban society continued to develop while Beduin society altered very little. The economic changes of the twentieth century have now intervened. The motor car spelt the end of Beduin wealth based on camel and horse breeding, and the rise of the oil industry has forced them into new occupations.

There have always been differences between the southern and northern Beduin. Those of the south dress differently, and in their migrations do not live in tents, but merely hang a sunshade from a tree, or go between mountain caves and camps.

The Beduin of the north ride their camels on saddles, while the southerners ride without saddles and much further back. The northern Arabs are believed to have adopted the saddle for use in war against their powerful neighbours, because it allows another warrior to be mounted behind the rider.

The aristocracy of the desert are the camel-rearing tribes. The sheep-rearing tribes were thought to be of lower social standing but, as the nomadic way of life has been eroded, any social disadvantage has now virtually disappeared.

Individuals or groups have always attached themselves to powerful persons or groups to obtain protection and the sheep-rearing tribes may have been clients who were not granted full right of membership in the more powerful tribes with which they had associated themselves for protection.

The economic basis of nomadic life lay in the utilization of resources difficult to exploit. Many scholars believe that it was not the weaker members of the tribe who were forced out of the oases and and fertile areas, but rather the strongest who launched themselves into the hostile desert.

It is clear that there are not and never were, nomads in Arabia who have had complete economic independence. They have always relied on the settled areas

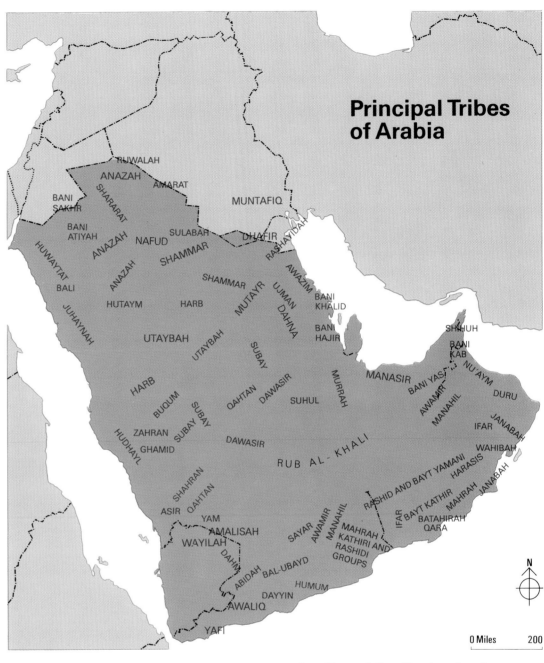

**Principal Tribes of Arabia**

*Tribal allegiance gives both character and meaning to life among Saudi Arabians, ensuring a sustained loyalty to locality, while allowing for the prevailing national unity.*

for an important proportion of their food.

H. St. John Philby has written of the unifying achievement of King ibn Saud by the mid-1920s: "The Arabia over which he was to rule for nearly three more decades was united as never before: . . . and the realm which he had carved out with his sword and his faith would descend intact to his successor. The vital factor . . . was his reputation for justice and resolution, which was seldom put to the test, and always vindicated when the rare need arose. For the first time in human memory Arabia had a single ruler whom all could, and did, respect."

(*See also* Social Life, p.232.)

*"The Arabia over which King Abdul Aziz ruled was united as never before . . . The vital factor was his reputation for justice and resolution, always vindicated when the need arose."*

# *Najd – "highland" – a secure and geographically isolated centre, was never a strong magnet for foreign invaders.*

## The People of the Central Province

THE Province of Najd is the heart and cradle of Saudi Arabia. Its inhabitants – Najdis – are a gifted and remarkable people. Adapting easily to the furious rate of change which prevails in Saudi Arabia today, they have proved their aptitude for jobs which were completely beyond the purview of their ancestors. Yet their basic conservatism and their attachment to traditional ways and ideals remain strong; they believe in treasuring the fundamental principles they have inherited, knowing that if they fail to do so, they will be left rootless. They cling to the flowing robes and headgear of their forefathers as an outward manifestation of this belief. Family allegiances are as strong as ever. Marriages arranged by parents for their offspring prove more durable and contented than marriages in the West. The spirit of Islam continues to permeate thinking.

Fully to appreciate their charm and strength of character, an outsider must visit them in Najd, and see how they rejoice in, and delight to share, the simple pleasures of life – love of the desert and the exhilaration of the chase, with falcons flashing down on the prey; horse races and camel races, the sword dance exalting the old martial prowess of the Arabs; the flow of conversation, spiced with cardamom-flavoured coffee and sweet tea; the banquet spread on a rug, with succulent mutton crowning a mound of rice, the poet reciting his rhymes; and the passing around of the incense burner when the time has come for guests to take their leave.

Najd (that is, "highland") has never been easy to reach from the outside. The mountain barrier of the Hijaz towered above the land to the west, and on the other three sides lay a wilderness of sand. But trails did thread their way into the interior, and resolute men followed them. Members of tribes calling themselves sons of Qahtan or southern Arabs moved northwards and intermingled with the sons of Adnan or northern Arabs they found there. The chiefs of Kindah, a southern tribe, founded a kingdom in the late fourth century of the Christian era, the first organized state known to have existed in Najd, but it was doomed to fall

after only a few decades. Men of Tayy, another southern tribe, went even further north to what is now called Jabal Shammar. The Najdis of today are in the main the offspring of these northern and southern stocks. In other parts of the Arab world Arabs have blended themselves with the indigenous peoples, but in Najd they have maintained a thorough Arabness which is perhaps their most distinguishing characteristic. In a sense they are Arab aristocrats, though their pride in this respect is tempered by the Islamic doctrine which proclaims piety rather than blood to be the true touchstone of nobility.

Najd had little to offer beyond the bracing air of the uplands, the stark beauty of landscapes, pastures for the grazing of herds of camels and flocks of sheep and goats, and scattered springs and wells. The pastures and the watering places helped to bring about the age-old dichotomy of Arabian society between the nomads and the settled folk. The nomads roamed from pasture to pasture and from source to source, while the denizens of the oases clustered together in spots where water flowed abundantly enough to irrigate their date palms and other plants. Neither element had much understanding of or sympathy for the

*The map shows, in black, the areas of central Arabia. The black tents (right) are woven of goat hair.* Far right: *Najdi craftsmanship is worked into the hilt of this National Guardsman's khanjar.*

other, and brawling often broke out between them.

The people of Najd have always loved eloquence, especially when cast in the form of poetry. During the century before Islam, there was an outpouring of magnificent verse in classical Arabic, much of it composed by men and women of Najd. This literature resembles a gorgeous tapestry depicting the life of that time and the ideals of Arab society. The poets held manliness and fortitude and honour to be supreme virtues. Men showed tenderness towards women, whom they pledged to protect with their lives. Frequent wars and feuds called for courage on the field of battle; death was never to be feared. Leaders and elders deserved respect, but could not and did not act autocratically. The harshness of existence in a largely barren land and the need of wanderers for food and shelter fostered the traditions of hospitality and generosity. Hatim, a poet of the tribe of Tayy, is still the paragon of open-handed giving throughout the Arab world.

As the new religion of Islam advanced in the Arabian peninsula, it met resistance in central Najd where, soon after the death of Muhammad the Prophet, a false prophet, Musaylimah the Liar, preached a heretical creed. To overcome him, Abu Bakr, the first Caliph, had to call upon his finest general, Khalid ibn al-Walid, the Sword of God. Once the Najdis came to understand the spiritual message and values of Islam, however,

they devoted themselves enthusiastically to its cause. As warriors and missionaries, countless Najdis left their homeland, many never to return. Carrying the gospel as far east as China and as far west as the Atlantic, these Najdis contributed largely to the expansion of the faith. Their old pagan fearlessness was now reinforced by the promise of eternal life in Paradise for those martyred in the path of God.

Najd, relatively secure in its geographical isolation and possessing few riches to be plundered, was not a strong magnet for foreign invaders. The bane of the region, however, remained for centuries civil strife and almost incessant feuding, town against town, tribe against tribe, nomadic bands against settled communities. This feuding militated against the formation of a powerful and durable state, and the absence of such a state meant that there was no authority to enforce effectively the Sacred Law of Islam and hold the people of Najd to orthodoxy. As time went by, backsliding became common. Many Najdis embraced innovations and beliefs abhorrent to the true spirit of Islam.

In the eighteenth century a religious scholar of central Najd, Sheikh Muhammad ibn Abd al-Wahhab, determined to bring Najd and the rest of Arabia back to the original and undefiled form of Islam as revealed through the Prophet Muhammad and upheld by the first generations of pious believers. To achieve this purpose he allied himself with Muhammad ibn Saud, the ruler of the oasis of Diriyah not far from Riyadh. This alliance survived in the person of the late King Faisal, who was descended on the paternal side from the ruler and on the maternal side from the Sheikh.

The reform movement inaugurated by the Sheikh relied for support principally on the townsmen. Contrary to the misconception common in the West, the townsmen in Najd far outnumber the Beduin; this appears to have been true during the past several centuries at least. Despite some checks in the nineteenth century, the reform movement is still alive and vigorous, commanding the allegiance of the people of Najd, who thus stand out in the Islamic world as

*The ancient skills of falconry represent one of the most sophisticated sporting activities in the world. Skilled falconers are to be found among all communities in the country outside the major cities. The game most often sought is Mac-Queen's bustard (hubara), sand grouse and stone curlew, dove, quail and courser. Falcons are kept hooded unless they are being worked. A skilled man will train a falcon in under three weeks. Of several varieties of falcon, the peregrine – shahin – is probably commonest: they are swift, bold and persevering. The saker falcon – hurr – is also favoured.*

*Men of Unayzah gather for a dignified but spirited traditional dance, com-* *bining skilful sword play with complex drumming.*

*The desert air is sweetest to many a Najdi. Watchtowers dot the landscape, sited on high ground, and built of clay and stone or a combination of both. Towns were once walled, and reinforced with towers: the bigger towns possessed administrative citadels, some of which remain. Inside homes have plastered walls, often with stylized floral decorations and geometric patterns carved in the plaster. Small niches for storage are cut into the walls of even the smallest houses.*

being among the foremost champions of conservative fundamentalism.

In the twentieth century the late King Abdul Aziz, popularly known as ibn Saud, found himself confronted with a problem of far-reaching implications. The reform movement, of which he was a devoted proponent, had as a cardinal objective the weeding out of all reprehensible innovations from Islamic society. So which new things were acceptable and which were not? Ibn

Saud took the liberal view that modern devices such as the automobile and the telephone, as long as they were useful to the community and not harmful to its religious beliefs, were acceptable. Various fanatical tribal chiefs rejected this view. They also chafed under the restraints ibn Saud placed on their raids against those Arabs they regarded as infidels in the neighbouring states of Transjordan and Iraq. Finally, they rose in revolt against their sovereign. After

much bitter fighting ibn Saud, who secured an even larger measure of help from the townsmen of Najd as the revolt went on, succeeded in crushing the rebellion. Since then tribalism has died out as a political force.

Today the loyalty of the Najdis to the House of Saud, a house sprung from the heart of their own region, is unswerving. At the same time, the old provincialism of the different parts of the Kingdom has been steadily waning. In the past Najdis

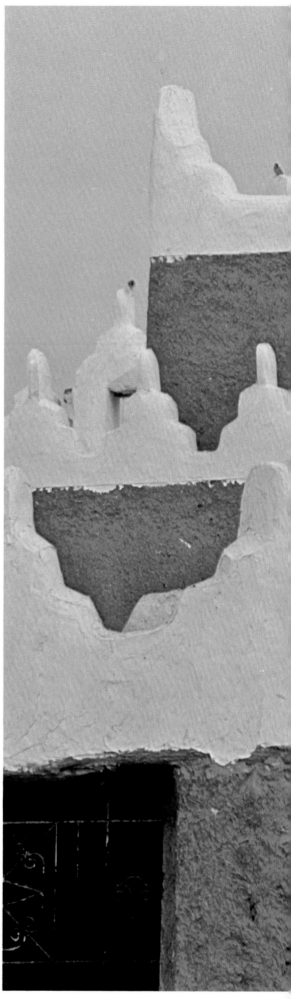

## Traditional House Styles

Traditional methods of building in Saudi Arabia are highly efficient. The unfired clay bricks, finished in plaster, which provide the basic material, give excellent insulation against the heat of the sun. Roof structures are usually of tamarisk. Mouldings, crenellations and finials beautify the exteriors, executed with grace and restraint.

*An instinctive sense of design prevails among the country's builders of traditional houses – as these examples from Burayda in the Qasim area indicate. Crenellations and rooftop edges are picked out in white. The windows and air vents, peepholes and hatches, by which occupants of houses can look out or inspect the arrival of visitors, are unfailingly worked into the overall design with confidence and panache. The triangular decorations of the doorway (centre picture) are widely found throughout the country. Family and social life may proceed at three levels – in the street, within the house itself, and on the level of the complex of roofs, parapets, and alfresco stairways.*

and Hijazis often looked at each other with a jaundiced eye, and Sunnite Najdis tended to disdain their Shi-ite neighbours in Hasa and Qatif to the east. Now they are all coming to think of themselves primarily as Saudi Arabs, fellow citizens of a state created, held together, and built up by two families of genius, the House of the Sheikh and the House of Saud.

The prevailing of ibn Saud's liberal view meant an era of great changes in Saudi Arabian society. The pace was slow at first. In the 1940s, two decades after the suppression of the recalcitrant chiefs, Riyadh was still a walled town built of mud-brick. The country had only a handful of paved roads, and modern airports were just beginning to be constructed. Since the 1950s the rising production of oil has helped to make the pace increasingly rapid and in recent years almost impossible to catalogue.

Yet life among today's people of the Central Province does retain its profundity and society its balance. The impact of modernism, the explosion of opportunities, the infusion of new wealth, have created strains, but manageable strains. Whereas in former times illiteracy was widespread in Najd, with the only formal instruction being in the religious sciences and the ancillary discipline of the Arabic language, the government now wages an anti-illiteracy campaign. Primary and secondary schools abound in the towns and villages, and in Riyadh, universities for both men and women with their *curricula* largely shaped on Western models, win the commendation of visiting Western academics. Young Najdis in growing numbers go abroad for postgraduate work and demonstrate their ability to hold their own with students from all parts of the world.

Not only in the sphere of education but in other spheres as well, modern Najdis are mastering new techniques and acquiring new outlooks. In the government of Saudi Arabia and in private business Najdis are proving their aptitude for callings, some of them highly technical, which a generation or two ago would have been unthinkable. All this pays tribute to the intelligence, innate skills, and versatility of this people who for long were cut off from the mainstream of modern industrial civilization.

(*See also* Sections 8 and 9)

**The Arabian Horse**

The legendary Arabian horse originated in the deserts of Saudi Arabia and through the centuries has been highly regarded for its extraordinary stamina and endurance.

The Najd pure-bred Arabian horse variously coloured bay, chestnut, grey or brown, stands from fourteen to fifteen hands in height. The head is larger in proportion than that of the English thoroughbred, the chief difference lying in the depth of the jowl. The ears are quite large but beautifully shaped, the eyes large and mild, the forehead wide and prominent, and the muzzle fine, sometimes almost pinched. The crest is slightly arched and the neck strong; the head is held high, the shoulders oblique, and the hoofs are round, large and very hard. The back is short and the croup longer and typically more level, with the tail set higher than in most other saddle breeds; indeed, Arabs have boasted that they could use them to hang their cloaks on.

For cross-breeding, the Arab stallion is notable for the transmission, to inferior stocks, of constitution, quality, intelligence and style.

It is written in the Qur'an that every man shall love his horse, while according to the *Hadith* the Prophet is said to have owned fifteen mares in his lifetime and to have quoted the following about them: "After woman came the horse, for the enjoyment and happiness of man."

*Traditionally, the people of western Arabia have linked the world of Red Sea and Mediterranean with the interior.*

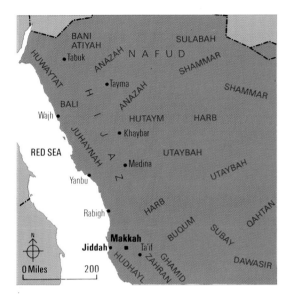

*Though water is relatively abundant in the mountainous west, the lore of the desert prevails among the tribesmen and makes men hardy and devout.*

**The People of the Western Province**

OF all the natural divisions into which the Kingdom may be reduced, the Western Province is the most diverse. It approximately corresponds to the region known immemorially as the Hijaz. It is an area of about 80,000 square miles extending approximately 200 miles inland from Haql in the north to Qunfidhah in the south.

It is a land of great variety where cultivated hilltops give way to seemingly endless desert, where steamy heat yields to bracing winds and frosts, and where townsmen live cheek by jowl with nomads. Over the whole area, the ebb and flow of many civilizations has left its impress on the people. Yet, out of all this diversity it is possible to identify a Hijazi, not by physical appearance or by way of life, but by a bond of historical and cultural associations. For centuries, the settlements have been linked by the passage of caravans bearing precious cargoes and communities of the devout performing the *hajj*, the years spent as an outlying province of the Ottoman Empire and fourteen centuries of provisioning and serving the *Haramayn*, or Holy Cities.

The origins and distribution of the Hijazi peoples have been strongly influenced by geography. North of a line from Jiddah to Ta'if is a land of deserts: arid mineralized mountains or great sweeps of sand and stone. Where the fortunes of geology have yielded water near the coast or at a few points inland, settled communities of farmers, traders, fishermen or sailors have formed. But where aridity prevails then man has adapted to a way of life based on movement. In consequence, the northern Hijaz has never been able to support significant densities of population, with the one striking exception of Medina, where water gushes out from beneath the great lava field of the Harrat ar-Rahah.

To the south of the Jiddah-Ta'if line is another world entirely. There, high above the foetid heat of the Tihamah, the ascending winds of the summer monsoon bring regular rains which have permitted the development of many hundreds of tiny farming hamlets. Outward and downward from the mountains aridity prevails, and settlements become fewer until the wandering way of life prevails once more.

Although the word "Hijaz" means "barrier", the history of the area and its peoples belies the term. The barrier referred to is the Great Escarpment which runs along, rather than across, the Hijaz, dividing it only from the interior plateaux. This same escarpment transforms the arid Hijaz into a natural corridor between the frankincense and myrrh country of Arabia Felix and the rich markets of the Fertile Crescent. Along this route a number of resting places and trading centres developed such as Makkah, Medina, Khaybar and Tabuk, where water was available to sustain a settled population. Into these settlements came the merchant adventurers of the past: the Nabataeans in their troglodyte city of Madain Salih; the Jews in their fortress towns of Yathrib and Khaybar; the Babylonians with their palace gardens at Tayma.

From pre-Islamic times the city of Makkah held a special place as a centre of pilgrimage and culture: a role which was greatly emphasized after the *hajj* brought new racial and cultural strains into the Hijaz and, as the word of the Prophet spread, so the diversity increased. Many who came stayed, while others brought

49

their skills to the service of the pilgrimage: from India came the grain merchants to Jiddah; from the Hadhramawt, the traders and importers; from Java the descendants of Muslim missionaries, and, from Turkey and Egypt, the soldiers to police the desert trails. Sometimes, as in Makkah and Jiddah, the ethnic types congregated into district *haras* or quarters of the city such as the Nusla Yamaniyya of Jiddah. Often, however, the individual groups were absorbed into the cosmopolitan embrace of the Hijazi way of life, only their names

*Al-Ula village near Madain Salih is typical of Western province architecture.*

distinguishing their origins: the al-Tunsis (Tunisia), the Daghestanis, the Yamanis (Yemen) and the al-Misris (Egypt).

Such are the demographic origins of cities like Jiddah, Makkah, Medina, Ta'if and Yanbu. In the smaller towns and oases of the north, a lasting symbiosis developed between, on the one hand, the itinerant Bedu such as the Bili, Huwaytat, Juhayna and the Harb, and on the other hand, the settled farmers of the agricultural oases. Very often the oases were dependencies of one or other Bedu group and were peopled by slaves and their descendants brought from Somalia, Eritrea and the *Suahil* (coast) of East Africa. This introduced a negroid

trait into the ethnic diversity which already existed, but, in general, brought none of the more pernicious aspects which accompanied slavery in the European Empires and Dominions.

In the south, along the coast, the African strain is strong and the Takarinah retain their distinctive thatched dwellings and racial features, though their African dialects have yielded to a universal use of Arabic. In the stone hamlets of the highlands, however, a Semitic homogeneity prevails, possibly because the farmers, pressed hard upon their pocket-handkerchief-sized farms, could neither use nor support a slave population.

The variety of landscape and habitat is reflected in the traditional social organization of the peoples. The Bedu form a complex skein of relationships based on common ancestry, so that lineage is not only a matter of great pride, and prodigious feats of memory, but also an entrée into a system of territorial rights, privileges and obligations. Binding this loose hegemony is a structure of, often hereditary, sheikhs wielding an even looser form of control. The villagers, on the other hand, may have some form of affinity by residence, but, in general, they belong to a wider community such as the Ghamid or Zahran tribes south of Ta'if. In the cities the situation is much more fluid. Some traditional sheikhly families are afforded their customary respect, but now they must compete with the great businessmen and traders, and an emerging group of technical and professional men.

Recent trends have accelerated many of the forces which shaped the population of the province. Most significant is the wealth created by the oil industry and the economic impetus it has given to the Hijaz, traditionally the commercial heart of the country. Following the boom years of the 1960s, increasing numbers of people began to flow into the Hijaz in several well-defined streams. At the same time, a clearly differentiated pattern of internal movement established and reinforced itself.

From Syria, Palestine, Egypt, Pakistan, Lebanon and Iraq have come the skilled and semi-skilled workers needed to fill the gaps left by sudden and rapid growth. They have concentrated mostly in the cities and towns, but some, notably doctors and teachers, have been sent into rural areas. This is seen by the Saudis as a stop-gap measure while the

*Intricate latticing and wood carving pay tribute to the skills developed over* *centuries of settled life in the Western highland city of Taif* (below).

# *The hill villages hold their own while the cities continue to burgeon.*

country trains its own qualified staff. Unskilled Yemenis have poured north to work on the building sites. Women from Ethiopia and Somalia have come seeking domestic employment.

Within the Hijaz the economic take-off has had no less an impact on the indigenous population. The Bedu have been fast quitting their traditional pastoral wanderings: exchanging the camel caravan for the Mercedes truck, the goathair tent for a breeze-block house on the outskirts of a town or city. Here too, job and origin are closely allied: find a taxi driver and you have found a Bedu.

The hill villages are just about holding their own and the cities continue to burgeon. The built-up area of Jiddah, for instance, expanded by 300 per cent between 1964 and 1971, and some 30 per cent of the city's population has moved in since 1970. Of the total Hijaz population of, perhaps 1,500,000, over 60 per cent are resident in the five main historic towns and there seems little doubt that the urban population is increasing both absolutely and relatively every year. The romance of the desert, if it ever existed, has yielded to the opportunities of the town. The rigours of subsistence farming in the mountains must now compete with the security of paid employment and an urban environment.

Yet all of the five major cities of the Western Province are of ancient foundation. Jiddah, commercial and industrial focus of the Western Province, has been an active port, certainly for 1,200 years, probably much longer. It is increasingly cosmopolitan. The other port of the region, Yanbu, until recently much sleepier than Jiddah, is also featured on the earliest maps and records of the west Arabian coast. Already, by the mid-1970s, it was beginning to take in new population in anticipation of the vital role planned for it in the country's economic blueprint.

Makkah, "the Blessed", lying at 2,000 feet in its hollow among the hills, is truly of the area, yet as the most venerated shrine in all Islam, is cosmopolitan in its spiritual role. So, too, Medina, also at 2,000 feet, centre of religious learning and site of the Islamic University's three colleges of Basic Religion, *Shari'ah* (Law), and Missions.

*Technical and engineering opportunities for citizens of the Hijaz multiply.*

The abundant wells of both cities have secured their survival over the centuries: both are growing fast today.

Lastly, Ta'if, by virtue of its high elevation (5,000 feet), became increasingly the annual refuge of those trying to escape the stifling summer heat of the lowland. Monarch, court and cabinet move to Ta'if in summer, making it for these months the second capital. For centuries Ta'if and its fine surrounding uplands have been the provider of fruit for the Hijaz, and of rosewater (*attar*), distilled from its vast acres of rose gardens, for the whole of Arabia, and, indeed, for Europe too.
(*See also* Sections 8 and 9).

**The People of the Eastern Province**
THE coastal strip of the Eastern Province is low with relatively plentiful water; it was here that oil was first discovered. The shore is sandy, with salt flats occurring in depressions. Sandy plains from Jubayl to Kuwait Bay, drifting sand and

dunes from Jubayl southward, a great belt of sand known as the ad-Dahna and a rock plateau called the Summan are the region's other main features.

For many years communication with other provinces in Saudi Arabia was negligible, apart from a rare caravan along the coast; but despite its reputation for bleakness and ferocity there was a steady movement of people into the region from the sea. Enterprising individuals came wherever social conditions allowed travel routes to develop, thus adding non-tribal sectors to the population and building up coastal centres. This polyglot population became socially integrated with other groups but remained politically subordinate to the tribal factions of the interior. Today, that subordination has been overtaken by the wealth and power of the coastal cities

and petroleum towns into which people from all over the country, but particularly from the region itself, are flooding. The recent expansion of the complex of towns encompassed by the port-city of Dammam, Al-Khubar and Dhahran (which is wholly comprised of the adjacent compounds of Aramco and the University of Petroleum and Minerals) is phenomenal.

Inland, the flares of unutilized gas – their smoke by day, their orange flame by night – pinpoint where industrial man has intruded upon the traditional lands of the tribe. Even so, there is always a "beyond" in Arabia; and beyond this intrusion the nomad does indeed pursue his life. The experience of the al-Murrah

*Football is the core of the Kingdom's new sporting endeavour.*

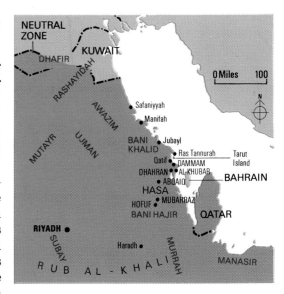

tribe, for example, along the northern edge of the Empty Quarter, is one of inescapable heat and shortage alleviated

*Herd of camels near Abqaiq* (above).
*Hofuf picnic* (left).

by space and freedom of movement. These tribesmen move their entire household in pursuit of grazing for their animals every few days throughout most of the year. They live largely on their animals' milk products and to a lesser extent on their meat, on dates, and on small amounts of rice and unleavened bread. Their inherited independence makes it difficult for them to fit into schemes of modern development.

The agriculturalist is generally better fed and better sheltered. The tribes of Bani Khalid and Bani Hajir live in the Haradh and Hofuf oases. The area in which Hofuf is situated bears the name Hasa, which signifies the "murmuring" of streams. The gardens of Hasa are magnificent, well tended groves amid colonnades of great palms. Standing back from Hasa, a striking natural feature pierces the skyline – Jebel Garrah, a mountain of soft rock that wind and occasional torrents have eroded into a fantastic complex of tunnels and spurs, hollows and pinnacles.

The oil industry has brought increasing prosperity to the whole province. Even deep in the hinterland tribesmen dress better and live more safely and satisfactorily than their grandfathers did. Oil turned the port of Dammam into the thriving centre of the region, and its neighbour al-Khubar – once a fishing village whose inhabitants supplemented their living with pearling – into the expanding centre of business. Fairly copious underground water is today supplemented by desalinisation plants (e.g. at Jubayl, Ras al Khafji, Al-Khubar, and Al-Uqair). The coastal population, amid their extensive groves of date palms, thrive. It is a region of very ancient settlement, at one time controlled from the islet of Tarut, now linked by a road to the mainland.

## The People of the North

NORTHERN Saudi Arabia is part of the great Syrian Desert of rock, gravel plains and lava beds. For thousands of years one of the most important trade routes connecting the Mediterranean and central Arabia passed through Wadi al-Sirhan and the oasis of Jawf.

Northern Arabia is typified by the Nafud, a great expanse of rolling red dunes which cover 22,000 square miles and reach almost to the Jordan border; their deep orange-red at dawn and dusk is offset by the grey-green of tamarisks here and there. Otherwise it contains few watering places and affords good grazing for camels, sheep and goats only in winter and spring.

To reach the Fertile Crescent and the Mediterranean, the southern Arabian merchants had therefore to enlist the Arabians of the north, who were masters of the desert. Only they knew the great wadi systems, the location of desert wells and pools, the oasis way stations, the best grazing, and the alliances and hostilities of the tribes. And only they were familiar with the efficient use of the camel, which alone made desert travel possible.

Chief amongst these, the Anazah, from whom Al Saud are in part descended, comprises many distinct tribal units, of which the largest is the Ruwalah, the most powerful tribe in the north Arabian

desert for centuries. Rivalling the Anazah – and once a challenge to Ibn Saud's power – is the great tribe Shammar, with the headquarters of its paramount sheikhs, the Ibn Rashid, at Hail. And to the west range the Huwaytat, with a tradition of enmity towards both; it was their paramount sheikh, Audah Abu Tayi, whom Lawrence called "the greatest fighting man in northern Arabia."

Amid the warring of these noble Beduin tribes, lesser shepherd tribes were left to rear their flocks in peace, providing they paid for the privilege. Below these in the social hierarchy of the desert in times past were the Sana, a blacksmith tribe, and the semi-gypsy Sulabar, a tribe of tinkers and trackers. Only the neutral Sulabar stay in the desert all year, for with their small donkey herds, they are able to use shallow wells.

Along with poems, stories and songs, camel-raiding was a favourite occupation for enhancing the reputation; herds that were too big to be guarded properly were attacked and spare camels were thus distributed about the desert.

King Abdul Aziz put a stop to the feuding and raiding of the Beduin in the late 1930s. He was the first ruler for centuries to be able to enforce his will on the Beduin tribes, who respected their powerful desert leader and became his most devoted subjects. Many have now abandoned their nomadic life to settle in the oases and cities. They are proving very adaptable, both in their willingness to settle to city life, and in their acceptance of new ways in the desert. Many families have abandoned herding camels. Sheep are more profitable, and grazing and water can be provided for them thanks to motor transport.

The tribes of northern Arabia believe that Beduin ways are best, and that the desert made the Beduin what they were: God sends the rain so that the herds will have pasture; from the herds they have milk to drink, hair for their tents, and young to sell for grain and coffee. Only in the desert is man truly free.

The slight winter rains fall in a different location every year and, after the star *Canopus* is visible in the night sky (October-November), everyone wants information on rain. From reports, which they check with everyone they meet, the herders can tell where the grazing will be, its quality and quantity.

Traditionally the Ruwalah have divi-

ded men into *hazar* (permanent house dwellers) and *arab* (people who live in the movable black tent); of the latter, the true Beduin are those who breed camels and for ten months live in the interior of the desert (see Beduin Life, Section 10). They eat twice a day, the main meal in the evening, a diet based on milk and supplemented by bread, coffee, dates and sometimes locusts. As the various tribes differ in dialect, so do they in dress. They all wear the same basic *thobe*, but of varying colours, cut and ornament. If a *Rwejli* sights a troop of riders in the distance, he can tell at once whether they are Ruwalah and of what clan.

A single family can manage forty to fifty camels, but it can survive on fifteen. Summer encampments on the high ground have been known to exceed 10,000 tents. The sheikh is the head of the tribe, chosen from the leading family for his courage, generosity and mediating skill. Today they deal with the government over concessions for the drilling of new oil wells, rents payable for pipelines crossing their grazing, jobs at the new administrative centres and vehicle licensing.

But northern Arabia is not all great red Nafud desert, and its people are not all nomadic Bedu. The main town in northern Arabia is Tabuk, whose busy main streets are modern dual carriageways taking the heavy traffic of container trucks bringing goods overland from Europe to the Kingdom. Graceful eucalyptus trees grow in Tabuk, and a Turkish fort, nearly 300 years old, stands on its edge. Then there are the oasis towns, founded on sources of perennial water, and supported by an economy of date palms and tribal markets, with a cultural life of their own. Dates were the staple food of the oases, and all other plants – fruit trees, vegetables, and alfalfa – were cultivated in their shade. And many oases established links with a local bedouin tribe who would defend them, and who may indeed have made their headquarters in the oasis town.

Typical of these is the ancient well-watered town of Jawf, some 220 miles north-east of Tayma and linked to it by a new asphalt road. The old town is sited on the slopes of a great basin surrounded by cliffs. Beside it stands the new town and both are dominated by a great castle, Qasr Mared. Its mosque, believed to have been founded by Caliph Umar, is one of the oldest in the land, and has a particularly beautiful minaret.

Beyond the crumbling stone walls of the old town, and the white concrete buildings of the new, stretch the palm groves, orchards, and even meadows of the oasis. Amid fields of grazing cows one might easily forget one was in the great Nafud. But around it all the red dunes stretch away to the horizon.

It is now linked by road to the next oasis way-station, Sakaka, famous for its lively rock carvings on the Jebel Burnus, an outcrop projecting from the near-vertical rock which is crowned by the Zabal fort. Continuing north from there, the next oasis town is Badanah, which is only thirty miles from the Iraqi border.

## The People of the South-West

THE traditional name for the south-west, Asir, means "the difficult region" – and so indeed it is, for the outsider. The range which, as one moves southwards, becomes the south-western massif of peaks and terraced valleys and plateaux at over 6,500 feet actually begins with the hills to the north of Ta'if and includes the hill of Arafat, known to all pilgrims to Mecca. But the route southwards through the foothills was indeed a difficult one, until the building of today's highway, and more difficult still from the west, where the great block of mountain rises precipitously from the low coastal plain, the Tihamah.

To the east, the Asir slopes more gently down into the largest sand-sea in the world, the Rub al-Khali. Southwards, these highlands of Saudi Arabia are

*In the settled and agricultural south-west, traditional veiling of women has not taken hold, and vivid colours and jewellery characterize the apparel.*
Right: *a similarly vigorous sense of colour is exploited in the interiors of lowland homes.*

*The heat of the charcoal is intensified by the bellows worked* (above) *by the craftsman's knee. The tradition of patterning by rows of fused beads* (bottom left) *is one that has survived from the Ancient World, and for which the Etruscans were famed. This technique of granulation is highly skilled, since it requires fusing minute metal beads at great temperature* (below).

## Metalcraft

The skills of silver-smithing (*right*) are not lost, nor the sense of design in, for example, these door handles (*left*). *Above:* an elder of the Asir region today wears his dagger for ceremonial purposes and (*far left*) intricate workmanship is evidenced in an elaborate sheath.

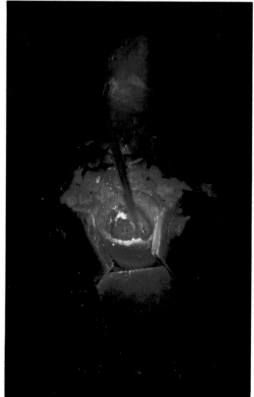

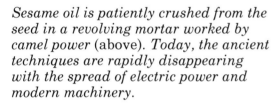

*Sesame oil is patiently crushed from the seed in a revolving mortar worked by camel power* (above). *Today, the ancient techniques are rapidly disappearing with the spread of electric power and modern machinery.*

separated by deep valleys and a rugged causeway of uplands from the mountains of northern Yemen. The people south of the border are different in appearance, custom, temperament and religious attitude from their Saudi neighbours. But both regions catch the monsoon rains.

The south-west is the one well-watered region of Saudi Arabia. The annual rains have cut deep gorges beneath the high peaks and valley walls. To hold the soil from the ferocity of the rains, the farmers have – for thousands of years – turned the valleys and bowls into beautifully contoured walled steps. In this ancient terrain grow every manner of cereals, fodder crops and fruit.

Likewise, to protect their dwellings, the people have evolved the unique practice of mortaring into the outer walls row upon row of shale louvres. In so fine a natural setting, a sense of design prevails. Homes are washed outside with colours that intensify the upland sunlight. Smithing abounds, as does the wearing of jewellery. Strong colours prevail among the women's dress. There is a celebrated grace and confidence among the highland people.

The south-west is not all highland. To the west, beneath the steep, sometimes vertical escarpment, lies the lowland Tihamah. And the Tihamah in turn presents two different aspects, the valleys, and a sandy plain stretching towards the Red Sea. Generally speaking, the people in the highlands are taller than those in the lowlands.

The heavier and relatively dependable rainfall has allowed south-westerners, for the most part, to live a settled life as cultivators of the soil and as herdsmen. The different regions are identified according to the tribal groups which inhabit them. The most important groups, from north to south, are Zahran, Ghamid, Hajr, Asir, Shahran, and Qahtan. When referring to a particular area one says for example, Bilad Zahran, "the land of Zahran", or Bilad Asir, "the land of Asir".

In the highlands, villages are found in clusters and the appearance of these differs often significantly from area to area. Thus between Bilad Dhahran and Bilad Hajr, the houses are built of stone, while southwards towards Asir, both stone and mud houses are found, the latter being more numerous. Before the expedition of the late King Faisal (then a Prince) some two generations ago, which brought it into the Kingdom of Saudi Arabia, this south-western area was a warlike region where feuds between villages were commonplace.

The disused watchtowers which dot the landscape everywhere are witnesses of that period.

Because of their altitude the highlands are cool in the summer with plentiful rain. This makes it a good region for agriculture. Indeed, the highlanders are an agricultural people, growing barley, millet, vegetables and fruit, but the date palm is not grown in the highlands. The terraced field, to be seen everywhere on the mountain slopes, is commonest of all. To ensure a better yield, irrigation is used in both orchards and non-terraced fields generally found in the drier and flatter areas. The water may come either from a water course swelled by rain, or from a well. In many areas where irrigation is mechanized, wells are drilled directly on the farm land, and pumps are placed in the old wells to replace muscle power.

The highland farms are compact, orderly and highly productive. Sophisticated marketing and excellent road and air communications today enable produce from the high Asir to reach Jiddah, Riyadh and the Gulf coast. The farmers enjoy a high standard of living, many of them owning cars or trucks or mechanized agricultural equipment. Yet, as is refreshingly true elsewhere in Saudi Arabia, new techniques and rising expectations and the advent of schools, hospitals, modern roads and dams, have not destroyed respect for traditional values and styles. For example, while some "functional" modern buildings have gone up in Abha, in the Asir as a whole homes are built in the highly distinctive, time-tested styles, with the encouragement of an enlightened regional administration.

Inevitably – and desirably – the highland people will be brought increasingly into contact with the "outside" world as a result of the certain growth in the tourist trade. Now that major roads have been opened from both north and south, and with the expansion of already efficient airline services to Khamis Mushayt, the flow of visitors escaping the summer heat of the lowland plateaux

will swell year by year, affecting both the economy and the outlook of the indigenous people.

At the southern end of the south-west region lies the oasis of Najran, below the highland chain. Although linguistically it must be considered part of Najd, geographically it is part of the south-west. The architecture, of mud and straw, belongs to the south-west and not to central Najd. Furthermore, the half-moon shaped windows of tinted glass above the main windows of the houses in Najran are Yemeni in style.

The oasis of Najran lies in sandy desert and in summer the temperatures are high. Since it is the sand desert in par-

ticular which supports nomadic life, Beduin come into close contact with the settled elements of the population of Najran. The main agricultural products are dates, as the climate allows the growth of the date palm, and grapes, which are famous in the south.

The clothing of the men consists of long shirt-like robes, like those of their counterparts in Najd, but here the width of the lower edge of the garment is greater. They may be white, blue or olive in colour. The headgear is usually a red and white checkered headcloth. The women wear long, waisted colourful dresses, often heavily embroidered. Stress is on individuality. In the Asir

region the peasant women wear broad brimmed sombrero-type hats. Women rarely veil the face.

In the Tihamah the population is of two types, sedentary people living in villages, and nomads. The sedentary population of the valleys is in close contact with the highlanders. There are dirt roads winding up the steep mountain passes separating the two regions. Today, the impressive Jizan highway is the most used link between these valleys and the flatter lands bordering the Red Sea.

A good example of a village of the valleys, the Tihamah, is Rijal, west of Abha. The village is of stone and built on two sides of a narrow valley. The way the houses rise on the slopes gives the impression of skyscrapers. Rijal used to be a trade centre, but the shops are now closed down as the Abha-Jizan road has diverted their trade. But the village is still renowned in the region for goldsmithing.

The interiors of the houses in Rijal are attractive. Even more than in Abha the walls are decorated with gay stylized designs painted by the women. For more decoration colourful imported enamelware adorns the shelves on the walls.

In the Rijal area agriculture is restricted to the sides of the valley. There is little terracing. The fields in the bottom of the valley have high retaining walls to protect them from the violence of flash floods. Higher up the slopes towards the highlands, where the climate is cooler, coffee has become a successful crop.

The other type of population found in the valley are the nomads who raise sheep and goats. They are unlike the Beduin of central Arabia. The men often

*The influence of Africa is seen in the conical homes of the southern Tihamah coast of the south-west* (left and below), *while characteristic Yemeni features are found in the south-western villages* (far left) *bordering on Saudi Arabia's mountainous neighbour.*

Below: *hats are worn by the women of the coastal south-west – a design reminiscent of Welsh hats in north-west Europe.*

61

go bare-chested, wearing a length of colourful cloth around their waists. Their side-arm is a sword-like curved dagger just under a metre long, a protection against leopards. Often their headgear is a tall, black, brimless hat with a flattish backward-sloping top. The women wear tall straw hats with brims, similar to the hats worn by South American Indians.

Coastal Tihamah is flat and sandy. The majority of the population is agricultural, growing mostly millet. In Wadi Baysh, about forty miles north-east of Jizan, is a vast expanse of millet covering about six hundred square miles. Much of this region is newly watered by rain floods stored in the massive Jizan dam, which is transforming a former wilderness into a significant grain-producing area, including an extensive experimental farm run by the Government. The visual impression of so much millet is strongly reminiscent of the endless maize fields of the American Mid-West.

Southwards down from the Red Sea coast, the influence of Africa is clearly to be seen among the people and their style of life. Conical houses are built in clusters behind high reed palisades. On the flats inland from Jizan, these villages present remarkable toothed silhouettes on the horizon. The single-chamber houses, lined with mud, are brilliantly painted inside with imaginative designs that reach to the pinnacle of the under-roof. Fishing is a major local industry, the Spanish mackerel being a principal source of protein food. The traditions of seamanship have maintained links with the Eritrean coasts across the Red Sea.

In the extreme south-west where the mountains rise sharply out of the plains, the lowland markets on the Saudi side of the frontier are frequently thronged with Yemenis with produce to sell. Higher Saudi standards of living bring higher prices.

In both the highlands and the lowlands the many markets constitute an important part of the people's life. The market in a village may be open every day or only once a week. If the latter is the case, market day is on a fixed day of the week, and, like anywhere else, that day is a social occasion for the people of the neighbouring villages. Often the name of the village incorporates the name of the day on which the market was customarily held. Thus: Khamis Mushayt, "the Thursday of Mushayt", Ahad Rufaydah, "the Sunday of Rufaydah", Sabt Tanumah, "the Saturday of Tanumah". Such places are usually referred to by the people of the region only by the name of their market day: Khamis, Ahad, Sabt. In some towns, where the market nowadays is open all week, as in Abha and Khamis Mushayt, market day sees more wares on display than other days of the week. On market day one may find nomads coming up from the

Tihamah to trade with the highlanders. In the markets, in addition to food and modern goods, one finds local products, such as straw baskets and hats, keys and nails made of locally mined iron, or, as in Najran, salt mined in the Empty Quarter.

The people of the south-west pride themselves on their hospitality. When a guest arrives, he is feasted by his host and various other members of the family who, on a more prolonged visit, take turns to entertain the guest. Besides the standard fare of lamb and rice, a dish offered to the guest is *arikah*, half-baked bread dough served in a big circular dish covered in brown honey. The guest fashions pieces of dough between his fingers into the shape of a spoon which he then dips into a side dish filled with white honey.

Weddings are a most important social occasion. Guests come, often from far away, to participate in the festivities.

There is dancing and singing on two separate days, one day for the men, and the following day for the women. On the men's day the guests dance in public in lines or circles, singing to the accompaniment of drums. There are also dagger dances.

On the women's day there are similar songs and dances performed in a marquee to the accompaniment of drums and pestle and mortar which serve as a percussion instrument. The women put on all their jewellery on such an occasion. Such ceremonial reflects the rich oral traditions of song and poetry of the people of the south-west.

(*See also* Sections 8 and 9)

*The highland south-west is today a sought-after resort during the heat of the lowland summer. A bluish wash gives a jewel-like quality to an Abha farmstead. The slate louvres ensure weather-proofing (left).*

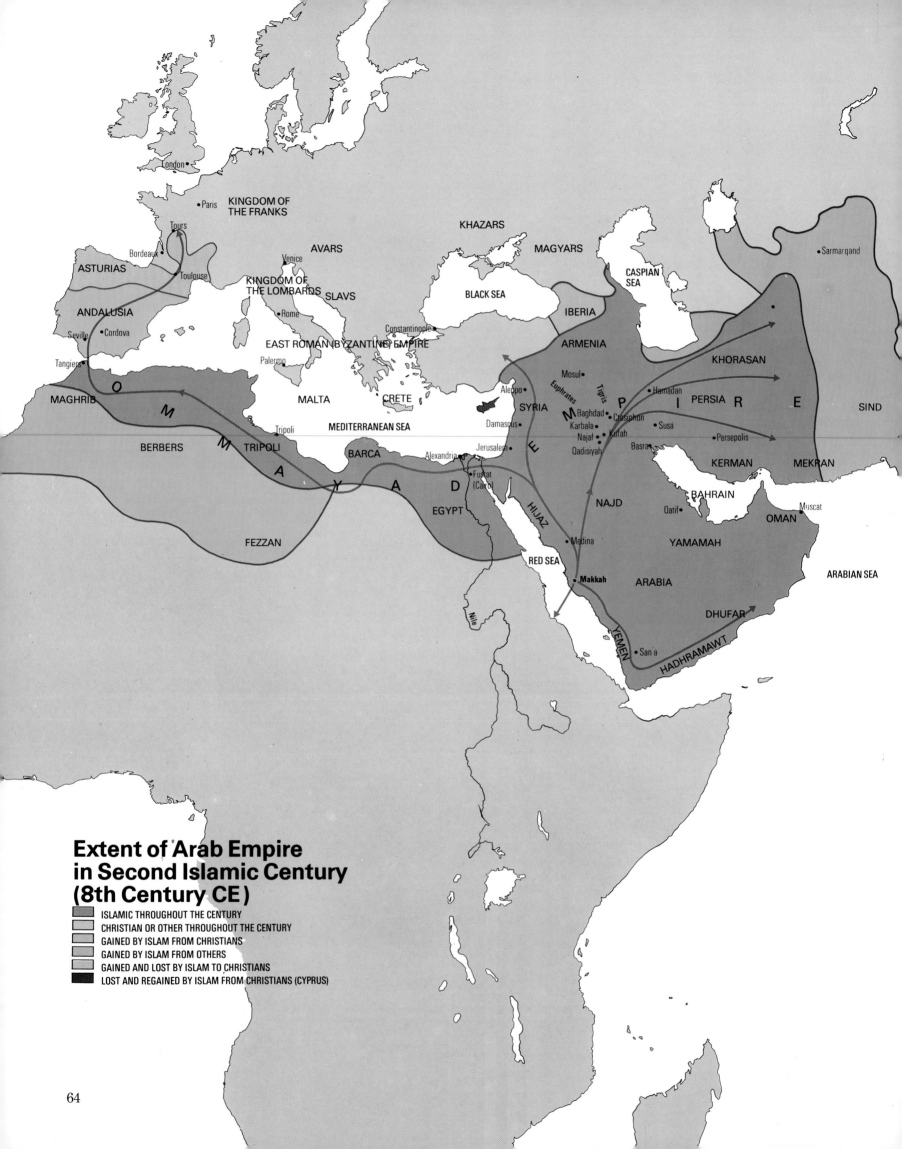

# Extent of Arab Empire
# in Second Islamic Century
# (8th Century CE)

ISLAMIC THROUGHOUT THE CENTURY
CHRISTIAN OR OTHER THROUGHOUT THE CENTURY
GAINED BY ISLAM FROM CHRISTIANS
GAINED BY ISLAM FROM OTHERS
GAINED AND LOST BY ISLAM TO CHRISTIANS
LOST AND REGAINED BY ISLAM FROM CHRISTIANS (CYPRUS)

London

KINGDOM OF
THE FRANKS

Paris

KHAZARS

MAGYARS

CASPIAN
SEA

Sarmarqand

AVARS

ASTURIAS

Venice

KINGDOM OF
THE LOMBARDS

SLAVS

BLACK SEA

IBERIA

ARMENIA

KHORASAN

Bordeaux

Tours

Toulouse

ANDALUSIA

Rome

Mosul

Euphrates

Tigris

Hamadan

PERSIA

Seville

Cordova

Constantinople

EAST ROMAN (BYZANTINE) EMPIRE

Aleppo

SYRIA

M

Baghdad

Ctesiphon

Susa

Tangiers

Palermo

MALTA

CRETE

Damascus

Karbala

Najaf

Kufah

Persepolis

SIND

MAGHRIB

O

M

MEDITERRANEAN SEA

Jerusalem

Qadisiyah

Basra

KERMAN

MEKRAN

Tripoli

M

A

BARCA

Alexandria

E

NAJD

BAHRAIN

BERBERS

TRIPOLI

Y

A

D

Fustat
(Cairo)

HIJAZ

Qatif

Muscat

OMAN

EGYPT

Medina

YAMAMAH

FEZZAN

RED SEA

Makkah

ARABIA

ARABIAN SEA

Nile

DHUFAR

YEMEN

San'a

HADHRAMAWT

64

PUNJAB

# 4 History

*From a pre-historic past whose civilizations are only today being revealed by archaeologists, the country became the illumined focus of countless people, from Spain to India, as the centre of swiftly expanding Islam. But a firmly unified Saudi Arabia was forged only on the third attempt, by the audacity and vision of King Abdul Aziz.*

*Liths bearing Aramaic inscriptions were found in Tayma (left). Scripts excavated in various parts of Arabia, as that in Himyaritic and Lithianic from the south and north (above), yield evidence of sophisticated civilizations reaching back some three millennia. The function of these fragments, which tell of priests and kings, was votive.*

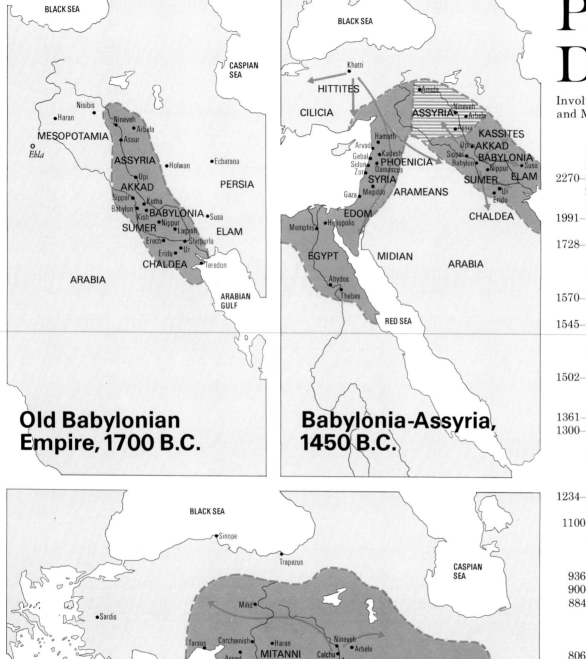

**Old Babylonian Empire, 1700 B.C.**

**Babylonia-Assyria, 1450 B.C.**

**Assyrian Empire, 7th Century B.C.**

# Pre-Islamic Datelist

Involving Arabs and Related Peoples of the Near and Middle East

**BC**

| | |
|---|---|
| 2350 | Sargon builds Akkad |
| 2300 | Ascendancy of Ebla (Tell Mardikh) |
| 2270–2233 | Reign of Naram-Sin of Sumeria |
| 2200 | Decline of Pharaonic Old Kingdom |
| 2000 | Zenith of civilization of Dilmun |
| 1991–1792 | 12th dynasty of Middle Kingdom of Pharaohs |
| 1728–1686 | Hammurabi reigns (founder of Babylon) |
| 1700 | Abraham leads migration to Palestine from Ur |
| 1570–1545 | 18th Egyptian dynasty founded in Thebes by Ahmose |
| 1545–1525 | Amenhotep of Egypt moves capital to Akhetaton (Tell al-Amarna) |
| 1530 | Hittites sack Babylon. End of first Amorite dynasty |
| 1502–1448 | Egyptian conquest of North Nubia and neighbouring Mediterranean coast under Thutmose III |
| 1361–1352 | Tutankhamun reigns |
| 1300–1200 | Rise of Sabaeans under the Queen of Sheba in South Arabia |
| 1280 | Treaty signed. North Syria recognized as Hittite, South Syria (Palestine) as Egyptian |
| 1234–1215 | Hebrews' exodus from Egypt |
| 1200 | Damascus gained by Aramaeans |
| 1100–888 | Rise of Sidonian state |
| 1020 | Saul anointed. First King of the Hebrews |
| 945 | Shishak of Libya ousts Pharaohs |
| 936–923 | Reign of Solomon |
| 900–842 | Rise of Damascus |
| 884–859 | Rise of Ashur-nasir-pal and an initial Assyrian conquest successful |
| 875 | Israel becomes a vassal of Damascus |
| 814 | Carthage founded by Phoenicians |
| 806–732 | Decline of Aramaean Damascus |
| 733 | Tiglath-Pileser of Assyria defeats Israel |
| 732 | Tiglath-Pileser overthrows Damascus, centre of Aramaean power |
| 727–722 | Shalmanese V of Assyria conquers Tyre |
| 722–705 | Sargonid dynasty. Ascendancy of Assyria |
| 705–681 | Sennacherib destroys Babylon |
| 671 | Tirhaka of Ethiopian dynasty in Egypt defeated by Assyrians under Esarhaddon |
| 600–593 | Phoenicians under Pharaoh Necho circumnavigate Africa |
| 605–562 | Reign of Nebuchadnezzar II. Restoration of Babylon and creation of the Hanging Gardens. |
| 586 | Nebuchadnezzar destroys Jerusalem, capital of Judah |
| 572 | Nebuchadnezzar conquers Tyre |
| 550–529 | Cyrus of Anshan in Elam founds Achaemenid dynasty in Persia |
| 546 | Cyrus overthrows Croesus and seizes Sardis |

539 Babylonians under Belshazzar
defeated by Persians
539–332 Phoenicia under Persian rule
529–521 Cambises of Persia conquers Egypt
521–485 Darius I establishes Persepolis
490 Darius loses Battle of Marathon to
Athenians
480 Spartans defeat Persians at
Thermopylae
480 Xerxes of Persia routed by Greeks at
sea battle of Salamis
446 Artaxerxes I makes peace treaty with
Greeks
330 Alexander the Great burns Persepolis
323 Alexander the Great conquers
Babylon and dies there
312–280 Seleucus I founds the Syrian
Kingdom
300 Petra becomes Nabataean capital
226 Parthians defeated by Sassanids
218 Hannibal of Phoenicia crosses the
Alps
202 Hannibal defeated by Romans
133 Attilid Kingdom creates extensive
province of Asia
169 Antiochus IV of Syria defeats
Ptolemy IV of Egypt
85 Nabateans take Coele-Syria from
Seleucids
69–83 Tigranes of Armenia makes conquests
in Macedonian Kingdom
64 Romans conquer Syria
51–30 Rule of Cleopatra in Egypt
48 Julius Caesar conquers Pompey at
Zela
44 Caesar murdered
30 Roman annexation of Egypt
37–4 Rule of Herod the Great of Judaea
6 Birth of Jesus (as calculated by
scholars)

**CE**
0–100 Himyarites migrate to Axum
(Abyssinia)
27 Death of Jesus
70 Titus, Roman Emperor, starves
Jerusalem into surrender
106 Romans destroy Nabataean Petra
114–116 Rome at war with Parthia
123 Hadrian renounces Euphrates
territory
195–199 Severus conquers Mesopotamia
226 Foundation of the new Persian
Empire
268–273 Palmyra conquers Syria,
Mesopotamia and parts of Egypt
330 Constantinople becomes seat of
Eastern half of Roman Empire
354–430 Life of Augustine
433–453 Attila, ruler of the Huns
525 Abyssinians conquer Yemen
568–572 Fall of Rome
571 Birth of Muhammad
575 Khosran I of the Sassanids expels
Abyssinians from the Yemen
586 Muhammad marries Khadijah of the
Quraysh tribe
610 Muhammad's first revelation outside
Makkah
614 Persians conquer Damascus,
Jerusalem and Egypt
622 Muhammad flees from Makkah to
Medina, the *hijrah* and official
beginning of the Moslem era
632 Death of Muhammad

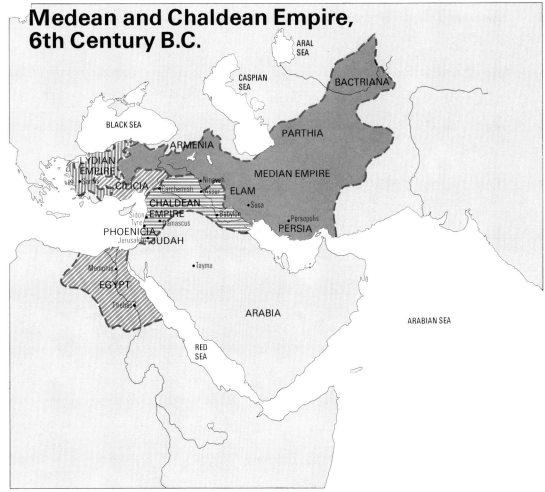

# Medean and Chaldean Empire, 6th Century B.C.

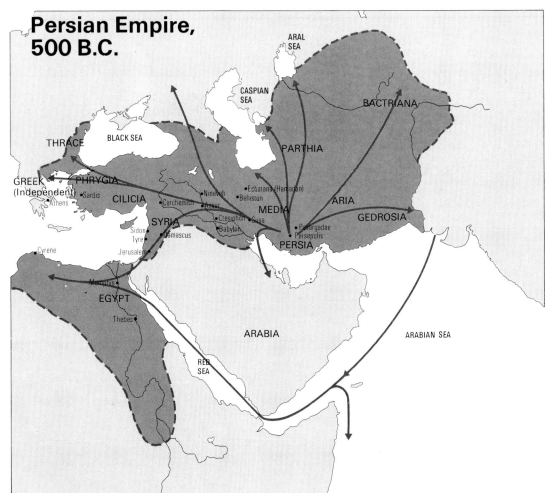

# Persian Empire, 500 B.C.

# The "Age of Darkness" to the Coming of the Prophet

SCHOLARS may disagree about the location of the cradle of the human race, but about the cradle of civilization there is no disagreement. It lies in the area called the "Near East" and is composed of the Fertile Crescent – Mesopotamia (modern Iraq), Syria, Palestine, Egypt, Anatolia (Asia Minor, Turkey) and Persia (Iran). At one time most of Europe and much of the Middle East was covered in ice, but to the south of this ice-sheet, Africa and Arabia were fertile with grass and streams flowing in what are nowadays dry *wadis*. The climate gradually changed, the ice-sheet retreated and the grasslands advanced.

International highways have always

linked Africa, Europe and Asia, and these continents provided the stage not only for the world's three great monotheistic religions but also for some of the earliest, most spectacular and enduring discoveries and achievements of man. The civilizations which developed in this area passed on to later generations a matchlessly rich heritage of science, art, literature and philosophy.

Civilization as we recognise it probably began in the vicinity of the basins of the Rivers Tigris and Euphrates in Mesopotamia, the River Nile in Egypt and the River Indus valley. From here it spread over the Middle East, while men in the rest of the world still lived in a primitive state. The area of the Middle East, originally a European geographical term loosely used to designate that part of south-western Asia nearest Europe, has a recorded history filled with drama – the rise and fall of empires, the growth and decline of great cities, the ascendancy and decline of great peoples, wars, invasions and deportations, kings and emperors, treachery, intrigue and disasters.

Long before written records existed

the people of the Middle East had developed urban life, with ordered governments, religions, and social and economic institutions. Earlier still, those who occupied the Fertile Crescent had discovered metal, realized its potential and worked it into tools and weapons which replaced the more primitive stone implements of preceding generations. Civilization first developed where it did because this was the one area of the globe which provided the climate, vegetation, and fauna necessary for the transition from a life of nomadic grazing and hunting to a settled existence. Through migration, invasion or cultural osmosis these remarkable accomplishments eventually found their way into the Eastern Mediterranean and the Aegean islands, and thence to the European mainland where they formed a prelude to the classical civilizations of Greece and Rome, parents to all Western civilizations. The full extent of the debt that Greece and Rome owed this area was hardly appreciated until recently, a debt which does not make the glory that was Greece less glorious, or the grandeur that was Rome less grand. In fact, it was not until the early nineteenth century that scholars began to rediscover the empires of Egypt, Babylonia and Assyria and to reconstruct their cultural institutions. As for the Hittites and their empire in Anatolia, the rediscovery began as late as the twentieth century. Historians and archaeologists disagree about some of the detail of pre-Islamic history but during the last century a great deal has been ascertained by exploration and excavation. Only since the 1960s has the role of what today is Saudi Arabia begun to be revealed by the discoveries of archaeologists.

The Sumerians created one of the earliest civilizations in an area adjoining Arabia. By 3000 BC they occupied their new homeland of Sumer at the head of the Arabian Gulf, at the watershed of the Tigris and Euphrates rivers. The principal city was Ur. Other cities founded then were Erech, Lagash and Nippur. Eridu was a burgeoning port on the coast, although its site is now some 130 miles inland, and the other cities are just mounds in the desert. Irrigation, trade, the use of money and codes of laws were all developed by the Sumerians, and their clay tablets of pictorial and syllabic writing became the cuneiform script widely used in the ancient Middle East. Our modern science of astronomy is derived from their advanced knowledge of the stars, supplemented by Babylonian, Greek and Islamic influences. They used wheeled vehicles, and built beautiful and imposing arches with dried bricks as a feature of their tower temples, known as *ziggurats*. Archaeologists have found good examples of utensils, sculpture and other remnants of the Sumerian way of life in the tombs which were con-

structed for each dead leader, and which habitually included all the men and women who had been his close servants in his lifetime.

But contacts between the rich lands of Mesopotamia and the coast of eastern Saudi Arabia were already vigorous during the preceding two millennia, the earliest traces beginning in 5500 BC and continuing through the rise of Dilmun (today's Bahrein and neighbouring mainland) during the third millennium, when the Arabian Gulf ports were of great importance, as excavations inland from Abqaiq have proved.

Traditionally the people known as the

Semites are thought to be descended from Shem, the eldest son of Noah. Their language was closely related to that of the Sumerians and they lived a nomadic existence north of Sumer, eventually filtering into central and northern Mesopotamia. Gradually they built up their own city states such as Kish and Mari, having for many years plundered their more advanced neighbours, the Sumerians. About 2360 BC the first empire of recorded history emerged, that of Akkad, in the area which became known as Babylonia. Akkadian influence spread beyond Mesopotamia to Arabia. This empire was destroyed after a couple of centuries, and, although Akkadian Sem-

*The exceptionally well-preserved rock tombs and dwellings of Madain Salih in north-western Saudi Arabia give vivid evidence of the civilization of the*

*Nabataeans who flourished two thousand years ago on the rich trade in frankincense and myrrh – the same Arab stock that built Petra, in Jordan. The*

*finely decorated façades and shrines carved out of the living rock show the unmistakable influence of Greece* (opposite above).

*Nabataean life was strictly controlled by an elaborate priesthood, occasionally depicted in stone relief (far right); temples served also as palaces. The Nabataean ancestors of today's Arabs were masters at extracting water from precipitation in the most forbidding of arid territories, and preserving it in underground cisterns hewn out of the rock. Pinnacles of soft rock (opposite) became natural citadels.*

ites continued to be one of the main elements in the population, other Semitic powers gained ascendancy, notably the invaders of Mesopotamia, the Amorites, who came from the present area of Syria.

The ancient city of Babylon was ruled in the eighteenth century BC by the Amorite, King Hammurabi. Basic laws were formalized and great progress was made in the fields of scholarship and science, especially mathematics and astronomy. The Hittites overwhelmed the Amorites in approximately 1600 BC. These tribes from Asia Minor absorbed Syria and made treaties with the Egyptians before they too were overcome by an invasion of barbarians from Europe in 1200 BC. The Kassite dynasty ruled Babylonia successfully for four hundred

years. Thereafter it came to be ruled by Assyria.

The Assyrians had settled in northern Mesopotamia; their capital was Assur on the Tigris, named after their national god. Nineveh later became the imperial capital, and the cultural ideas of the Babylonians and the Sumerians were developed by the Assyrians with their own characteristic variations. Very active commercially, they used stamped silver bars for money, employed letters of credit and originated the practice of lending money to neighbouring people at an interest rate of twenty or thirty per cent. They constructed huge libraries for cuneiform documents and great palaces and temples. From the tenth to the seventh centuries they remained

*Madain Salih, though built by Nabataean Arabs, was strongly influenced by the architecture of Greece. This north-western Arabian twin of Petra was built to forestall the Romans in their attempt to take over the spice and frankincense trade, which the Nabataeans controlled until 106 CE.*

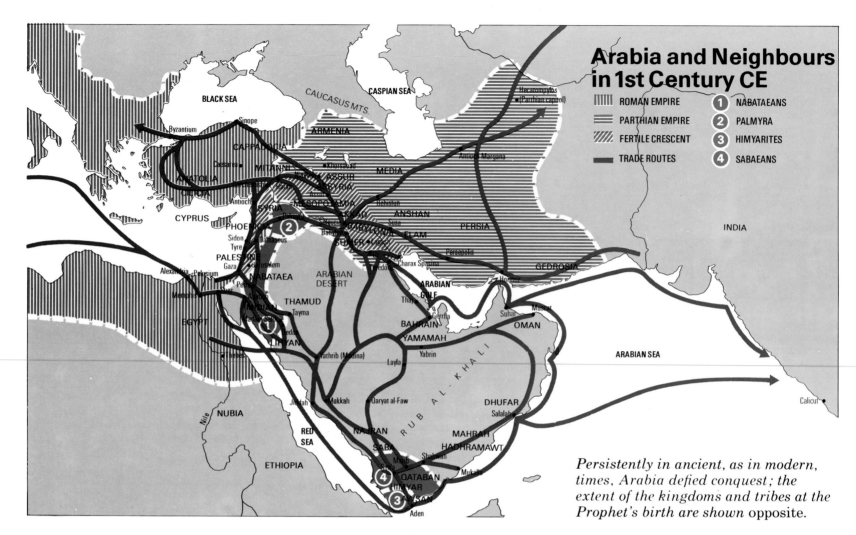

## Arabia and Neighbours in 1st Century CE

|||||| ROMAN EMPIRE  ① NABATAEANS
≡ PARTHIAN EMPIRE  ② PALMYRA
///// FERTILE CRESCENT  ③ HIMYARITES
▬ TRADE ROUTES  ④ SABAEANS

*Persistently in ancient, as in modern, times, Arabia defied conquest; the extent of the kingdoms and tribes at the Prophet's birth are shown opposite.*

powerful, employing iron weapons to arm their bellicose formations of infantry, cavalry and archers. Eventually in 612 BC the Assyrians were overthrown by a combination of Medes, Babylonians and Persians, and Nineveh was destroyed.

Babylon continued to be powerful and remained a centre of scholarship. The city was destroyed by the Assyrian conqueror Sennacherib as a punishment for rebellion, but was rebuilt by his heir, Esarhaddon. It later became the capital of an empire known as Babylonia, which was created by the Chaldeans, who included both Aramaeans and Arabians. Nebuchadnezzar was the greatest of its kings; he conquered a reviving Egypt, destroyed Jerusalem in 586 BC and rebuilt Babylon with greater grandeur. The famous Hanging Gardens became one of the seven wonders of the world. Two chariots could race abreast on the city walls. Palaces and temples combined to make Chaldean Babylon one of the most remarkable capitals the world has ever seen. Nebuchadnezzar carried many of the people of Judah into exile in this city. When Babylon fell to Cyrus, the Persian conqueror, in 539 BC,

some remained, while others returned to their native countries.

The Persians had a number of great emperors – Cambises, Darius, Xerxes – and their strategies conquered a vast region extending from Asia Minor and Egypt as far east as India. These conquests and the ensuing advance of the Persian empire were finally arrested at Marathon, in 490 BC, by the Greeks, who after a setback at Thermopylae and the sacking of Athens in 480 BC forced the Persians to return to Asia.

An efficient and stable administration enabled the Persians to perfect a system of fast communication by horse. They spoke an Aryan language and practised a version of Zoroastrianism. Some two centuries later, Alexander the Great finally conquered the Persian or Achaeminid Empire in 334–323 BC. Having conquered the whole of the civilized world from Macedonia to India, he died in Babylon in 323 BC. Greek culture was influential in other Middle Eastern countries through the Seleucids in Syria and the Ptolemies in Egypt, and through the later Byzantine and Roman Empires until the dawn of Islam.

The Persian Empire was revived by

the Parthians between 250 BC and 226 CE, and later by the Sassanids from 226 BC to 650 CE. There was at this time a close relationship between the Arabian Gulf and Mesopotamia, and in the latter fertile area was the site of Ctesiphon, the Persian capital when the Sassanids were conquered by Muslim Arab armies in the *jihad* or holy wars of 637–650 CE.

The Hebrews as well seem to have developed first as semi-nomadic tribes, brought together under a common traditional patriarch, a system characteristic of some Beduin tribes today, for whom the desert life is only now beginning to change. The Old Testament was probably finished while the Hebrews were in captivity in Babylonia. They were much influenced by the Canaanites of Palestine, part of whose land they conquered and inhabited. The time of Moses and the Exodus from Egypt is thought to have been early in the thirteenth century BC. The Hebrews were never an important people politically and the great empires of Egypt, Mesopotamia, Greece and Rome ruled them successively, although occasionally the Hebrews gained independent control of their so-called "pro-

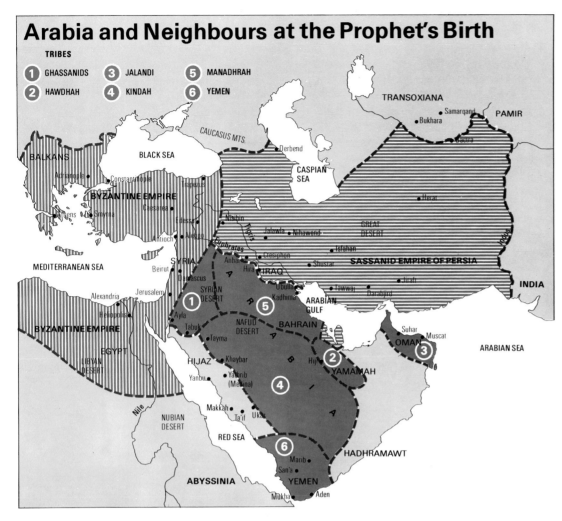

## Arabia and Neighbours at the Prophet's Birth

**TRIBES**

① GHASSANIDS ③ JALANDI ⑤ MANADHRAH
② HAWDHAH ④ KINDAH ⑥ YEMEN

ern and southern kingdoms. During this time the 365 day calendar was devised. This was followed by the dynastic era in which the two kingdoms were consolidated and Egyptian power expanded into Syria and Palestine. The Old Kingdom saw the building of the pyramids, followed by further conquests in Nubia during the Middle Kingdom, although there was some disintegration between these periods. Then came the Empire, during which the Hebrew Exodus from Egypt took place. Under Ikhnaton father-in-law of Tutankhamun, sun-god monotheism was practised temporarily. Sovereignty over Egypt changed hands from a Libyan to a Nubian Dynasty, but was returned to the Egyptians during the Lower Empire. Rome was the last power to rule Egypt before the Arab conquests of the seventh century CE.

Although the Arabian Peninsula now has valleys and alluvial plains as fertile as those which originally encouraged settlements in the Fertile Crescent and in Egypt, its oases have also been populated for many thousands of years. During the Ice Ages which rendered so much of Europe uninhabitable, the Arabian region had enjoyed a temperate climate and evidence remains of numerous watercourses. The earliest Arabs were divided by custom into the nomads of the north and the city dwellers of the south, although some integration had occurred by the time of Muhammad. (To this day the vast deserts of the Peninsula are peopled by the Beduins, whose early raids into civilized territory led to cultural exchange across the area). The Hebrews, Aramaeans, Assyrians and other Semitic peoples migrated in large numbers to underdeveloped territories, and it is likely that they set up the Hyksos dynasty of Egypt in the eighteenth century BC.

Not long after the time of the Nile and Mesopotamia civilizations the southern part of Arabia became a populated commercial centre specializing in the production of frankincense and myrrh, both of which were in great demand from the Romans. The region also traded in the silks and spices and jewellery which were brought from the Indies and East Africa to the Eastern Mediterranean. Northern civilizations were supplied with precious metals, of which a quantity of gold and copper was mined in Arabia itself. Goods were transported by camel from one trading centre to another along a network of caravan routes

mised land" for brief periods of not more than forty or fifty years between their arrival there under Joshua in the thirteenth century and their final futile rebellions which were cruelly put down by their Roman overlords in 66–70 CE and 132–135 CE.

The Phoenicians, the northern Canaanites who originated in what is now the Lebanon and the coast of Syria, became the greatest Semitic seafarers and traders during a period of growth which started in the twelfth century BC. Through their far-flung voyages they disseminated their cultural influence. Their alphabet, and the resulting great improvement in communication, was a major development which took place in the Semitic territory between Sinai and Syria, the homeland of the Phoenicians. Several other forms of alphabetic script were devised; pictographs of Egyptian type gave rise to alphabets which are still used in the Middle East, and are the basis of the European alphabet and those of India and Mongolia. The Minoans of Crete had led the civilized world in seafaring but were replaced by the more adventurous Phoenicians, who traded in tin from Western Europe, silver from

Spain, and Tyrian purple dye from the Mediterranean and tropical seas. Carthage was their great colonial possession, situated in north Africa, not far from present-day Tunis. Other homeland cities included Tyre, Sidon and Jubayl. Carthage almost defeated Rome in the three Punic (Phoenician) Wars of the third and second centuries BC, but was finally destroyed by the Romans in 146 BC.

Parallel with the existence of the Hebrew Kingdom was that of Syria, whose capital was Damascus. The Syrians, known earlier as Aramaeans, fluctuated between alliance and war with the Hebrew people. Their close links with the Phoenicians included a similar alphabet and language, which survived as the language of the people of Palestine until it was replaced by Arabic a millennium later. They were equally successful in spreading their commerce abroad.

Of all the very early civilizations the one which left the most splendid cultural legacy was Egypt. The predynastic period had its beginnings in the days of the rise of Mesopotamia, when its provinces, known as *nomes*, were united into north-

*Acceptance of the Prophet's message transformed the Eastern world from the Atlantic shores to the Indus and, later, beyond. The threads of earlier cultures were drawn together and under the inspiration of Islam a new and confident civilisation flowered.*

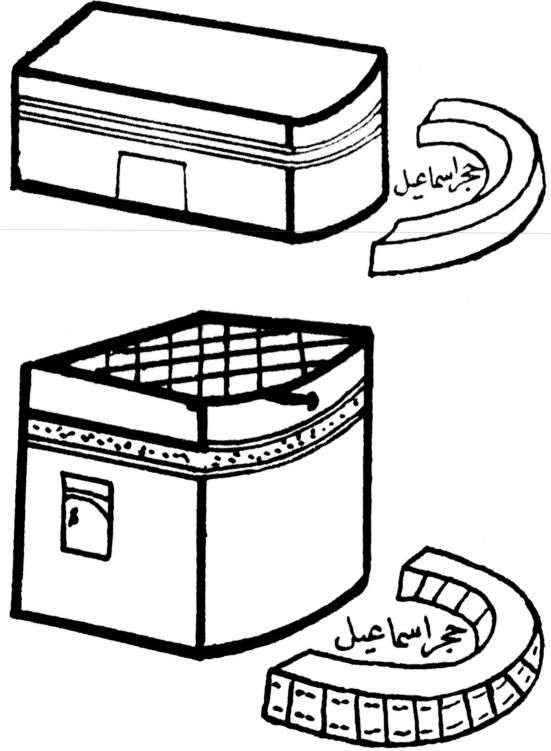

*The reconstruction of Abraham's Ka'bah* (top) *and the Ka'bah of the Holy Prophet Muhammad* (above), *as calculated from ancient chronicles, demonstrate the consistency of design throughout the immense period – nearly five thousand years – of its existence as the holiest of shrines.*

fanning out from Arabia to Egypt and Babylonia. Some of these routes are still used by pilgrims to Makkah and Medina, although the camel is no longer the most popular method of transport. Agriculture was difficult, but a sophisticated system of irrigation included the building of dams to retain flood water for the dry season. One such dam was at Marib, built of limestone and so well designed that it stood intact almost up to the birth of Muhammad.

The Kingdoms of Southern Arabia were subject to frequent change and internecine warfare. Ma'in and Saba, the probable domain of the Queen of Sheba, were two of the earliest which rose to power. Others included Awsan, covering approximately the area now known as Aden, Qatabah to its north-east and Hadhramawt to the east of Qatabah. The powerful tribe of Himyar in the south-west gave its name to contemporary civilisation there. Oman had been a centre of trade and ship-building for many centuries, and Dhofar the source of frankincense, a major commodity of international commerce.

Some time after the first settlements, the northern portion of the country was taken over by the Nabataeans. The Nabataean capital was al Petra, but their southernmost stronghold at Madain Salih, in north-western Saudi Arabia, was of great importance in controlling the trade routes. The influence at Madain Salih evident in the fine façades of the tombs, with their pilasters and pediments, is wholly Hellenistic. The Nabataeans, too, controlled the trade route to the Greek and, later, Roman worlds from the northern Gulf through al-Sawf. Their remarkable technology involved the construction of dams, rock cisterns and irrigation systems, some of which are usable today. With the rise of Rome, the Peninsula's commercial wealth came under military threat, but an invasion launched by Aelius Gallus in 24 BC ended in failure. Having overcome one hurdle, however, south-western spice trade routes based on such cities as Dedan, Yathrib (modern Medina) and Najran, fell at another. Trade began to decline when the Greeks and

## "Blessed" Makkah and "Radiant" Medina were the sites of the first converts.

Romans discovered the Arab methods of sailing to India on the monsoon winds, and the people of the once-prosperous south migrated northwards. Once-prosperous towns along the trade routes that withered include that of Qaryat al-Fawr, recently excavated by the University of Riyadh, on the way from the south-west to the east, skirting the Rub al-Khali.

In the fourth and sixth centuries CE, south-western Arabia fell under Abyssinian rule, and it was during the year 571, when Makkah successfully rebuffed an attack by the Abyssinian Abraha, that the Prophet Muhammad was born in the Holy City.

The birth of Muhammad was a momentous event in history. The followers of Islam today number some five hundred million. Muhammad was the son of Abdullah and Aminah, of the tribe of Quraysh; he became an orphan when still young and spent part of his boyhood among the Beduins of the desert. At twenty-five years of age he married Khadijah, also of the Quraysh tribe, and entered a life of meditation. Soon after, in 610 CE, he experienced his first revelation and began his role as a prophet spreading the message of the one, all-powerful God and the day of judgement to come.

The early converts were few and slow to follow his teachings, but the turning point came in 622 CE when two hundred followers eluded the vigilance of the Quraysh and slipped into Medina. Seventeen years later the *hijrah* migration was described by the Caliph as an essential part of the Muslim experience. The Prophet assumed the role of warrior, judge and civil administrator, winning several victories against the Qurayshis and their supporters, among them the Medinese Jews. From being a religion within a state Islam became the State.

Although an unschooled man he was responsible for the Qur'an, regarded by Muslims as their spiritual and behavioural guide. Within his life span Muhammad established a religion that replaced Christianity in most of Asia and Africa, and laid the foundations of an Empire that was soon to embrace a large part of the then civilized world.

### Early Islamic cartography

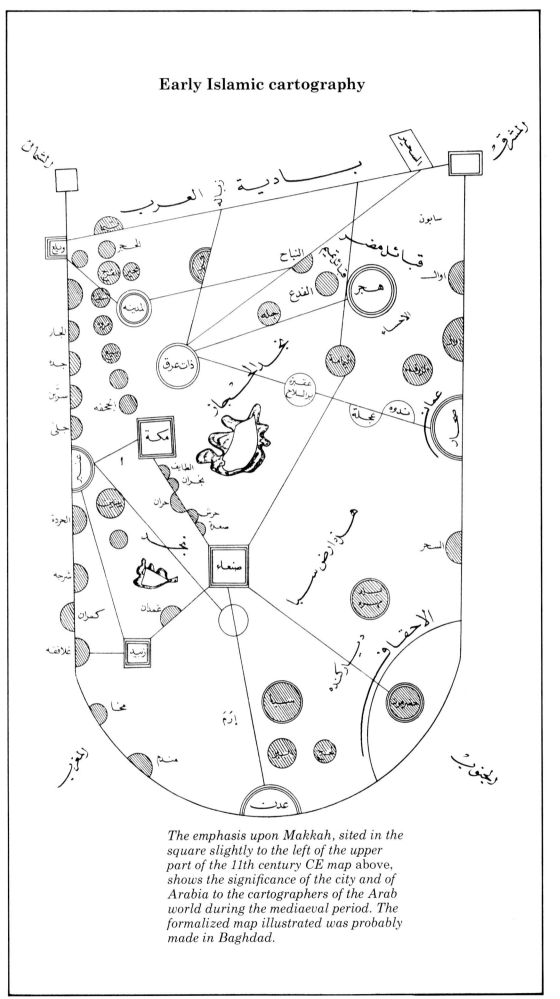

*The emphasis upon Makkah, sited in the square slightly to the left of the upper part of the 11th century CE map above, shows the significance of the city and of Arabia to the cartographers of the Arab world during the mediaeval period. The formalized map illustrated was probably made in Baghdad.*

# The Rise of Saudi Arabia to the Mid-20th Century

THE modern state of Saudi Arabia began to develop in the Najd region of central Arabia some two hundred years ago. From the start of the Islamic era to the middle of the eighteenth century CE Arabian history is made up of the separate stories of a number of individual regions. Despite contacts between these regions and the unifying force of Islamic civilization, the political and religious development of Arabia was by no means uniform. More information is available about the important coastal areas – the Hijaz, Yemen and south Arabia, Oman and Hasa on the Gulf – than about central Arabia, the heartland of the future Saudi state.

Until the European expansion into the Indian Ocean after the fifteenth century, the Hijaz – the region containing the two main sanctuaries of Islam, those of Makkah and Medina – was the area of significance to the outside world. For reasons of prestige, as well as for the financial benefit which accrued from control of the annual pilgrimage, powerful Muslim rulers frequently sought to establish their ascendancy over it. In the tenth century CE a descendant of the Prophet declared himself Sharif of Makkah, and the Sharifate thus founded survived, sometimes independently, sometimes under outside control, until ibn Saud conquered the Hijaz in 1925. Most frequently it was the ruler of Egypt who controlled the Sharifate, and after 1517, when Egypt became part of the Ottoman Empire, the governor of Egypt was recognized as having authority over the Hijaz on behalf of the Ottoman sultan.

Yemen too, because of its position at the mouth of the Red Sea, was of interest to the rulers of Egypt, who on occasions exercised political control over the area. From the early ninth century CE a number of independent dynasties established themselves in the Yemen, and at the end of the century two competing schools of thought in Shi-ite Islam, Isma'ilism and Zaydism, won support among some sections of the population. The Makramid dynasty of Najran, which arose in the eighteenth century and with whom the Saudi rulers came into conflict, espoused a form of Isma'ilism, but ultimately it was Zaydism which prevailed in most of Yemen. In 1636 CE, following an Ottoman withdrawal, the Zaydi Imam occupied San'a and united the greater part of Yemen under his authority. Despite the breakaway of the southern part of his territories, including the port of Aden, at the beginning of the eighteenth century CE, the Zaydi Imamate in the Yemen survived into the twentieth century.

Oman has a similar history, being ruled for much of the period by a non-Sunni Imam, and subject to tension between the tribes of the interior and the towns of the coastal region. The Imams

## Venerated Places

Almost equal in sanctity to the two Saudi Arabian cities of "Makkah the Blessed" and "Medina the Radiant" is Jerusalem, and its Qubbat as-Sakhra, Mosque of 'Omar *pictured here* and al-Aqsa Mosque. Sites in Damascus and in Baghdad, both seats of the Caliphate, are also revered. It was in Damascus and Jerusalem that the Omayyid built their mosques. Apart from its very ancient Arab association, Damascus was associated with the relic of John the Baptist, and Jerusalem with Solomon, Jesus and Muhammad's ascensional vision.

followed the Ibadhi Kharijite form of Islam. They established their power in the ninth century and, ruling from the interior, managed to maintain it with interruptions down to the sixteenth century. In 1507 CE the Portuguese captured Muscat, the main port, but in the middle of the next century the Omanis recovered it. In the succeeding period the division between the coastal region, centred on Muscat, and inner Oman intensified. The Saudis were sometimes able to establish their authority in inner Oman by way of Buraymi.

The region of Hasa on the Gulf came at times under the authority of powerful rulers in Iraq, and at other times had independent rulers. From the late ninth to the late eleventh century Hasa was the centre of an Isma'ili state which, at its height, became involved in Iraq and Syria and for a while even removed the Black Stone from the Ka'bah. In 1591 CE the Ottomans brought Hasa under their rule, but in 1669 a local family, the Banu Khalid, drove them out, and between 1694 and 1709 actually took control over the emirate of Diriyah away from the Saudi family. By the end of the eighteenth century, however, the tables were turned and the Saudi rulers of Diriyah were able to defeat the Banu Khalid and install their own nominee in Hasa as a preliminary to taking over the region completely.

Information about the pre-Saudi history of Najd and inner Arabia is fragmentary. For the outside world Najd was important because of the pilgrim route which crossed it from the Gulf to the Hijaz, but the area remained largely independent. The population was mainly nomadic, but here and there conditions did allow the growth of sizeable settlements. One such area was that of Wadi Hanifah near Riyadh, where, by the fifteenth century CE, a number of independent emirates or principalities had established themselves. Here the Saudi state had its origins.

The Saudi family traces its descent from Mani ibn Rabia al-Muraydi, who came, about the middle of the fifteenth century CE, from Hasa to settle in Wadi Hanifah. By the beginning of the seventeenth century his descendants had established themselves as rulers of a small emirate centred on Diriyah to the north of Riyadh. Shortly before 1720, Saud ibn Muhammad, the eponymous founder of the family, became ruler.

He was succeeded, on his death in 1725, by his son Muhammad. It was under Muhammad that the Wahhabi form of Islam was espoused, and the expansion of the emirate began.

Wahhabism takes its name from Muhammad ibn Abd al-Wahhab, who was born in 1703 CE into a family of religious scholars at Ayayna, the centre of another emirate in Wadi Hanifah, to the north of Diriyah. He was brought up to follow the Hanbali Law School, the most rigorous of the four law schools of Sunni Islam, and from an early age was noted for his strictness. In the course of his education he became influenced by the ideas of ibn Taymiyya, a theologian and jurist who died in 1328 CE and who had argued for a purification of Islam from what he considered to be accretions to the primitive faith. His ideas had some influence, especially among followers of the Hanbali Law School, and ibn Abd al-Wahhab came to believe that the essential monotheism of Islam had been compromised by excessive veneration of the Prophet Muhammad and other "saints". This veneration was most commonly expressed in pilgrimages and visits to minor sanctuaries and to the tombs of holy men; so ibn Abd al-Wahhab preached against these. He also insisted on the stricter implementation of penalties – such as death for adultery – fixed in the Qur'an, and he forbade certain innovations, notably the smoking of tobacco.

In 1745, after setbacks elsewhere, ibn Abd al-Wahhab settled in Diriyah, where he was favourably received by Muhammad ibn Saud. This event marks the beginning of a seventy-year period of expansion for the Diriyah emirate, the first of three distinct phases in the history of the Saudi state. Modern Saudi Arabia is the product of the third of these phases. Wahhabism seems to have provided the Saudi power with an ideological basis for expansion which the competing emirates lacked. It appealed equally to the tribes and to the settled population – the latter provided the main support for the dynasty in the first two phrases, and the tribes were crucial in the third.

By the end of the eighteenth century CE the emirate of Diriyah had extended its authority over the Najd, finally gaining control of Riyadh in 1773. This extension of political power was accompanied by the spread of Wahhabism and the implementation of its teachings.

Tombs of holy men raised above the ground more than about thirty centimetres and other minor sanctuaries were destroyed. By 1792 when ibn Abd al-Wahhab died, his ideas had already proved more directly influential than those of ibn Taymiyya ever were.

The rapid expansion of the Saudi emirate inevitably provoked fear and hostility in neighbouring non-Wahhabi states. The Sharif of Makkah undertook a series of expeditions against the Saudi state which now bordered his in the Hijaz, but these expeditions were unsuccessful, and in 1803 CE, shortly before the death of Abdul Aziz, who had succeeded his father Muhammad in 1765, a Wahhabi army brought Makkah under Saudi control. Two years later Medina was taken. In the north the Ottoman governors of Iraq supported the anti-Wahhabi tribes on the border between Iraq and Arabia, but they too were unable to hold back the Wahhabi forces. In 1802 Wahhabi raids into Iraq reached a climax when the tomb at Karbala of Husayn ibn Ali, the Prophet's grandson, whom most Muslims regard as a martyr, was sacked, together with its neighbouring town. However, the Wahhabis were not strong enough to take and hold the towns of Iraq.

The sack of Karbala provoked the hostility of most Muslims, Sunni and Shi-ite, and the occupation of the Hijaz brought the Saudi state into direct conflict with the Ottoman sultan, who regarded himself as the guardian of the Holy places for the whole Muslim world. At first the sultan was unable to act, but in 1811 CE the Albanian, Muhammad Ali, having secured control of Egypt, organized, at the sultan's command, an expedition against the Wahhabis. In 1812 forces from Egypt, led by Muhammad Ali's son Tusan, took Medina and in the following year Makkah. Abdul Aziz had been assassinated in 1803, probably by a Shi-ite Muslim seeking vengeance for the sack of Karbala, and was succeeded by his son Saud. Saud himself died in 1814, and his successor, his son Abdullah, had to conclude a truce with Tusan, ceding control of the holy towns to Muhammad Ali. In 1816, however, fighting began again, an army from Egypt invaded Najd, and in 1818 CE Diriyah was taken. Abdullah was sent in captivity to Istanbul, where he was executed. This was the end of the first distinct phase in the history of the Saudi state.

The second stage ran from 1824 CE, when Turki, the son of Abdullah ibn Muhammad, seized Riyadh from Muhammad Ali's forces, until the last two decades of the nineteenth century, when the Saudi state was taken over by the Rashidi rulers of Ha'il in Jabal Shammar. Riyadh now became the capital of the Saudi state, and from there Turki extended his authority over

own rule over the Saudi state. Between 1838 and 1843 CE Faisal's rule in Riyadh was interrupted when Muhammad Ali again sent a force to invade Najd and set up another member of the Saudi family as ruler under the supervision of Muhammad Ali's agent in Riyadh. Faisal himself was taken prisoner to Cairo, but escaped and re-established his rule with the help of Abdullah ibn Rashid.

time an independent sheikhdom.

It was Abdul Aziz ibn Abd ar-Rahman, usually called simply ibn Saud, who initiated the third phase in the history of the Saudi state, lasting from the beginning of the twentieth century CE until the present day. In 1902 he was able to take advantage of the weakness of the Rashidi power, following the death of Muhammad ibn Rashid in 1897, in order

## Western Travellers in Arabia

The dangers of desert travel and Arab caution towards foreign intruders deterred Westerners until quite recently. In 1761 Carsten Niebuhr, a German in the service of Denmark, travelled in portions of Western Arabia. So, too, did the Swiss J. L. Burkhardt in 1814. The British explorer Richard Burton, setting out in 1853, like Burkhardt followed the *hajj* route. Starting in Alexandria, he landed at Yanbu. Later he travelled in Midian. At much the same time another Englishman, Charles Doughty, was travelling in northwestern and west central Arabia (1875–78). First to enter the "cradle of the Arab race", as Lady Anne Blunt called the Najd, was the Finnish professor Wallin, reaching Ha'il in 1848. The Levantine Italian Guarmani started from Jerusalem in 1863, with a commission to buy horses, and reached Tayma, Burayda, Ha'il and Jawf. Later the Jesuit missionary Palgrave travelled to Ha'il and Riyadh in 1864. The Blunts reached Ha'il in 1879. Of all the subsequent outstanding travellers in Arabia – Alois Musil, T. E. Lawrence, Bertram Thomas, Wilfred Thesiger among others – none covered half as much territory as

*Richard Burton's (1821–90) famous journey on the pilgrim route took place in 1853.*

*Charles Doughty (1843–96) wrote his* Travels in Arabia Deserta *after travels in the Hijaz.*

*Gertrude Bell (1868–1926), a fine Arabist and tribal expert, reached Ha'il in 1912.*

*Bertram Thomas (1892–1950) crossed the Rub al-Khali in 1931, from Salala to Qatar.*

*St. John Philby (1885–1960) explored and mapped more widely than any other.*

St. John Philby. Setting off in 1917, he crossed Arabia from Uqair in the east to Jiddah, travelling the following year through the Aflaj to Sulayyil. From then on he travelled extensively, journeying through the Rub al-Khali in

1932 and south from the Tihama to Mukalla in the Hadhramawt in 1936. His last journeys in the early 1950s took him north through Wajh and Tabuk.

*Wilfred Thesiger (b.1910) made several journeys in the Rub al-Khali in the 1950s.*

the whole of Najd, inner Oman, and Hasa, which had been occupied for a time by Muhammad Ali's forces. Abd ar-Rahman ibn Hasan, a grandson of ibn Abd al-Wahhab, was appointed by Turki to be *qadi* of Riyadh, and he, together with his son, Abd al-Latif, was largely responsible for the continued development of Wahhabism in the nineteenth century.

In 1834 CE Turki was assassinated in a dispute between members of the Saudi family, but his son Faisal managed to wrest power from the rebels who had seized Riyadh. In the following year Faisal appointed Abdullah ibn Ali ibn Rashid to be his governor in Ha'il. Rashid's descendants were eventually to extend their power and establish their

Faisal's death in 1865 CE was followed by a struggle for power between two of his sons, Abdullah and Saud; a conflict which enabled the Ottomans to win back Hasa and the ruler of Ha'il, Muhammad ibn Rashid, to extend his power over the Saudi state, while ostensibly seeking to uphold the rights of Abdullah. By the time of Abdullah's death in 1889 CE, the Saudi state was no more than a province of the territory ruled by the Rashidis from Ha'il. Two years later Abdullah's son and successor, Abd ar-Rahman, was expelled from Riyadh by Muhammad ibn Rashid who appointed a puppet governor there. Abd ar-Rahman and his family, including his young son Abdul Aziz, who had been born about 1880, fled to Kuwait, which was at this

to recapture Riyadh with the help of what was really no more than a raiding party from Kuwait. The following ten years were spent in inconclusive fighting against the Rashidis, who received support from the Ottomans, and it was not until 1912 CE that ibn Saud took a step which was to prove decisive – the inauguration of the *Ikhwan* movement. During his exile in Kuwait and the fighting with the Rashidis, ibn Saud had come to see the military potential of the nomadic tribes if their customary resistance to state control could be overcome. Realizing that he must settle the tribesmen and give them a motive for uniting, he organized them into a religious brotherhood (*Ikhwan* means "brethren"), the aim of which was the militant

# The House of Saud

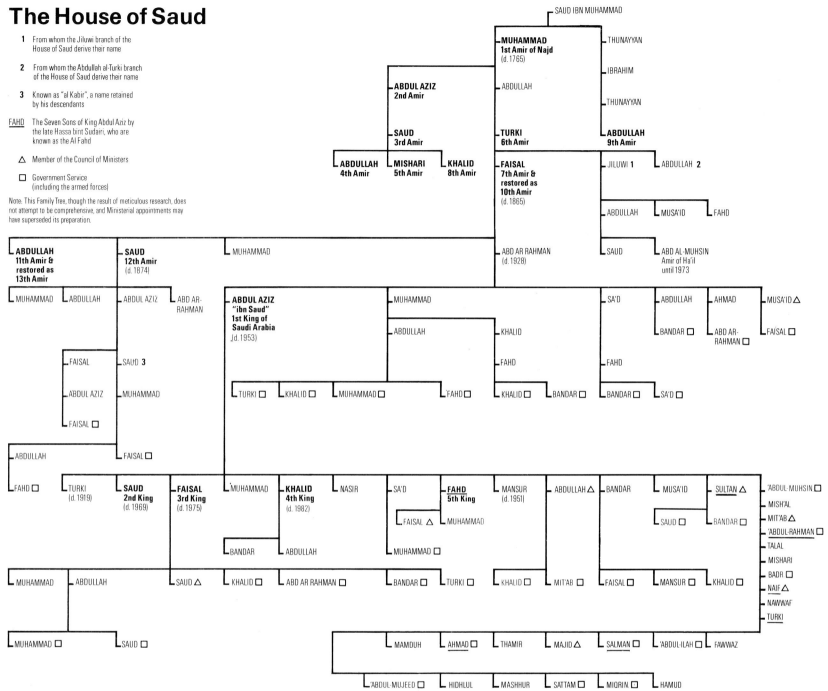

1  From whom the Jiluwi branch of the
   House of Saud derive their name

2  From whom the Abdullah al-Turki branch
   of the House of Saud derive their name

3  Known as "al Kabir", a name retained
   by his descendants

FAHD  The Seven Sons of King Abdul Aziz by
   the late Hassa bint Sudairi, who are
   known as the Al Fahd

△  Member of the Council of Ministers

☐  Government Service
   (including the armed forces)

Note: This Family Tree, though the result of meticulous research, does
not attempt to be comprehensive, and Ministerial appointments may
have superseded its preparation.

expansion of Wahhabism. The members of the movement were to settle in military encampments called *hijrahs*, just as at the time of the Arab Conquests the tribesmen had abandoned their nomadic way of life in Arabia for the garrison towns of the conquered territories. The first *hijrah* was founded at Artawiyya in 1912. Nobody knows the exact number of *hijrahs* which were established, but it may have been as high as two hundred. The number of warriors in each of them varied between ten and ten thousand.

With the help of the *Ikhwan*, ibn Saud took Ha'il in 1921 CE and the whole of the Hijaz, including Makkah, in 1924–25. Any further expansion in Arabia or its border areas would entail a clash with Great Britain, which was involved as protector or mandatory power in all of the territories now bordering the Saudi state. Indeed clashes had already occurred. To the *Ikhwan*, such political considerations appeared a betrayal of the doctrine of holy war against all infidels (i.e. non-Wahhabis) with which they had been inculcated. Relations between ibn Saud and the *Ikhwan* deteriorated rapidly in the late 1920s as the *Ikhwan* began to act more independently. In 1929 they massacred a party of Najdi Wahhabi merchants, and the revulsion which this act aroused among the settled population of the Najd, as well as among several of the tribes, strengthened ibn Saud's hand sufficiently for him to take action against the *Ikhwan*. At the battle of Sabalah in March 1929 ibn Saud put the *Ikhwan* to flight, and their power collapsed. Early in 1930 a number of their leaders surrendered to the British authorities in Kuwait, whence they were extradited by ibn Saud. He spared their lives but imprisoned them in Riyadh. This marked the end of the power of the *Ikhwan* as a force independent of ibn Saud. Some of their *hijrahs* continued to exist, but were now under government control. Eventually the *Ikhwan* were incorporated in the National Guard.

After 1930 ibn Saud began the transformation of the state which is still continuing. The battle of Sabalah marked the end of the era in which the history of Saudi Arabia can be discussed only in traditional terms.

# From Abdul Aziz to the Present Day

*Saudi Arabia's stability owes much to the fact that a single dynasty has governed since Abdul Aziz ibn Saud established the Kingdom in 1932. King Fahd succeeded his brothers, Khalid, Faisal and Saud in 1982 to become the fifth king. Born in 1921, he too is the son of the kingdom's founder, Abdul Aziz.*

TODAY'S Saudi Arabia under King Fahd – energetic, swiftly developing, yet profoundly respectful of tradition – is the direct heir of the Saudi Arabia created by Abdul Aziz ibn Saud. King Fahd is the fifth king in the present dynasty of Saudi rulers, succeeding his brothers Khalid, Faisal and Saud. It is easy to overlook the fact that he is only one generation away from the founder of this stable, forward looking state.

King Fahd's father Abdul Aziz ibn Saud, is remembered by all who knew him for characteristics which distinguished him among the Arabs of his generation. Physically, he was outstandingly tall; self-disciplined to be hardy, he relished battle and was indifferent to injury. Spiritually, his faith dominated his life; he was deeply devout, and steadfast in upholding the puritanism preached to his forbears by the eighteenth century Islamic reformer, ibn Abdul al-Wahhab. Mentally, he was a master of politics; his appraisal of men and their capacities was shrewd, and his grasp of world affairs astounding in one who during his long life paid only three brief visits outside his native Arabia, and never left the Arab world. Lastly, his basic instincts – integrity, a sense of honour, of justice, of humour – added up to a nature that brought him success despite early vicissitudes in his chequered life.

He was born in or about 1880 CE into a family – the Saudis of southern Najd – that had formerly been great but was then living in penury and exile after defeat by its northern rival, the Rashids of Ha'il. He spent his childhood in Kuwait, dreaming of restoring his family's fortunes. At twenty-one, he took advantage of some leisurely skirmishing between Kuwaitis and Rashidis to slip inland with forty picked companions and, in a night of surprises and sharp sword thrusts, to recapture his home town, Riyadh. This exploit brought him his first acclaim, and to this day Riyadh, in all its other buildings fashionably modern, preserves at its heart the old mud fort that is his people's memento of his daring. In 1902 his father, glad to reward determination allied to piety, named him Emir of Najd and Imam of its puritanical brand of Islam.

Thereafter, he simultaneously spread religious reform and Saudi power, sometimes in battle, sometimes in the name of Wahhabism (a movement which appealed for a return to the true teaching of Islam), sometimes through persuasiveness or through respect for his military success. By 1926 he had captured the Holy Cities of Makkah and Medina and the whole Red Sea coastal province of the Hijaz. He declared himself King of Hijaz and Najd, and in 1932 renamed his kingdom Saudi Arabia.

As always happens, conquest brought complications. He owed to his belligerent *Ikhwan* the conquests that enabled him to dominate Arabia, yet was obliged to suppress them, because he could not condone their wish to carry Holy War abroad. Again, although Wahhabism had become a matter of course in the austere climate of Najd, it was less acceptable in the more sophisticated and easy-going Hijaz. In overseas Islam, too, the thought of Wahhabi fanatics in charge of Makkah and Medina caused deep disquiet. These misgivings he was within two or three years able to dispel, partly by ensuring the safety of the pilgrimage, partly by his handling of the *Ikhwan*, partly by the tact and moder-

*The great Abdul Aziz ibn Saud* (right) *was swift to perceive the potential of his country's oil wealth and to encourage prospecting by foreigners like the early American oilman* (above), *robed for the desert.*

ation that he showed to anxious visitors. Equally tactfully, he slowly introduced his own people to innovations that they saw as heresies, but which he knew must come if his country was to grow great – concessions sold to infidels, the telephone, pilgrimage by motor transport, wireless telegraphy. But it was in his dealings with great powers that he best showed the acumen, and the awareness of Arab limitations, which made him

an outstanding diplomat. For instance, though he hated the two Hashimite brothers whom the British had installed as rulers in neighbouring Iraq and Transjordan, he punished tribal or religious forays into their territory. Again in 1934 when armies led by his sons were on the verge of conquering Yemen, to their chagrin he ordered them to withdraw, because he realized that their approach to the confines of Aden and the coast of Eritrea was antagonizing both Britain and Italy. He was always circumspect with the British, surrounded as he was by their sea power, their mandates and their dependencies. Yet he was friendly; even during the darkest days of the Second World War, he warned them of local pitfalls and backed them to win in the end. Only on the subject of Palestine did he censure them, then and later. As he listened, conscious of Arab impotence, to broadcasts about the British handling of Palestine's dismemberment, tears, it is said, poured down his cheeks.

At home, the greatest boon that he gave his people was internal security. Until his reign, all towns were walled, all gates barred at nightfall, all desert journeys undertaken at risk from raiders or feuding tribes. At the sight of strangers, friend could be told from foe only by some conventional gesture such as waving a headcloth or throwing up sand; if no such sign were given, the safest course was to gallop out of sight. Ibn Saud put an end to these hazards. His ways of doing so were to appoint trusted Najdis as regional governors, usually members of his vast family or of related stock – as-Sudayris, al-Jiluwis or ath-Thunayyahs; these outposts he furnished with the mobile wireless trucks that enabled him to keep a watch – miraculous to the tribes – on desert behaviour; he also travelled widely and frequently among them, often cementing loyalties as he went by arranging a marriage between some sheikhly family and his own. By the time of his death, town walls were a thing of the past; he had induced the *Ikhwan* survivors to settle in agricultural colonies, and a traveller could stop and pray at the lawful hour or camp at nightfall without fear of molestation, as he can today.

When ibn Saud won his kingdom, it was pitifully poor. It produced only the bare necessities of life; its so-called roads were tracks; it had no ports; its sole source of foreign exchange was pilgrim-

*The first decisive act in the restoration of the Saudi dynasty was the capture of Riyadh by Abdul Aziz in a raid of astonishing daring, on January 15th, 1902 CE, with a handful of men.*

*A memorial of Abdul Aziz' capture of Riyadh's Musmak Fortress* (above) *remains in the spear-tip lodged in the woodwork of the door* (right).

age dues. Religious learning apart, education was scanty; he had to resort to foreign Arabs as his advisers. All but one of his immediate entourage were literally advisers, for though he listened to information, he took all decisions, however trivial, himself. The exception was the one Najdi among them – his Minister of Finance, Abdullah Sulayman. Ibn Saud, though the equal of anyone in political skill, negotiation or paternalistic power of decision, hated administration and was not good at it. As the business of his kingdom swelled and paperwork piled up, he was fortunate in having at his elbow for over twenty years one Najdi possessed of executive ability. When the outbreak of the world economic crisis of the early 1930s seriously reduced the numbers making the pilgrimage, the repercussions magnified beyond management his kingdom's endemic poverty. At this moment of crisis, a stroke of fortune relieved his plight.

In 1932, oil was discovered in Bahrain,

an island visible from the Saudi mainland. Mining geologists suspected that oil deposits might underlie the mainland also. An American oil company, offering to pay gold for prospection rights, enabled the desperate King and Finance Minister to round a tight corner. So began the exploration and discovery that, once the Second World War was over, turned Saudi Arabia's oil production into the most promising and wealthiest venture in an oil-rich peninsula.

Ibn Saud was abstemious throughout his life. His tastes were simple. Prayer and reading the scriptures took up many hours of each day; late in life he composed his own anthology of religious wisdom, sayings and proverbs. He rejoiced in family life; children and grandchildren were his delight; a cluster of them surrounds him in every informal photograph. Since at his death he left behind him forty-seven living sons (the youngest under seven) and unnumbered daughters, children were always in plentiful supply. He could be irascible, but not for long. Among his greatest pleasures were desert life and pursuits, camping for part of every year, hunting, hawking, tests of horsemanship, camel racing. Whether in tent or palace, his mornings were spent giving audience in a *majlis* open to all his subjects, hearing grievances, righting wrongs, dispensing reward and punishment. Duty done, he

*The fort wall in Hofuf* (right); *it was walls such as these that Abdul Aziz and his Saudis scaled in 1913 to found their Kingdom.*

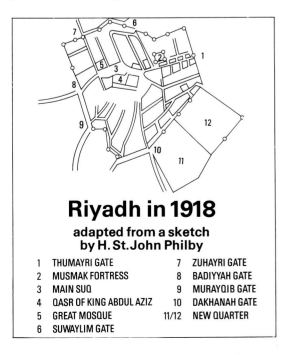

## Riyadh in 1918

### adapted from a sketch
### by H. St. John Philby

| | | | |
|---|---|---|---|
| 1 | THUMAYRI GATE | 7 | ZUHAYRI GATE |
| 2 | MUSMAK FORTRESS | 8 | BADIYYAH GATE |
| 3 | MAIN SUQ | 9 | MURAYQIB GATE |
| 4 | QASR OF KING ABDUL AZIZ | 10 | DAKHANAH GATE |
| 5 | GREAT MOSQUE | 11/12 | NEW QUARTER |
| 6 | SUWAYLIM GATE | | |

83

liked to spend his afternoons in the peace of the desert, on some restive horse when in his prime, travelling by car in old age. A tremendous talker, his evenings were spent in discourse; topics on which he liked to dwell were theological niceties, such as the distinction between pure and impure belief; desert genealogies, which he had at his fingertips and the details of old campaigns. He was a devout man who consistently relished the gift of life.

Legend and anecdote sometimes tell more of a man's character than a recital of fact. It is said that when he captured Ha'il in 1921, a traitorous defender let him into the town by one of its five gates; he honoured the captains of the other four and punished the traitor. He handed out judgement with assurance and well-remembered imagination – summary execution for a villain, coupled with compassion for the victims of his crime, the shaving off of the beard and moustache of a young man who had simply been pert. Until crippled by arthritis, he liked to join in fun or horseplay; part of his personal success with his subjects was the spontaneity with which he rubbed shoulders with a crowd or joined in a war-dance. He loved an apt quip.

topped twenty-five million tons, his health had deteriorated. An old eye trouble worsened; old wounds generated arthritis; unwillingly, he took to a wheel chair; inch by inch he lost his grip as he fought a long last illness. He grew unequal to controlling leaks of revenue. He had named his son Saud as Crown Prince. When the old king died in 1953, Saud became king. It was a difficult period for the Middle East. It was characterised by a fashionable republicanism and wild radio propaganda from abroad. Nasser was the new hero of the market place. The sudden influx of wealth in Saudi Arabia found the country without an infrastructure to cope with its opportunities. Many a ruler might have faltered in such circumstances. King Saud built hospitals, opened schools, initiated the education of girls. A programme of road building was begun.

Yet it was not until a decade later that the Prince fit to meet the situation succeeded, as King Faisal, to the throne.

Statesmen blessed with ibn Saud's moral stature, high principles and common sense are rarities; by any standards, he must be reckoned among the greatest in the first half of our century.

*King Saud bin Abdul Aziz succeeded his father at a difficult period.*

Once, chatting tête-à-tête with a British envoy, he mentioned the contrariness of his English friend, St. John Philby. The envoy countered with the story of the British mum watching the Guards march by: "Everyone's out of step but my Johnnie." The king laughed till his sides ached. Philby, often described as his "British adviser", was never this, but rather his walking encyclopaedia and verbal sparring-partner.

By 1950, in which year Petromin and Aramco recorded that oil production

*Up to the First World War, Turkey claimed a sovereignty over Arabia that was never more than nominal, and not even that so far as King Abdul Aziz was concerned. The war affected Arabia principally in the Hashemite area of the Hijaz, where T. E. Lawrence came to fame – not least in his role in the destruction of the Turkish-controlled Hijaz railway, of which some relics (left) survive in the desert to this day. Hashemite rule did not long survive the Great War. By December 1925 Medina and Jiddah were Abdul Aziz', and in January 1926 the principal citizens of Makkah offered their allegiance to Abdul Aziz.*

"From log cabin to White House" was a phrase once coined by an American author to epitomize the life of Abraham Lincoln. From desert obscurity to world status is no less a shift of fortune, and perhaps the more remarkable of the two in that it sums up the career not of one man – the late King Faisal of Saudi Arabia – but of a whole nation.

Changes of this magnitude within the span of a lifetime are seldom wholly due to the worth or character of a single individual. Outside agents such as a freak of timing, or the unwisdom of others – or a simple stroke of luck – often play their part. Yet King Faisal ibn Abdul Aziz ibn Saud made a great personal contribution to his own rise to fame and power. When historians come to assess him, they will refer first to the spiritual reserves underlying the inner calm which enabled him to bide his time when things were not going his way, and secondly to the cautious reasoning and balanced judgement that made him a first-class negotiator. Add to these assets a presence marked by a fine bearing, inborn dignity and grace of manner, and you have the outlines of a portrait that is filled in by the story of his life.

He was the fourth son of a father who had won back from a rival – the Emir of Ha'il – the family patrimony of Najd in central Arabia, after almost a generation of exile in Kuwait. At Faisal's birth, Riyadh, the capital which ibn Saud had recovered less than four years before, was hemmed in by the enemies of its puritanism and its claim to spiritual superiority. The Rashids of Ha'il lay to its north, the Turks in the coastal province of Hasa to its east, and their myrmidon the Sharif of Mecca on the Red Sea coast to its west. Riyadh was in those days a dour place, dependent for life on dates and herding; its gates clanged shut at dusk and at the hours of prayer; at night, no glimmer of light revealed its existence except when, in Ramadan, a huge arc lamp was hoisted above the palace flagpole to signal the breaking of the fast. Faisal was educated by the customary *qadi*, and knew only family pleasures – hunting, horse and camel racing, hawking, picnics in the gardens of the neighbouring *wadi*. Desert excursions were unsafe, except for in well-armed bands, owing to the prevalence of raiders, tribe against tribe.

But before Faisal was out of his 'teens, this state of isolation had begun to

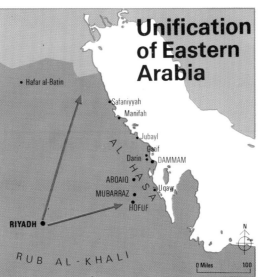

By 1920, the fortresses of eastern Arabia (illustrated this page) *had all fallen to Abdul Aziz. But the Turkish hold on the area had been broken on a moonless night in April 1913 when Abdul Aziz, with 600 men, scaled the walls of Hofuf and surprised the defenders.*

change. His father the Emir ibn Saud had chased the Turks out of Hasa province (1913), had established treaty relations with the British in the Gulf (1915), and had conquered Ha'il (1921). He had made large tracts of the desert safe for travellers and when, in 1919, his new friends the British offered a member of his family a trip to England as a reward for services in the First World War, he chose Faisal for the treat. Maybe he picked a boy of only fourteen because his eldest son, Turki, had died in the influenza epidemic of 1918 (as had his favourite wife and some 25,000 of his people); anyway, he reckoned Faisal to be the child most likely to profit from a new experience. Faisal justified the choice. With the dignity that was to mark him throughout his career, he exchanged swords with King George V and, in the freezing cold of a post-war December, gravely accepted the visits that were thought suitable to his years – to the Zoo, to the Greenwich telescope and to *Chu Chin Chow*.

By 1925–1926, when his father overpowered the Sharifian family and conquered the Holy Cities of Makkah and Medina, he was thought old enough to command an army. He brought up the reinforcements for which his father sent in order to capture the sea port of Jiddah. Later, still only twenty-nine, he was to prove his military capacity more conclusively by commanding the most successful of the armies used by his father on the last of his campaigns – that of 1934 – by means of which he settled his frontier with the Yemen. Faisal's army, which sped down the coastal plain of the Red Sea, was the spearhead of this operation.

For all his success in the field, it was in the council chamber that Faisal's talents showed up best. Makkah and Jiddah once

*The decisive incorporation of the southwest (top pictures: Abha's fortress) into the young kingdom was assigned by Abdul Aziz to his young son Faisal (later King) pictured opposite, while he himself subdued the last strongholds in Hijaz (above) and to the north, including Ha'il and Shenanah (far right).*

conquered, ibn Saud proclaimed himself king of the Hijaz and Najd; but he could not be everywhere at once and he appointed Faisal his Viceroy in the Hijaz, with his seat in Makkah. Here the responsibilities were great, for the whole of the Islamic world outside Arabia was exercised, if not aghast, that its Holy Cities should have passed into the hands of unlettered desert religious reformers who might in their zeal destroy the essential features of the pilgrimage and tamper with the seats of Islamic learning at Makkah and Medina. For several years after 1926 anxious delegations poured in from more sophisticated lands –

Egypt, India, Indonesia, Iran, Iraq. Whenever possible, ibn Saud received and reassured these delegations himself. When he was there, his sons, if they appeared at all, took the customary place behind his chair. But at times he was forced to be absent because of the demands of Najd, where his warriors were champing to carry their Holy War into Iraq and needed curbing. In his absence, visitors to Makkah were received by Faisal.

Faisal was likewise his father's deputy in many dealings with non-Islamic states. In 1926, he was sent to Europe to broaden his mind in Britain and France, and five years later he embarked on a wide-ranging tour that included Soviet Russia. (Saudi-Soviet relations at the time were good, for Soviet Russia, with its own Muslims in mind, had been one of the first foreign states to recognize the new King and his Kingdom.) Ibn Saud throughout his life continued personally to handle dealings with foreigners if they

## Murabba Palace

Abdul Aziz' Palace of Murabba in Riyadh is today preserved as a memorial to his achievement – with its traditional decoration and weaponry, it is characteristic of the period.

It was here at Qasr al Murabba that the ailing King spent the last years of his life, yet maintaining his strict routines of life.

A selection of flintlock rifles, used by King Abdul Aziz' soldiers in the early days of the unification of the Kingdom, are preserved at the Palace (*above*).

came to Arabia – for instance, to negotiate frontiers or seek concessions, but
abroad he left everything to Faisal,
whom he appointed as his Foreign
Minister.

The Second World War changed the
status and outlook of most Arab lands.
They joined forces in a League; they
gained admission to the United Nations;
they gave new forms of expression to
their nationalism. Some began to earn
income from the oil that had been discovered before the war; most planned to
use this new wealth for development and
welfare. Looking back, it is odd to
remember that, at this stage, the states
which made all the running in the Arab
League were Egypt, Iraq and Syria;
Saudi Arabia's contribution to the
League's budget was seven per cent of
the total as against Egypt's forty-two

*King Faisal ibn Abdul Aziz combined
inspirational leadership with sound
management, and respect for the past
with sagacious innovation.*

per cent. Only from 1950, when it made its "fifty-fifty" arrangement with the Arabian-American Oil Company (Aramco), did Saudi Arabia throw off its image of barren desert, backward inhabitants and poverty.

Faisal, who during the war had further broadened his experience of the world by visiting the United States with his half-brother Khalid (later King Khalid), became a figure of note in world conclaves. At the San Francisco Conference which inaugurated the United Nations, at meetings of the Arab League, in the United Nations Assembly, his dignified figure and graceful robes (he never wore Western dress) singled him out for attention. His father, smitten from 1950 with the sad illness of which he died in 1953, became wholly dependent on the two eldest of his thirty-five surviving sons – Saud, the Crown Prince, who had inherited touches of ibn Saud's humour and gaiety, and Faisal, who was more like him in his piety and austerity, and in his grasp of human foibles.

When the old King died and Saud succeeded him, the younger, graver brother became Prime Minister as well as Foreign Minister. At the time, Saudi Arabia lacked the institutions and the administrative framework that were becoming necessary if it was to handle its mounting revenue and play its potential role in Arab affairs. Faisal responded to the challenge and, with the assistance of a devout and cautious Pakistani financier, set up the Saudi Arabian Monetary Agency (SAMA).

When King Saud's health deteriorated in 1963, Faisal picked up the reins of power, and in 1964 Crown Prince Faisal became King of Saudi Arabia.

The role was not easy. To the right of him, the *ulama* and the more pious members of his family were pressing for a return to the austerity of his father's day; to his left, and in the forces, young men who had been abroad urged "modernization" and less rigorous adherence to the strict rules of religious extremists. Faisal, as was his wont, steered towards compromise. He permitted television but not the cinema; he promoted secular and technical education for boys, but kept girls' education under the jurisdiction of the Sheikh al-Islam – the chief religious authority. His middle way was not everywhere popular. Whatever his personal inclinations (and he cannot have enjoyed the glare of lighting for

the television cameras that he permitted even during audiences) he never forgot that it was the *ulama* who had helped him to restore the kingdom to its proper course.

Foreign policy, too, presented its problems. Nasser's Egypt, the most powerful of his neighbours, had to his consternation taken up arms in support of the republicans against the royalists in Yemen; Aden, which the British were about to leave, was a hotbed of left-wing parties fanned by Egyptian propaganda; Syria and a newly-republican Iraq were flirting with his bugbear, Soviet Russia. He sought to create for himself a new base by visiting Islamic countries and establishing an Islamic summit that would include Iran and Pakistan. But this plan foundered because the Islamic states had differing political priorities. It won him little beyond the respect he already commanded as Defender of the Faith and guardian of its Holy Places.

The Palestine War of 1967 abruptly changed his role in foreign affairs. Egypt, till then a rival, was humiliated and truncated. So was Jordan. Jerusalem, the third holiest city of Islam, fell into Israel's hands. Faisal set about providing financial support for the states on Israel's borders. Nasser's death in 1970, and the passing of Egypt's presidency to a less dominant figure, Anwar Sadat, opened Faisal's way to the leading role in Arab affairs which, with his usual dignity, he now assumed. Though in his late sixties and often far from well, he made long journeys to Arab summits in order to have his say.

To him Zionism and Communism were twin evils, and he warmly approved when, in the summer of 1972, Sadat dismissed his Soviet advisers. Now nothing stood in the way of the full-blooded alliance that was capable of dominating the Arab scene – the marriage of Saudi wealth with Egyptian manpower and technical superiority. In July 1973 King Faisal gave the world an idea of what was in his mind when for the first time he publicly mentioned his country's power to cut back oil deliveries if President Nixon did not modify his support for Israel. The Arab oil embargo that accompanied the general oil price-rise during the October War of 1973 was applied only with his customary caution, but a repetition could be all-important since Saudi Arabia owns forty per cent of the world's known oil reserves.

At the time of Faisal's death, his country was one of the richest in the world in liquid funds. Riyadh, seventy years earlier a village, was a city throbbing with activity, besieged by salesmen and technical experts out for contracts to fulfil the developments he had in mind, pierced by dual carriageways, humming with traffic, twinkling at night with the lights that outline mile on mile of ribbon development, yet with *suqs* that fall quiet, empty of their menfolk, at the hour of prayer.

Saudi Arabia's government is highly centralized. Though competent and well trained Saudis are now available to run it, King Faisal personally took most of the important decisions. On the Prophet's birthday, 1975, one of his scores of nephews, the son of a much younger half-brother, slipped into his audience chamber and fired three shots at the King over the shoulder of the Kuwaiti Oil Minister whom the King was receiving. Perhaps we shall never know whether the assassin struck out of vengeance for the death of a puritanical brother who had, some years back, tried to tamper with a television mast, and been shot by guards in the course of a scuffle at its base; or whether he acted out of radical notions picked up while he was sampling three American universities without much success; or whether a mixed-up kid was prompted by both these ill-assorted motives. What we know for sure is that his bullets deprived his countrymen of a leader with a store of wisdom and experience.

The stability of the Kingdom stood the test of this capricious act. King Khalid, next in line, moved naturally into the role of leader of the nation. His own wide experience and the talents of the immediate family – exemplified by Prince Fahd, the Crown Prince as First Deputy Prime Minister, and Prince Abdullah ibn Abdul Aziz, Second Deputy Prime Minister and Head of the National Guard – ensured the smooth continuance of government. Within six months, King Khalid launched the monumental second five year plan.

Like his father, Khalid honoured the essentially Arabian quality of his roots. He was at home in the desert and trusted by the tribes. With his father he took part in several expeditions during the unification of the country. In 1932 he was appointed Governor of the Hejaz, and in 1934 Minister of the Interior. As a young man he represented the Kingdom on various missions abroad with his brother Faisal (e.g. to Britain in 1939 and 1945, and the US in 1943.)

As Faisal's First Deputy Prime Minister he moved to the centre of the affairs of state, was party to all major decisions of policy and frequently travelled abroad. When he became King in 1975, Saudi Arabia was already committed to carefully planned development on a massive scale. Fahd was by his side as First Deputy Premier, dynamic and involved in the day-to-day administration of government. Khalid's heart disease, twice alleviated by open heart surgery, precluded sustained strenuous public duties. Yet it was remarkable what he achieved, repeatedly travelling at home and overseas in his kingly role, and playing a vital personal part in Arab and Islamic affairs.

Khalid's intervention halted – for a while – the Lebanese civil war in the late 1970s; he brought Muslims together in the historic 38-nation summit in Taif and Makkah in 1981, and that year launched the six-nation Gulf Co-operation Council.

He was a man of generosity of heart and personal modesty. He had little time for the panoply of power. When he died in Taif on June 13, 1982, at the height of Israeli aggression in Lebanon, his people mourned a wise, fatherly and devoted leader. (He is pictured on the right.)

For many years King Fahd, his successor, had above all others exemplified Saudi Arabia's unprecedented evolution into modern statehood – as a substantial contributor to world stability and cool-headedness, and as a country shaping for its own cleanly defined needs the benefits of modern technology in a strictly Islamic framework.

King Fahd was born in 1921. Recognition of his abilities came early: in 1953, in his early thirties, he took the education portfolio and was responsible for the first expansion in schools throughout the Kingdom. In 1962 he became Minister of the Interior, and Second Deputy Prime Minister in 1967.

After appointment as Crown Prince and First Deputy Prime Minister on King Faisal's death, he acted as viceroy during King Khalid's absences, and remained at the heart of the daily affairs of state throughout his brother's reign.

Thus he came to power as a man already well known and profoundly respected in the world, no less than in his

own Kingdom, as a man of vision, experience, authority, accessibility and consistency of policy. Internationally he has always upheld Arab solidarity. He has established Saudi Arabia as a steadying factor in world affairs, skilful in the use of the Kingdom's economic strength to preserve equilibrium during a period of global recession. Domestically he is intent on building a Saudi Arabia whose prosperity will endure by means of painstaking planning, diversification, conservation of resources, and devotion to Islam.

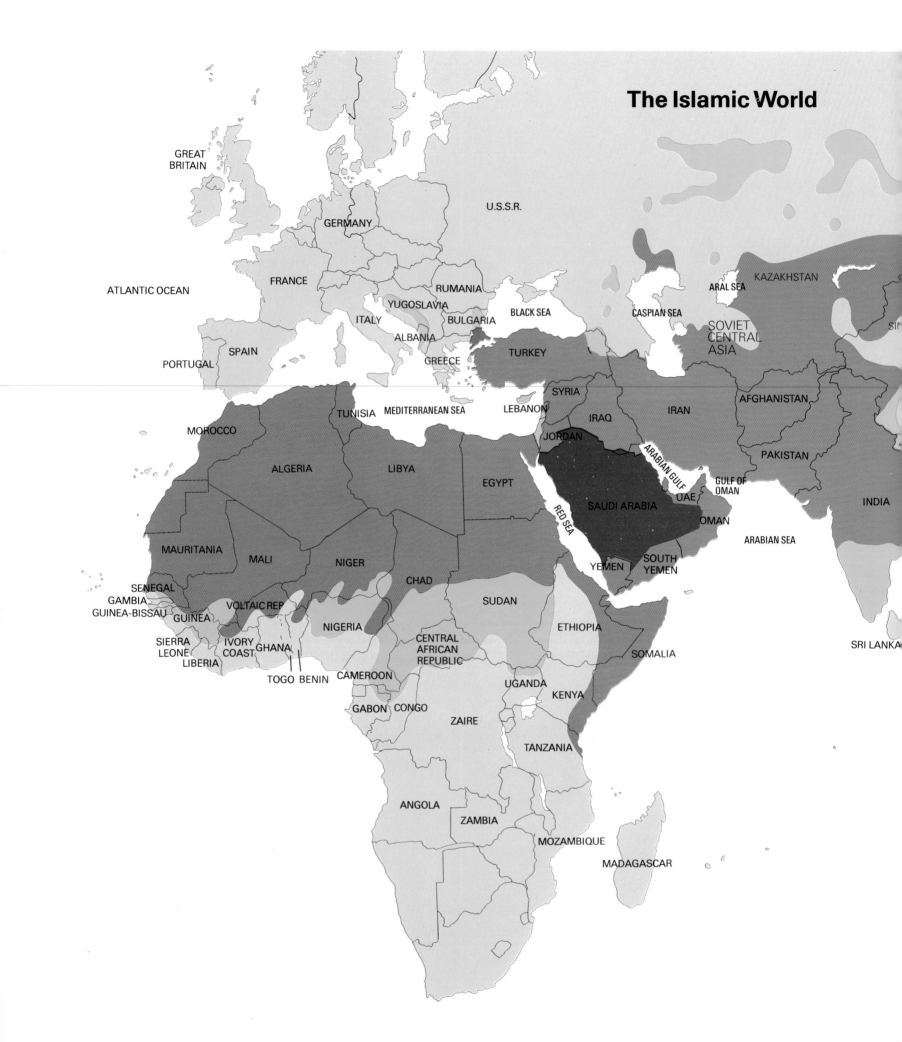

# The Islamic World

GREAT BRITAIN

ATLANTIC OCEAN

GERMANY

U.S.S.R.

FRANCE

RUMANIA

YUGOSLAVIA

ITALY

BULGARIA

BLACK SEA

CASPIAN SEA

ARAL SEA

KAZAKHSTAN

SOVIET CENTRAL ASIA

ALBANIA

GREECE

TURKEY

SPAIN

PORTUGAL

TUNISIA

MEDITERRANEAN SEA

SYRIA

LEBANON

IRAQ

IRAN

AFGHANISTAN

MOROCCO

JORDAN

ALGERIA

LIBYA

EGYPT

ARABIAN GULF

UAE

GULF OF OMAN

PAKISTAN

SAUDI ARABIA

OMAN

INDIA

RED SEA

ARABIAN SEA

MAURITANIA

MALI

NIGER

CHAD

YEMEN

SOUTH YEMEN

SENEGAL

GAMBIA

GUINEA-BISSAU

GUINEA

VOLTAIC REP

NIGERIA

SUDAN

ETHIOPIA

SOMALIA

SRI LANKA

SIERRA LEONE

IVORY COAST

GHANA

LIBERIA

TOGO BENIN

CAMEROON

CENTRAL AFRICAN REPUBLIC

UGANDA

KENYA

GABON

CONGO

ZAIRE

TANZANIA

ANGOLA

ZAMBIA

MOZAMBIQUE

MADAGASCAR

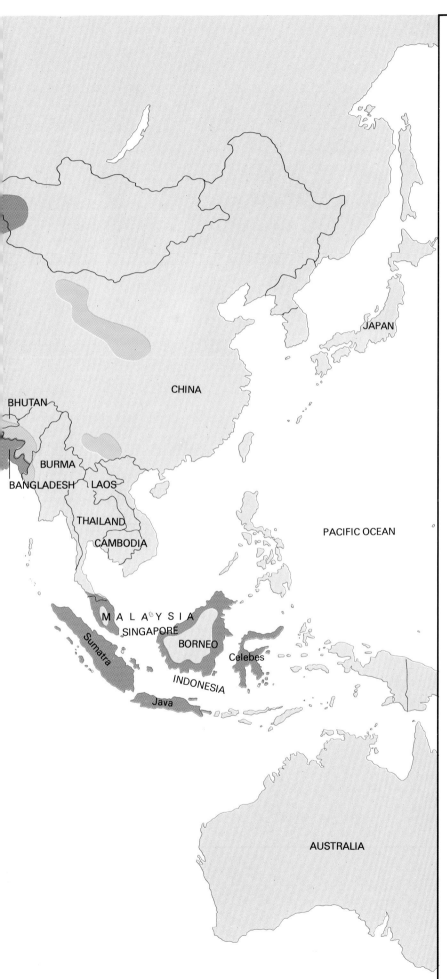

# 5
# Islam

*To Saudi Arabia, the holy cities of Makkah and Medina are a sacred trust, exercised on behalf of all of Islam. To the fountainhead of their faith every year flock pilgrims in their hundreds of thousands, to offer their "submission", as is the meaning of Islam, to God's will as revealed through the Prophet Muhammad.*

BHUTAN

JAPAN

CHINA

BURMA

BANGLADESH  LAOS

THAILAND

CAMBODIA

PACIFIC OCEAN

M A L A Y S I A

SINGAPORE

Sumatra

BORNEO

Celebes

INDONESIA

Java

AUSTRALIA

*From its foundation in the Arabian heartland, Islam today circles the globe and is the accredited faith of some 500 million people. It is constantly making new converts among those without belief.*

# Saudi Arabia as the Heartland of Islam

THE religious pre-eminence of Saudi Arabia in the Muslim world is vouchsafed by the fact that it contains the two cities of Makkah and Medina, where Islam was born and where it matured under the Prophet Muhammad himself, and where the Qur'an was revealed. Makkah also has the Ka'bah, Islam's central shrine, while the tomb of the Prophet and his mosque are in Medina. The Saudi regime earned the gratitude of all Muslims by ensuring the safety of pilgrims under the strong hand of King Abdul Aziz ibn Saud, who enforced the strict Shari'ah rules of law and order. The late King Faisal brought a new political dimension by pursuing a policy of Islamic solidarity, as distinct from pure territorial nationalism.

Islam is a world-wide faith. There exists today a world Muslim community about seven hundred million strong (some Muslim agencies put the number at around eight hundred million) which, despite sectarian differences, feels bound together in one faith: every Muslim must recite the profession of faith, "There is no God but Allah, and Muhammad is his Prophet", with awareness of its meaning and full consent from the heart. The first proselytizers were, of course, the Arabs themselves, and rightly so. The Qur'an repeatedly states that it is "a Reminder *for the whole world*", that differences of tribes and peoples, of tongues and skin-colour, are signs of God's power and mercy, but that real rank in God's sight depends on piety and virtue, and that the Prophet himself was "sent only as a mercy *to all mankind*". This universal character of the Islamic teaching was also strongly underlined in the Prophet's Farewell Pilgrimage sermon, which declares the religious ideal to be indifferent to racial and other natural differences.

The fact remains that Islam's origins lie in an Arab milieu and that it has a clear Arab base. Muslim thinkers have considered this point and given explanations to rationalize it. Thus, ibn Khaldun holds that the Prophet had to be born in Arabia, whose people were not primitive, yet were close to the natural state of man and therefore possessed of natural manly virtues and minds unencumbered by preconceived notions. Indeed he had to be born among the Makkan tribe of Quraysh, who, once converted to Islam, had the necessary power and prestige to protect and propagate it. It is, of course, historically true that when Makkah joined Islam, the rest of Arabia followed. Shah Walig Allah of Delhi adds that it was part of the divine plan to replace the older Middle Eastern civilizations with a new civilization which would have a moral freshness and virility that could be supplied only by the Arabs, once they had been nurtured by Islam.

Be that as it may, there was undoubtedly a religious ferment in Makkah and Medina prior to the appearance of the Prophet. While the Jews of Medina longed for a Prophet to make them victorious over the Arabs there (*Qur'an* II,83), Arab intellectuals in Makkah having accepted neither Judaism nor Christianity, desired a new Arab Prophet so that "they may be better guided" than the Jewish and Christian communities (*Qur'an* XXXV, 42; VI, 157; XXXVII, 168). When the Makkans opposed the Prophet, the Qur'an repeatedly reminded them that he had been raised up "from among themselves" and that they knew him well because he had lived among them for so long. Even more emphatically, the Qur'an time and again states that it is revealed in a "clear Arabic tongue" (*Qur'an* XVI, 103; XXVI, 195; also XII, 2; XIII, 37; XX, 113), for "if We had made it a non-Arab Qur'an, they (the opponents) would have said, 'Why are its verses not clearly set out?'" (*Qur'an* XLI, 44). This last statement refers to the belief of the Arabs that the Arabic language is the most expressive and eloquent.

That the Prophet, since he was an Arab himself, should communicate to his people in Arabic, and that they should be the first addressees of Islam, was, of course, natural. But the statements of

*Focus of the annual pilgrimage of hundreds of thousands of devout Muslims is the Ka'bah of Holy Makkah which pilgrims circle seven times – the first three times preferably hastening round three of the sides.*

**The Way to Makkah**

Twelve miles north of Jiddah, the new King Abdul Aziz International Airport, covering 40.5 square miles, is one of the wonders of the modern aviation world. Some 1.2 million pilgrims are expected to arrive by air in 1985, and the figure is expected to double by the turn of the century. The award-winning design of the roof of the Hajj terminal (above) is spectacular; based on that of the tents of the desert, it is a striking reminder of the pilgrim past. It has the world's largest fabric roof – 210 white fibreglass "tents" (left) as high as ten stories above the terminal floor at their peaks. Pilgrims approaching from Ta'if may refresh their spirits at a mosque (right) on the edge of the Haram.

the Qur'an about its own nature go much further, since it regards itself as miraculous and challenges its opponents – those Arabs who were proud of their literary perfection – to produce anything like it (*Qur'an* X, 38; XI, 13; XXVIII, 49). In these verses, the Qur'an is emphasizing that its source is Divine, and cannot be the composition of a human mind, even that of the Prophet himself; and it is, indeed, clear that the speech of the Prophet, outside of Revelation, is of a different quality from that of the Qur'an. Muslim theologians early deduced the doctrine that the Qur'an is "inimitable" and hence untranslatable. Many Western scholars also think that it is not really translatable – which is why Arthur J. Arberry called his English rendering *The Qur'an Interpreted*, rather than *The Qur'an Translated*. For centuries, the religious scholars of Islam did not allow the Qur'an to be translated. This law has been quite recently relaxed in the interest of the wider dissemination of Qur'anic teaching; but they still insist that no translation be published without the Arabic text.

The second major source of Islamic doctrine and practice – particularly in the field of Law, which stands at the centre of the entire Islamic system – is the Sunnah (Example or Model) of the Prophet – that is his precepts and conduct, both in private and public activity. The Sunnah interprets and elaborates the teaching of the Qur'an, and is embodied in certain authoritative works. These do not only include what the Prophet actually said or did. At a very early stage, the Muslim jurists decided that the entire body of Arab practices and customs to which the Prophet had not explicitly objected and *hence had tacitly approved of, is part of the Prophetic Sunnah*. This concept of the "tacit (*sukuti*) Sunnah" thus sanctified the entire gamut of Arab life – essentially Makkan and Medinan after its reform by the Qur'an and the Prophet. In its outward expansion and during its long development it was certainly modified, elaborated and changed (on the basis of the principle of *ijtihad*, or fresh thinking), but it always served as the normative base of reference. In the outermost regions of Islam, such as Indonesia, much of pre-Islamic custom (called *Adat*) still prevails, but the religious leaders there have been exerting steady pressure to change the situation.

Besides being the birthplace of Islam,

*A fully-serviced tented city accommodates the pilgrims on their arrival for their approximately week-long ritual of contrition and worship.*

Makkah is the object of the annual pilgrimage (*hajj* – q.v.) undertaken by Muslims to the Ka'bah Sanctuary (the Haram), also called the "House of God (*bayt Allah*)". A pre-Islamic Arab site, it was officially adopted by Islam in the year 1 AH (622 CE), after reforms purging it of idolatrous practices and implications. It is, for all Muslims, the most holy place, where the Divine comes into special touch with the earth. Muslim mystics (Sufis) in particular developed a mystique of the Ka'bah, regarding it as the earthly manifestation of a metaphysical Divine reality. Throughout the centuries, almost every Muslim, no matter how distant his abode, has aspired to visit Makkah, thus rendering it the metropolis of Islam, and the *hajj* the greatest living religious epic on earth. Scholars and saints – side by side with common folk – have usually visited Makkah, often more than once in their lifetime, to meet scholars and spiritual leaders from other parts of the Muslim world. Many stayed on in Makkah for

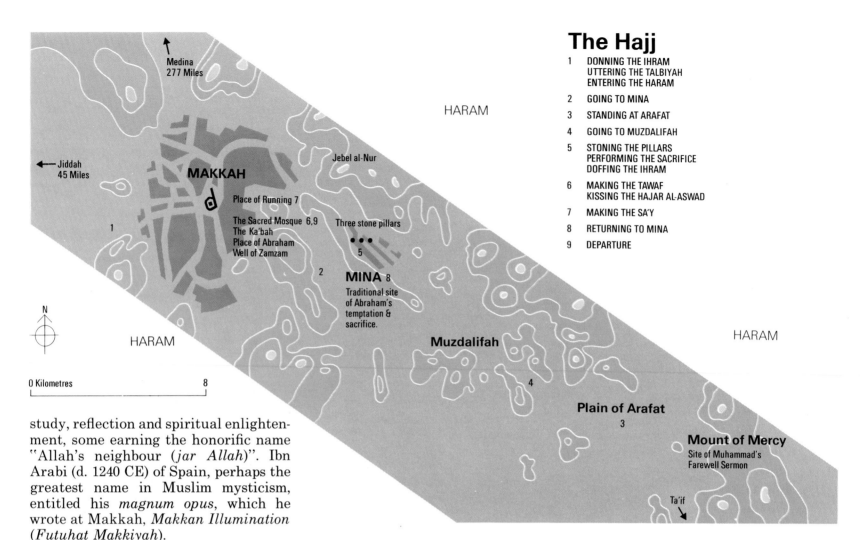

# The Hajj

1 DONNING THE IHRAM
  UTTERING THE TALBIYAH
  ENTERING THE HARAM

2 GOING TO MINA

3 STANDING AT ARAFAT

4 GOING TO MUZDALIFAH

5 STONING THE PILLARS
  PERFORMING THE SACRIFICE
  DOFFING THE IHRAM

6 MAKING THE TAWAF
  KISSING THE HAJAR AL-ASWAD

7 MAKING THE SA'Y

8 RETURNING TO MINA

9 DEPARTURE

study, reflection and spiritual enlightenment, some earning the honorific name "Allah's neighbour (*jar Allah*)". Ibn Arabi (d. 1240 CE) of Spain, perhaps the greatest name in Muslim mysticism, entitled his *magnum opus*, which he wrote at Makkah, *Makkan Illumination (Futuhat Makkiyah)*.

Since 1925 CE, the quantity of pilgrims has increased immensely. Whereas at the *hajj* in the summer of 1925 the number of pilgrims was estimated at one hundred thousand, at the *hajj* celebrated in 1977 there were two million. This increase is partly due to the fact that more Muslims can now afford to go on the pilgrimage, but the main reason lies in the development of Saudi Arabia. The Saudi regime has acquitted itself admirably as protector of the Holy Cities. King ibn Saud's primary task was to put an end to the lawlessness which deterred Muslims from performing the *hajj* for fear of robbery and murder. Inheritor to the puritanism of his ancestors he strictly enforced the penal law of the Shari'ah, which ordains severe punishment for theft and murder. At the same time there have been steady improvements in air travel, roads, water, electricity and the availability of better and more hygienic accommodation, until today the handling of what is now an influx of millions of pilgrims, all at once, in the performance of the *hajj*, is an annual feat of astonishing organization. Profiteering is non-existent. Traffic is controlled by helicopter. There are no

scrums, no shortages. Yet the techniques of control do not obtrude upon the mood of devotion.

The prestige of Saudi Arabia in the international Muslim community has grown gradually but tangibly. Although the new Saudi regime has never made theocratic or caliphal claims, its policies represent a broad-based Islam and a robust realism which have won for it the respect both of peoples and of governments. Turkey, which had been alienated since World War I and had virtually banned Turks from performing the pilgrimage, removed these restrictions in 1965, and at the pilgrimage in December 1974 the Turkish contingent was the largest from outside Arabia. Due primarily to the religious basis of the state, the Saudi monarchy is the only one in the world to eschew the use of such symbols of worldly power as the crown and the throne; an egalitarian practice much respected by all Muslims, whether Arab or non-Arab.

King Faisal, in particular, brought a new dimension to the Saudi rule by his active policy of pan-Islamic solidarity – a policy sustained by King Khalid (e.g. over bringing peace to Lebanon). The

acute crisis created by Israel's occupation of Arab lands and particularly by her takeover of Jerusalem presented him with a special challenge. After the incident in 1969, involving Aqsa Mosque in Jerusalem. King Faisal played a central role in organizing the Islamic summit meetings held in Morocco in 1969 and in Pakistan in 1974. A permanent Islamic Secretariat has been established, with headquarters in Jiddah, and financed by Saudi Arabia, to bring about closer co-operation among Muslim governments. At semi-official level, the Saudi government had already set up an important organization called The World Muslim Congress (*Rabitat al-Alam al-Islami*), with which many other Muslim organizations all over the world have become affiliated or associated. In April 1974, 158 Muslim national and international organizations, big and small, held a meeting in Makkah under its auspices. While the Congress discusses religious problems and socio-political issues arising from them, the Secretariat addresses itself to matters of politics and intra-Muslim development.

*Statistical sources:* Ministry of Pilgrimage & Waqfs and Ministry of Planning.

# The Hajj

*"And complete the* Hajj *and the* Umrah *in the service of God. But if you are prevented (from completing it) send an offering for sacrifice such as you may find. And do not shave your heads until the offering reaches the place of sacrifice. And if any of you is ill or has an ailment in his scalp (necessitating shaving) he must in compensation either fast or feed the poor or offer sacrifice."*

HOLY QUR'AN, II

*Medical facilities* (top) *and nourishment* (centre) *are available to pilgrims as they adopt the simple* Ihram *garb of two pieces of white towelling.*

AFTER belief in the one God (Allah), the performance of regular, ritual prayers, fasting during the month of Ramadan and the giving of fixed alms (*Zakah*), the *hajj* is the fifth pillar of Islam, a fundamental duty which a Muslim, male and female alike, must perform at least once in his lifetime if he or she has the material means to do so.

Long before the Prophet Muhammad began to preach Islam and summon the Arabs and all mankind back to the worship of the One True God, indeed since time immemorial, the barren valley of Makkah had been a place of pilgrimage venerated by the Arabs, both settled and nomadic. It had been associated with the Patriarch Abraham, the Friend of God, who was the first to establish there a house to the glory of God. In the Holy Qur'an (II, 122–123) we read: "And lo! Abraham and Ishmael raised the foundations of the House saying: 'Oh Lord! accept this from us. Thou art, indeed, the All-Hearing, the All-Knowing. Our Lord! and make us submissive to Thee and of our progeny a nation submissive to Thee and show us our rites and turn to us in Mercy. Indeed, Thou art the All-Forgiving, All-Merciful. Our Lord! send amongst them a Messenger of their own who will recite to them Thy signs.' "

Again we read (III, 91–92): "Indeed, the first House (of worship) established for men was at Bakka (Makkah), full of blessing and guidance for all men. In it are clear signs, the Station of Abraham. Whoever enters it shall be safe. Pilgrimage thereto is a duty men owe to God, all those who can afford the journey. But if any reject this, God is in no need of any of His creatures."

And so the ancient pilgrimage to Makkah became incorporated in Islam; the guiding lines of its performance were laid down by the Holy Qur'an (II, 193 ff.): "And complete the Hajj and the Umrah in the service of God. But if you are prevented (from completing it) send an offering for sacrifice such as you may find. And do not shave your heads until the offering reaches the place of sacrifice. And if any of you is ill or has an ailment in his scalp (necessitating shaving) he must in compensation either fast or feed the poor or offer sacrifice. And when you are in safety again, if anyone wishes to continue the Umrah on to the Hajj he must make an offering such as he can afford. But if he cannot afford it he should fast three days during the Hajj and seven days on his return, making ten days in all. This is for those whose household is not settled in the Sacred Mosque. And fear God and know that God is strict in punishment. The Hajj is in well known months (Shawwal, Dhu'l-Qa'dah and Dhu'l Hijjah). If anyone undertakes that duty in them let there be no obscenity, nor wickedness, nor quarrelling in the Hajj. And whatever good you do God knows it. And take provision for the journey. But the best of provisions is fear of God. So fear him, all you who are wise."

The pilgrimage is made to Makkah, the most sacred city of Islam, where the Prophet Muhammad was born, where his mission was first revealed to him and where he began preaching Islam. In the centre of Makkah stands the Sacred Mosque (Al-Masjid al-Haram), a large open courtyard enclosed by cloisters, rebuilt and enlarged many times.

*"The Pilgrimage is in months well-known; whoso undertakes the duty of Pilgrimage in them shall not go in to his womenfolk nor indulge in ungodliness and disputing in the Pilgrimage. Whatever good you do, God knows it. And take provision; but the best provision is godfearing."* HOLY QUR'AN, II

Roughly in the centre of the Sacred Mosque stands the Ka'bah, the House of God, towards which all Muslims turn their faces in their daily prayers, no matter where they may be. The Ka'bah, as its name denotes, is a cube-shaped building of stone, the front (north-east) and back (south-west) sides being forty feet long, the other sides being thirty-five feet and the height fifty feet.

In the east corner, about four feet above ground level, is set the Black Stone in a silver frame. This stone (eight inches in diameter) is believed to be the only remnant of the first mosque built by Abraham and to go back even before him to the time of Adam. The Ka'bah has been rebuilt many times in the course of the centuries, once in the lifetime of the Prophet, before his mission, when he was chosen by chance to place the Black Stone in its position. In the north-east wall of the Ka'bah close to the corner in which the Black Stone is set and some

seven feet above the ground is the door to the Ka'bah which is opened at special times. There is nothing inside the building, which was cleansed of its idols when the Prophet returned in triumph to Makkah early in 630 CE. The Ka'bah is covered with a black pall decorated with verses from the Qur'an. This is the *Kiswah* (garment) which from the Middle Ages was made in Cairo and brought ceremoniously to Makkah every year by the Egyptian pilgrims. It is now made by local craftsmen.

The two remaining shrines inside the Sacred Mosque are the Station of Abraham (facing the door) where the Patriarch bowed down in prayer and the Well of Zamzam, north-east of the Ka'bah, which sprang up when Hagar was desperately seeking water for the infant Ishmael.

*Pilgrims gather on the Mount of Mercy, the site of Muhammad's farewell sermon, to watch in prayerfulness as the sun descends over the Plain of Arafat.*

Just outside the Sacred Mosque is the Mas'a (running place) between the rocky hillocks of as-Safa and al-Marwah, a distance of 440 yards. The Mas'a, which was until recently an ordinary street with shops, is now covered over and paved with marble flags. It was between these two hills that Hagar ran distractedly seeking water.

Pilgrimage to Makkah is of two kinds. There is the *umrah*, the Lesser Pilgrimage or Visit, which can be performed at any time of the year and is confined to worship at the places mentioned above. Then there is the *hajj* proper, which combines the rites of the *umrah* with others outside Makkah and takes place only once a year in the first part of the month of *Dhu 'l-Hijjah*, the last month of the Islamic lunar calendar.

Again, the *hajj* and the *umrah* can be performed together (*Qiran*) or separately (*Tamattu*). The latter is chosen by pilgrims who arrive in Makkah some days before the ninth of the month, which day is the culmination of the pilgrimage. *Tamattu* entails either sacrifice at Mina or fasting during the pilgrimage and on return home.

Nowadays, with frequent and easy means of transport, the number of pilgrims to Makkah during the pilgrimage

*"When you press on from Arafat, then remember God at the Holy Waymark, and remember Him as He has guided you, though formerly you were gone astray. Then press on from where the people press on, and pray for God's forgiveness; God is All-forgiving, All-compassionate. And when you have performed your holy rites remember God, as you remember your fathers or yet more devoutly. Now some men there are who say, 'Our Lord, give to us in this world'; such men shall have no part in the world to come."* HOLY QUR'AN, II

*"Indeed, the first House (of worship) established for men was at Bakka (Makkah), full of blessing and guidance for all men. In it are clear signs, the Station of Abraham. Whoever enters it shall be safe. Pilgrimage thereto is a duty men owe to God, all those who can afford the journey. But if any reject this, God is in no need of any of His creatures."*

HOLY QUR'AN, III

*Children count for no less than adults in the eyes of Allah, and throughout Islam, children at an early age are able to recite large portions of the Holy Qur'an.*

month is very large, sometimes exceeding a million. Organizing such a vast number of people, seeing to their health and other needs, is a formidable task which the Saudi Government performs with great efficiency.

Most foreign pilgrims arrive either by sea or by air through Jiddah, the port of Makkah, and there the Government has a special *hajj* Administration. From Jid-

dah they go by bus to Makkah (some fifty miles away), each group of pilgrims being assigned according to their rites (Hanafi, Shafi'i, Maliki, and so on) to a *mutawwif* in Makkah. A *mutawwaf* is a special guide and mentor whose duty it is to see that the pilgrims under his wing perform the rites of the pilgrimage correctly, have no difficulties while in the Holy Land and return to their homelands happy and satisfied, having gained the blessing of the pilgrimage properly performed. Each *mutawwif* has under him a number of assistants whose duty it is to accompany groups of pilgrims. Of course, a pilgrim who knows the language and is familiar with Makkah can do without a *mutawwif*, relying on one of the many guides to the *hajj* printed in Arabic or other languages.

Before entering the sacred territory around Makkah – indeed, sometimes from the start of his journey – the pilgrim puts himself in a state of sanctity by ablution, prayer and donning the pilgrim's dress (*Ihram*), which for a man consists of two unsewn towels, one worn wrapped around the lower part of the body, the other thrown over the upper part, and unsewn sandals. There is no special dress for a woman except that her face must remain unveiled, no matter what her local customs may be. The reason for these regulations is to emphasize the equality of all pilgrims, high and low, before God.

On and off during his journey and until he enters Makkah the pilgrim chants a short formula of acceptance of the pilgrimage duties (the *Talbiyah*). This is: "Here I am in answer to Thy call, O God, here I am! Here I am! Thou hast no associate! Here I am! All Praise and Favour and Kingship are Thine! Thou hast no associate!"

The rites of the *umrah* are *Tawaf* (circumambulation of the Ka'bah), *Sa'y* (running between as-Safa and al-Marwah) and shaving of the head or clipping of the hair. On arrival in Makkah the pilgrim performs *Wudu* (ablution before prayer) and goes straight away to the Sacred Mosque which he enters preferably by the Bab as-Salam (Gate of Peace). Around the Ka'bah is a paved area (the *Mataf*) on which the pilgrim performs his *Tawaf*, beginning at the Black Stone and going around the Ka'bah seven times in an anti-clockwise direction. The pilgrim makes the first three rounds of the Ka'bah at a fast pace and the remainder at walking pace, all the while glorifying God and supplicating His favour and mercy in set phrases generally repeated after his guide. As the pilgrim passes the Black Stone he either kisses it, or touches it or simply makes a motion of his hand towards it. As the throng making *Tawaf* is generally very large, the last is by far the most common. A policeman is posted on either side of the Black Stone to keep the pilgrims on the move. It is a remarkable fact that the *Mataf* is never free from pilgrims, night or day, except at the times of congregational prayer. Muslims in no wise worship the Black Stone. They kiss or touch it because it is known that the Prophet Muhammad did so and thereby they establish a physical link between themselves and the Prophet. And he did so because it was a link between himself and Abraham. *Tawaf* is the first and last religious act of the pilgrim to Makkah.

After performing his *Tawaf* the pilgrim then proceeds to the Station of Abraham and there performs two cycles of individual prayer. Before going out from the Sacred Mosque to the Mas'a he may drink some water from the Well of Zamzam. This water is slightly brackish but is drunk in large quantities by the pilgrims, who often fill their water bottles with it to take home.

The second rite of the *umrah* is *Sa'y* (running) between as-Safa and al-Marwah. For this the pilgrim leaves the Mosque by the Bab as-Safa (Safa Gate) and mounts the rocky hillock of that name. After a short prayer he proceeds at walking pace towards the second

*"Thus We appointed you a midmost nation that you might be witnesses to the people, and that the Messenger might be a witness to you. Turn thy face toward the Holy Mosque; and wherever you are, turn your faces towards it."*

HOLY QUR'AN, II

*An historic picture of Makkah, dating from the 1950s, shows the prevailing architecture backed by the so-called Black Hills. A minaret of the Great Mosque is seen in the foreground.*

*"And when We settled for Abraham the place of the House: 'Thou shall not associate with Me anything. And do thou purify My House for those that shall go about it and those that stand, for those that bow and prostrate themselves; and proclaim among men the Pilgrimage, and they shall come unto thee on foot and upon every lean beast, they shall come from every deep ravine that they may witness things profitable to them and mention God's Name on days well-known over such beasts of the flocks as He has provided them: "So eat thereof, and feed the wretched poor." Let them then finish with their self-neglect and let them fulfil their vows, and go about the Ancient House.'"*

HOLY QUR'AN, XXII

hillock, al-Marwah, all the while saying prayers and supplications. The second fifth of the distance between the two hillocks, between two marker posts, is covered at a fast pace.

Having performed the *Sa'y* between the two hillocks seven times the pilgrim ends up at al-Marwah where he has his head shaved or, more commonly nowadays, his hair cut, which is the third rite of the *umrah*. With this he has completed the *umrah*, and if he has come before the ninth of the month with the intention of separating his *hajj* from *umrah* (*Tamattu*), he is now free to put off his *Ihram* dress, have a bath and put on his ordinary clothes, entering into the social life of Makkah. If on the other hand, his intention was that his *hajj* and *umrah* should be joined (*Qiran*), then he remains in *Ihram*.

On the eighth of the month of *Dhu'l-Hijjah* the pilgrims prepare for the culmination of the pilgrimage to Makkah. Those who have performed the *umrah* separately bathe and put on their *Ihram* dress again and go to the Mosque to perform *Tawaf*. Then the whole mass of the pilgrims and even inhabitants of Makkah move to Mina, four miles away, arriving for noon prayers. Mina is a remarkable place: for five or six days of the pilgrimage month it is thronged. For the rest of the year it is a ghost town.

Later, on the eighth or early on the ninth of the month, the pilgrims move to the Plain of Arafat, some thirteen miles south-east of Makkah and outside the sacred territory, where the *mutawwifs* have set up their thousands of tents, each with its distinctive flag, arranged in streets. On the morning of the ninth of *Dhu'l-Hijjah* the pilgrims move about freely, talking with other pilgrims and making new friends from many distant lands. Noon and afternoon prayers are combined at mid-day and the Imam gives a short sermon from the pulpit of Namirah Mosque on the Jabal al-Rahmah (Mount of Mercy), a distinguished landmark of Arafat, on which the Prophet gave his Farewell Sermon in which he summarized the duties of a Muslim.

The whole of the afternoon of the ninth is spent in prayer on the Plain of Arafat. This is the *Wuquf* (Standing), which is the culmination and cornerstone of the pilgrimage to Makkah. Whoever misses it cannot be said to have performed the pilgrimage. In *Wuquf* the pilgrim stands bare-headed all the afternoon in the open air glorifying God, reading the Qur'an and crying aloud "*Labbayka 'llahumma Labbayka* (Here I am, O God, here I am!)." The infirm may sit or seek shade during their devotions but it is considered more meritorious to remain standing all the time.

As soon as the sun sets the whole immense throng gets on the move, making for Muzdalifah, an open plain about half way between Arafat and Mina. There the pilgrims say their sunset and night prayers combined. Controlling the movement of over a million human beings, in all forms of transport, is a supreme feat of administration by the Saudi police. The pilgrim spends the night under the stars at Muzdalifah and gathers seventy pebbles, each about the size of a chick-pea. Early the next morning (the tenth) after prayer he proceeds to Mina, where the pilgrimage is concluded.

In Mina are three stone pillars surrounded by low walls called *jamrahs*. At the one nearest Makkah (Jamrat al-Aqabah), on the morning of the tenth day, the pilgrim casts seven of his pebbles calling out each time "*Allahu Akbar* (God is most Great)". This is symbolic of man's casting out evil from himself. Then, if necessary, the animals are sacrificed and some of the meat given to the poor. The pilgrims must then return to Mina, for it is there that the pilgrimage ends. With a final shaving of his head or symbolic clipping of his hair the pilgrim emerges from the state of *Ihram* and his pilgrimage is concluded. He bathes, puts on new clothes and looks forward to returning to his home a *hajj* or *hajji*. He must, however, spend the two or three days after the tenth day of Dhu'l-Hijjah in Mina, cast his remaining sixty-three pebbles at all three *jamrahs*, and perform *Tawaf al-Ifadah*.

Having completed his pilgrimage the pilgrim is generally eager to be on his way, but there are many who linger in Makkah for days, weeks or even months, some for the rest of their lives. Delay also arises from the difficulty of arranging transport for such a vast multitude. When the day of his departure is fixed the pilgrim goes to the Sacred Mosque for the last time and performs a final *Tawaf* (*Tawaf al-Wida* or Tawaf of Farewell). He leaves the House of God walking backwards all the time, praising and thanking God and praying that this may not be the last time he enjoys the grace and favour of visiting His Holy House and goes out from the Sacred Mosque by the Bab-al-Wida (Gate of Farewell). Then with joyful heart he sets

*On the approach to the final act of worship, the pilgrim passes through the city of Makkah to the proximity of the Great Mosque. Regular prayer, five times daily, proceeds as usual.*

*Since the photograph below was taken, the floor of the Great Mosque has been paved throughout.*

## "God has appointed the Kaaba, the Holy House, as an establishment for men."

HOLY QUR'AN, V

*Islamic dignitaries from home and abroad are permitted to enter the Ka'bah* (far left and below), *which contains a spare and unadorned chamber, with no intervention of human artifice needed to add to its unique sanctity. Most pilgrims wish to kiss the Black Stone* (bottom left) *and to worship at the shrines of the Station of Abraham* (left) *and the Well of Zamzam.*

## " 'Take to yourselves Abraham's station for a place of prayer.' " HOLY QUR'AN, II

off on his journey home.

But since it is vouchsafed to the vast majority of Muslims to make the pilgrimage to Makkah only once in their lifetimes most pilgrims combine their pilgrimage with a visit to Medina, sometimes before, but generally after the pilgrimage. There they visit the Prophet's tomb and those of the early Caliphs in the Sacred Mosque. They usually spend several days in this second city of Islam – the city to which the Prophet Muhammad fled from persecution in his native city, where he established the Islamic State and where he lies buried with so many of his noble companions.

The pilgrimage to Makkah used to be an arduous and often perilous adventure, but today it is done in comparative comfort and perfect safety. Nevertheless, owing to the vast numbers of pilgrims, it is still a challenging enterprise, especially when the pilgrimage season falls in the summer months. Yet, when the *hajji* is safe at home with his family and when the month of the *hajj* comes round again he feels that there is nowhere he would rather be than with countless thousands from all corners of the earth thronging the Sacred Mosque and the streets of Makkah or standing in prayer on the Plain of Arafat.

## Medina the Radiant

*Second only to Makkah in sanctity is the city of Medina, whose night-time profile is dominated by the Great Mosque with its green dome and exquisite interior. It was to Medina that the Prophet fled (in 622 CE) when his teachings were resisted by his fellow citizens in Makkah. Medina, whose ancient name was Yathrib, lay on a principal north-south caravan route. Its essentially Arabian character largely survives today.*

# Islam in Today's World

"SURELY in the creation of the heavens and earth and in the alternation of night and day there are signs for men possessed of minds who remember God, standing and sitting and on their sides, and reflect upon the creation of the heavens and the earth: 'Our Lord, Thou has not created this for vanity. Glory be to Thee! Guard us against the chastisement of the Fire.' "
*Qur'an* III, 187

### Islam and Knowledge

"Hast thou not seen how that God sends down out of heaven water, and therewith We bring forth fruits of diverse hues? And in the mountains are streaks white and red, of diverse hues, and pitchy black; men too, and beasts and cattle – diverse are their hues. Even so only those of His servants fear God who have knowledge."
*Qur'an* XXXV, 26

"Say: 'Are they equal – those who know and those who know not?' Only men possessed of minds remember."
*Qur'an* XXXIX, 12

". . . God will raise up in rank those of you who believe and have been given knowledge."
*Qur'an* LVIII, 12

These verses are but a small sample of the many in the Holy Book of Islam, the Qur'an, where knowledge and men of knowledge are given such a high place. From them we can see that Islam looks at knowledge – including science – not just as a friend of faith and of God-fearing men, but, more important, as the right way to piety; hence the special position of the 'men of knowledge'. Islam not only encourages people "to seek knowledge from the cradle to the grave" (as the Prophet Muhammad has instructed his followers), but considers fact-finding and scientific discovery as a form of worship, provided no evil is intended. In fact, the

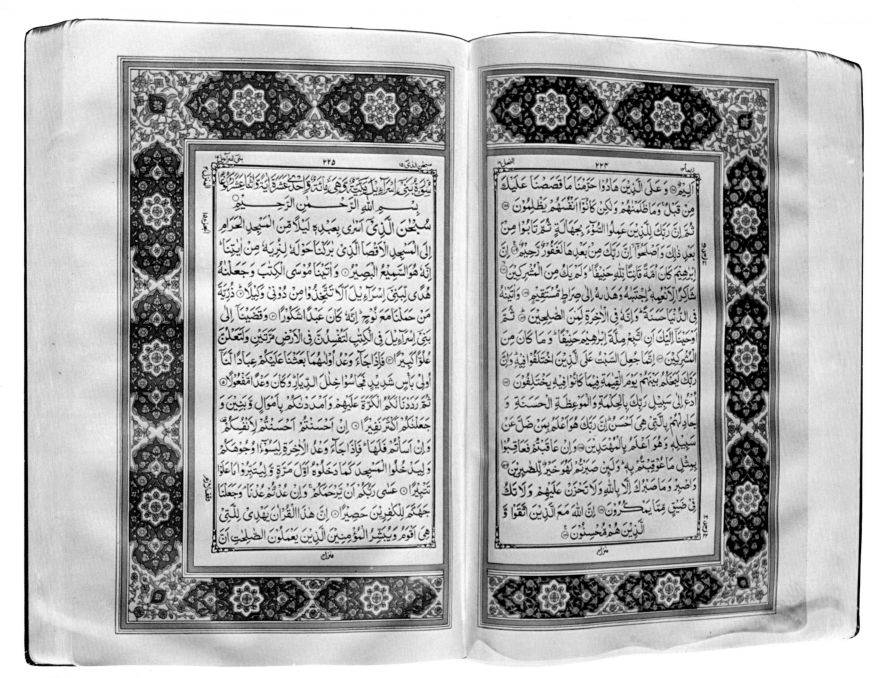

Prophet Muhammad is reported to have said, "To seek knowledge is obligatory on every Muslim, male and female." He also said, "Whoever takes a road in search of knowledge God will ease for him a way to Paradise." The first verses revealed by Almighty God to the Prophet Muhammad were directly related to the question of knowledge and the search for it. The revelation of the Holy Qur'an began with the words "Recite: In the Name of thy Lord who created, created Man of a blood-clot. Recite: And thy Lord is the Most Generous, who taught by the Pen, taught Man, that he knew not" (XCVI, 1–5). Reading and the pen – the basic tools in the search for, and dissemination of, knowledge!

The road to knowledge which leads to Paradise has many landmarks, and the Qur'an has much to say about them.

On the liberation of the mind from the shackles of convention, tradition and every sort of prejudice that may affect one's judgement, we read in the Qur'an: "And when it is said to them, 'Follow what God has sent down,' they say, 'No; but we will follow such things as we found our fathers doing.' What? And if their fathers had no understanding of anything, and if they were not guided?"

In another part we read: "And when it is said to them, 'Come now to what God has sent down, and the Messenger', they say, 'Enough for us is what we found our fathers doing.' What, even if their fathers had knowledge of naught and were not guided?" (V, 104). These and other verses express the Qur'an's strong condemnation of blind imitation and the mere acceptance of traditions inherited from others, even from one's own father. The Qur'an actually gives mention to "thinking", the "mind" and synonymous expressions in no less than three hundred places.

Contemplation and observation are of equal importance: the Qur'an has instructed Muslims to take advantage of the gifts of mind and time provided to them by their Bounteous Lord. They are encouraged to go through the land and observe the marvellous and intricate systems in the skies as well as on earth, animate and inanimate. "Surely in the creation of the heavens and earth and in the alternation of night and day there are *signs for men possessed of minds*" (III, 195). "What, do they not consider how the camel was created, how heaven was lifted up, how the mountains were

*The Qur'an, holiest of the Islamic scripts, is believed by Muslims to have originated from God himself, dictated to the Prophet Muhammad. Binding not only in the faith but as a way of life, it has become perhaps the world's most influential book. It is recited frequently by believers and is constantly under study by scholars, as in a library of Medina (above).*

hoisted, how the earth was out-stretched?" (LXXXVIII, 17–20). "*Hast thou not regarded* thy Lord, how He has stretched out the shadow? Had he willed, He would have made it still. Then We appointed the sun, to be a guide to it . . . It is He who appointed the night for you to be a garment and sleep for a rest, and day He appointed for a rising. And it is He who has loosed the winds, bearing good tidings before his Mercy; and We sent down from heaven pure water so that We might revive a dead land, and give to drink of it . . ." (XXV, 46–50). "What, have they not *beheld* heaven above them, how We have built it, and decked it out fair, and it has no cracks? And the earth – We stretched it forth, and cast on it firm mountains, and We caused to grow therein of every joyous kind for *an insight and a reminder* to every penitent servant" (L, 6–8). There are many more examples; out of more than six thousand verses in the Qur'an no less than seven hundred deal with natural phenomena.

One of the necessary steps in the search for facts is the process of comparing and contrasting the evidence. Scores of Qur'anic verses teach us to do just that. "Not equal are the two seas; this is sweet, grateful to taste, delicious to drink, and that is salt, bitter to the tongue" (XXXV, 13). "It is He who sent down out of heaven water, and thereby We have brought forth the shoot of every plant, and then We have brought forth the green leaf of it, bringing forth from it close-compounded grain, and out of the palm-tree, from the spathe of it, dates thick-clustered, ready to the hand, and gardens of vines, olives, pomegranates, like each to each, and each unlike to each. Look upon their fruits when they fructify and ripen! Surely, in all this are signs for a people who do believe" (VI, 98).

The Qur'an teaches man to be careful and enlightened in his judgements, and to base these judgements on a foundation of knowledge, rather than mere guess-work. It teaches: "And pursue not that thou hast no knowledge of; the hearing, the sight, the heart – all of those shall be questioned of" (XVII, 38).

Humility also is a key feature of Qur'anic teaching. In order that we may

*The essential simplicity of the faith is upheld by Saudi Arabia – in its village mosques* (right), *and in the adherence to the rules of regular prayer* (far right).

110

not think that we know everything (and become arrogant or ignorant), the Qur'an tells the Prophet: "They will question thee concerning the Spirit. Say: 'The Spirit is of the bidding of my Lord. *You have been given of knowledge nothing except a little*'" (XVII, 87). "He knows what lies before them and what is after them, and *they comprehend not anything of His knowledge save such as He wills*" (II, 257).

### The Views of Islamic Scholarship

Though the reaction of the Muslim masses to the scientific and techno-logical achievements of the present age is a mixed one, ranging from the dazzled and bewitched to the sceptic or non-chalant, it seems that the scholars of Islam agree on the following points.

Science and technology are not the property of any one person or nation, and they are not the products of any specific religion or ideology. So there is nothing wrong in accepting and contri-buting to them. In fact, whatever is beneficial to man in science and tech-nology is recommended for a Muslim. For the Prophet of Islam said: "Wisdom is the believer's lost camel, wherever he finds it he has the greatest right to it." The Holy Book of Islam tells us that scientific investigation leads to the dis-covery of the marvellous works of our Creator; therefore, it should be appreci-ated and encouraged. This explains the great contributions made by Muslim scholars who bore the torch of know-ledge during the Middle Ages when science and scientific investigation were

regarded with suspicion elsewhere, particularly in the West.

Science and technology are a means of discovery. Neither they nor man are creators or substitutes for the Creator, because science only unveils what is already present in the universe. Therefore, scientific achievements, however marvellous, should not lead us to atheism; the two things are unrelated.

The Qur'an tells us that whatever is in the skies and whatever is on earth were made serviceable to man by his Lord and Master, Almighty God. "Have you not seen how that God has subjected to you whatsoever is in the heavens and the earth, and He has lavished on you His blessings, outward and inward?" (XXXI, 19). We are also told that man was created to be "On the earth a viceroy

## "From whatsoever place thou issuest, turn my face towards the Holy Mosque."

(of God)" (II, 28), and that man has been honoured by God and given preference above many of God's creation (XVII, 70). Accordingly, we must not be slaves to things material, and we should be above the pursuit of sheer animal satisfaction. Man should take his responsibility seriously, remembering his proper place in the universal scheme.

Since science and technology are amoral, they can be used both to the advantage of man and to his disadvantage and destruction. The only way we can guard against the evil misuse of the scientific achievements of this age is by reviving religious consciousness and by

adhering to the moral values of Islam, values which preach man's responsibility to God, on the Day of Judgement, for the security and peace of his fellow men.

Science and technology can help man only in matters material. Faith alone can help him achieve spiritual satisfaction and psychological well-being. As the Qur'an puts it, "It is in the remembrance of Allah that hearts may find serenity and peace." (XIII, 28).

Renderings of the Qur'an from *The Koran Interpreted* by Arthur J. Arberry, published by Oxford University Press.

# 6 The Cultural Heritage

*What men recite and sing, what they forge and fashion, have been determined above all by the genius of holy scripture and the demands and joys of life in the desert and oasis. But the cities have seldom lacked an infusion of ideas and skills from the wider world.*

*The dagger is of typical formalistic Arabian design, avoiding direct representation.*

*The superb craftsmanship of the Makkan veil (left and far left) in gold and pearls dates from the last century.*

THE truest culture of Arabia rests not in things but in words, in the language. This is not only because in the nomadic life a man can possess no more than he and his camel can carry, but because the Holy Book, the Qur'an, is the fount of his culture as it is of his faith, and the verbal richness of the Qur'an is without parallel.

As Islam became established throughout Arabia, the followers of the Prophet drew on the heritage of Arab tribal thought. Adherence to the Holy Law constituted the primary act of faith. The absence of a priesthood meant that no clear distinction arose between the religious and the secular. No part of a man's daily life, or his thought, or his culture, lay outside his religion.

The religious scholars who chronicled the early centuries of Islam incorporated in their works the sagas and genealogies of tribal life as well as the career of the Prophet and the Community of the Faithful. The traditions they recorded became precedents for the legal and social fabric of Islam. This body of writing emphasizes the significance of human lives and human acts. It contributed to the forming of a self-aware Islamic culture in the Land of the Prophet.

For its part, the Holy Qur'an itself, in its style, not only took into consideration the poetic traditions of the Beduin, but also challenged their literary talent. Before the appearance of the Holy Book, the Beduin had no written

code of law, and only the custom of the blood vendetta ensured the protection of a man's life. Leaders had to rely on their own merits for their authority: it was necessary for such men to demonstrate the qualities which entitled them to their position. The spare nomadic life of the Beduin offered little chance for the development of the material arts. Only those forms which could survive the harsh demands of their existence were cultivated.

The nomad jealously nurtured his language as his single unalienable good. By nature he was, and is, a rhetorician. The poet, the man of eloquence, was prized almost above all others in the community. His gifts and powers, believed to have been inspired by spirits, had already

## Weaponry

*Brass, wood and leather are the traditional materials for decorated shields. The leather is of camel hide, and the wood is often tamarisk.*

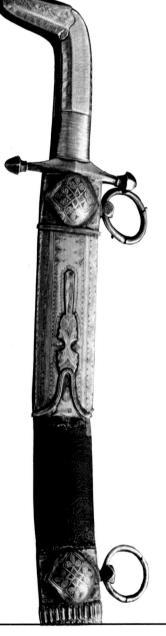

*Powder horns (above) take their design with surprising literalness from the shape of ram's horns. The silversmith's craft in Arabia has for centuries been lavished on the hilts of swords (left) and daggers, and their sheaths.*

Although skilled smiths plied their trade in every permanent settlement, the development of intricate workmanship in precious metals was largely confined to major centres such as Makkah, Jiddah and the Gulf ports. Metal work was often imported from Oman and Yemen. On the other hand, distinctive designs evolved in central Arabia itself, and regional styles emerged in, for example, Qasim and Sudayr. Until the second quarter of this century, it was customary for every male to regard himself as properly dressed only when he was also armed – either with dagger or rifle or both – if for ceremonial rather than strictly defensive purposes.

evolved a complex art form. Poets sang of their lives, loves and land, but they also served as promulgators of the virtues and merits of their own tribes. The obligations of social values such as hospitality, generosity and courage were a matter of honour. Failure to uphold this unwritten code resulted in insult, and it was in this respect that poetic panegyrics possessed an enormous moral force for the Beduin, and had a regulatory effect within the community. The Prophet himself had to contend, through Muslim poets, with opponents who used the gift of poetry against him in Medina.

The first revelations to Muhammad were spoken in rhymed prose consisting of short phrases. These were taken down during his lifetime and were grouped into chapters which became collectively known as the Recitation, or Qur'an.

There is no trace of Arabic prose before Islam, and although examples in the same form may have existed before, they were never written down. It was only the special nature of Muhammad's messages which caused them to be recorded. The Holy Book's concern was not to produce a literary work, but to communicate the meaning which formed itself in it. To do this, the Qur'an initially employed a forceful, rhythmic and rhyming prose, for example:

"We have taught Muhammad no poetry, nor does it beseem him to be a poet. This is but a warning, an eloquent Qur'an to admonish the living and to pass judgement on the unbelievers."
*Qur'an XXXVI, 69*

Islam gathered in not only the poetic traditions but the practice of pilgrimage. Makkah's sanctity, reaffirmed and redefined by Muhammad, had attracted pilgrims from very ancient times. The last stopping place on the route from the south, lying somewhere between Ta'if and Makkah, was the fabled town of Ukaz. Here, during the four-month season of the "holy truce", travellers gathered to meet their fellows, to trade, to recuperate for the last leg of their journey, and to recite.

Poems were composed in honour of the powerful and were paid for in gold and silver. Swift fame was guaranteed to the

## Embossing

*Influences from Oman and Turkey have mingled with traditional Arabian techniques to produce a variety of designs for dagger-hilts and sheaths* (shown here).

*With the introduction of firearms in the late eighteenth century, metal-smiths turned their skills to the decoration of rifles.*

successful poet. Here first developed the *Qasidah*, the ode in celebration of desert heroes – "appearing with Homeric suddenness", as Philip Hitti, the historian, has written, "and surpassing the Iliad and Odyssey in metrical complexity and elaboration."

Unquestionably, the poetic rhythms have been influenced by the gait of the camel. First to emerge was the rhythmic prose of the sages and travelling poets. From such prose grew the *Rajaz*, the four or six beat metre, rhymed prose for the father and a song for the mother, spoken or sung to the lilt of travel by camelback.

And so eloquence was, and has been ever since, allowed its place in Arabian culture. The flow of poetry and well-turned precepts has continued down the centuries, sagas of battles, journeys, loves and loyalties, moral tales and aphorisms as guides to the conduct of life, passed by word of mouth, from generation to generation, sometimes sung or chanted, sometimes accompanied by the stringed *rababa*.

The pure doctrine discouraged dancing and licence, and any extravagance of display or decoration. Yet no group in Saudi Arabia are without their traditions of communal rejoicing. And the sense of elegant design and craftsmanship is evident from the meanest artefact or utensil of daily life to the finest and most intricately wrought of garments or weapons.

The nomadic life of the desert has always existed in interdependence with the settled life of the oasis, or well-watered south-west, or the cities and ports. No Saudi Arabian settlement is without its craftsmen of ancient tradition – bronze-smiths, brass-smiths, gunsmiths and swordsmiths, potters and weavers and dyers, makers of incense burners and coffee mortars, makers – and players – of musical instruments. In the earlier past would have been found fletchers and bowmakers, and specialists in the manufacture of intricate bird traps. And in the ancient past – revealed today in the new Riyadh Museum established by the Director of Antiquities – elegant stone tools were worked by the Neolithic inhabitants of the Rub al-Khali and Eastern Province.

## Home Utensils

Amid the onrush of 20th century technology, Saudi Arabia is taking decisive steps to preserve its ethnological history. Riyadh has a fine Museum of Archaeology, both for the public and for research. Six further local museums are planned by the Department of Antiquities – at Hofuf, el-Awda, Tayma, al-Jawf, Najran and Jizan.

*Incense burners are used in tents and houses to pervade the atmosphere with fragrance.*

*Metal inlays of this perfume container show influences of Damascus or Turkey.*

*This elegant water jug is used for rinsing the right hand before eating.*

*Pots and pitchers are widely made, both on wheels and by coiling the clay.*

*The singing voice is often accompanied by the one-stringed rababa.*

*In the preparation of coffee, beans and cardamom are pounded in mortars.*

*Highly decorated brass-bound chests are a distinctive product of the Gulf area. Such chests were in the past part of the dowry of a newly-wed bride.*

The main centres, above all Makkah, would attract those with the finer skills: calligraphers and illuminators of holy manuscripts, ceramicists and workers in gold and silver thread, fine leather-workers, cabinet-makers and chest-makers (this was a speciality of the Gulf, with its sea-faring tradition), and those skilled in embossing and engraving, especially of guns.

Many of these crafts, in humbler form, were carried on within the tribe. Today they are indeed challenged by the importation of mass-produced goods from abroad. But the day of the craftsman in Saudi Arabia is not yet ended. For the market remains. Those things that are essentially "Arabian" are constantly sought by the discerning.

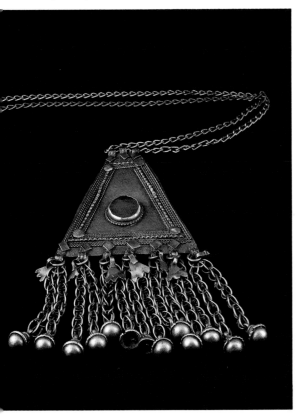

*Characteristic of fine Beduin jewellery, often supplanted by modern trinkets.*

*Throughout the country, doors are often finely carved and studded, while in the Eastern Province, a tradition has persisted of decorating doors with elaborate designs in natural paints. The wood is often imported from India. Elaborately devised locks are locally made, to deter intruders.*

# The Government of Saudi Arabia

KEY TO
ABBREVIATIONS

| | |
|---|---|
| Min. | Minister |
| Dep. Min. | Deputy Minister |
| Asst. Dep. Min. | Assistant Deputy Minister |
| D.G. | Director General |
| Asst. D.G. | Assistant Director General |
| Gen. | General |
| Cttee. | Committee |
| Admin. | Administration |
| Org. | Organisation |
| Tech. | Technical |
| Govt. | Government |
| Agric. | Agriculture |

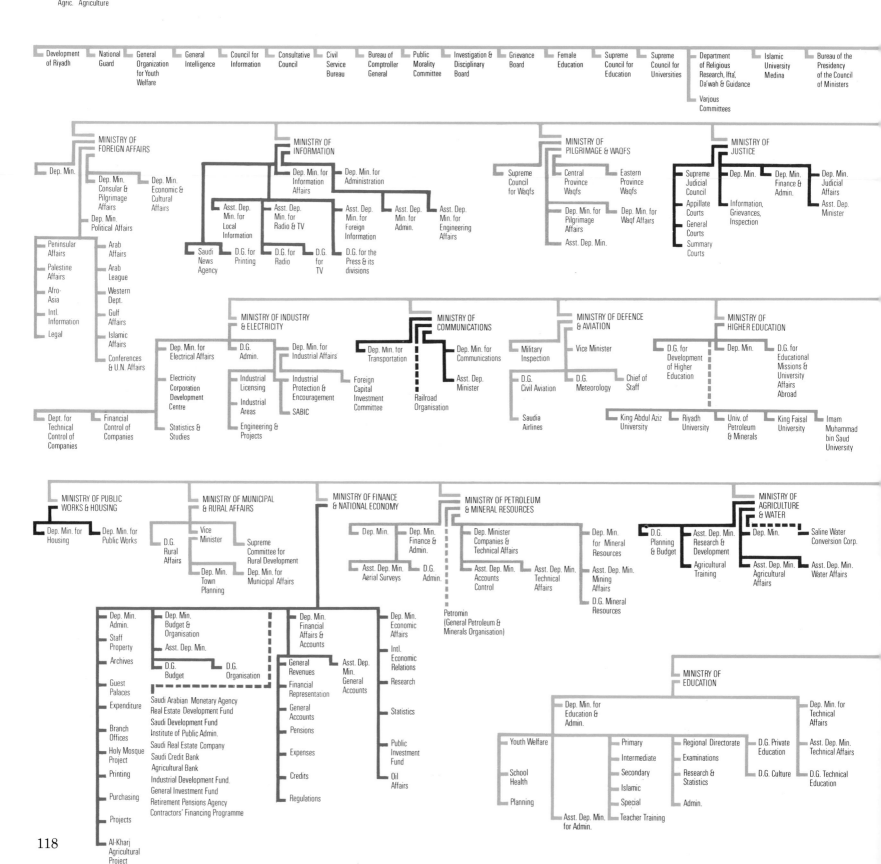

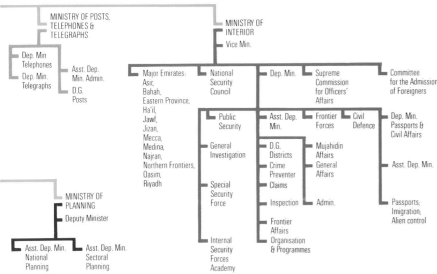

**HIS MAJESTY THE KING**

Supreme Commander of Saudi Arabian Armed Forces
President of the Council of Ministers
President of the Consultative Council
Chairman of the Supreme Committee for Administration Reform

- Secretariat General for Committee of Senior 'Ulema
- Office of Beduin Affairs
- Supreme Committee for Administration Reform

**Presidency of Council of Ministers**

Premier His Majesty the King
1st Deputy Premier HRH Crown Prince Abdullah bin Abdul Aziz
2nd Deputy Premier HRH Prince Sultan bin Abdul Aziz

Secretariat General of the Council of Ministers

- Royal Commission for Jubayl & Yanbu
- Ports Authority
- Supreme Petroleum Council
- Agency for Technical Cooperation
- Experts Division
- Military Section

**MINISTRY OF POSTS, TELEPHONES & TELEGRAPHS**
- Dep. Min. Telephones
- Dep. Min. Telegraphs
- Asst. Dep. Min. Admin.
- D.G. Posts

**MINISTRY OF INTERIOR**
- Vice Min.
  - Major Emirates: Asir, Bahah, Eastern Province, Ha'il, Jawf, Jizan, Mecca, Medina, Najran, Northern Frontiers, Qasim, Riyadh
  - National Security Council
    - Public Security
    - General Investigation
    - Special Security Force
    - Internal Security Forces Academy
  - Dep. Min.
    - Asst. Dep. Min.
      - D.G. Districts
      - Crime Preventer
      - Claims
      - Inspection
      - Frontier Affairs
      - Organisation & Programmes
  - Supreme Commission for Officers' Affairs
    - Frontier Forces
    - Civil Defence
    - Mujahidin Affairs
    - General Affairs
    - Admin.
  - Committee for the Admission of Foreigners
  - Dep. Min. Passports & Civil Affairs
    - Asst. Dep. Min.
    - Passports; Imigration; Alien control

**MINISTRY OF PLANNING**
- Deputy Minister
  - Asst. Dep. Min. National Planning
  - Asst. Dep. Min. Sectoral Planning

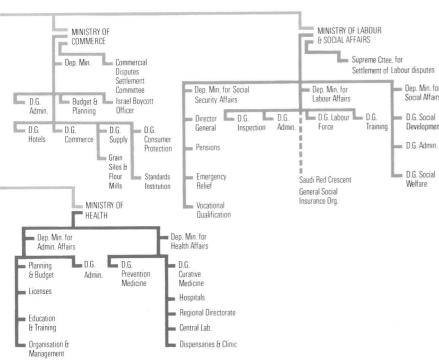

**MINISTRY OF COMMERCE**
- Dep. Min.
  - Commercial Disputes Settlement Committee
  - D.G. Admin.
  - Budget & Planning
  - Israel Boycott Officer
  - D.G. Hotels
  - D.G. Commerce
  - D.G. Supply
    - Grain Silos & Flour Mills
  - D.G. Consumer Protection
    - Standards Institution

**MINISTRY OF LABOUR & SOCIAL AFFAIRS**
- Supreme Cttee. for Settlement of Labour disputes
- Dep. Min. for Social Security Affairs
  - Director General
  - D.G. Inspection
  - D.G. Admin.
  - Pensions
  - Emergency Relief
  - Vocational Qualification
- Dep. Min. for Labour Affairs
  - D.G. Labour Force
  - D.G. Training
- Dep. Min. for Social Affairs
  - D.G. Social Development
  - D.G. Admin.
  - D.G. Social Welfare

Saudi Red Crescent
General Social Insurance Org.

**MINISTRY OF HEALTH**
- Dep. Min. for Admin. Affairs
  - Planning & Budget
  - D.G. Admin.
  - D.G. Prevention Medicine
  - Licenses
  - Education & Training
  - Organisation & Management
- Dep. Min. for Health Affairs
  - D.G. Curative Medicine
  - Hospitals
  - Regional Directorate
  - Central Lab.
  - Dispensaries & Clinic

# 7 Government

*A monarchy built upon consultation and consent has proved flexible enough to sustain benevolent and enlightened rule in a period of unprecedented change. The Qur'anic foundation has held firm, supporting the complex structures required to govern a modern state.*

*The lines of authority and rule, evolved from the days of King Abdul Aziz, but formalized under the late King Faisal, give to Saudi Arabia a coherent and effective Government structure; the diagram opposite should be reviewed in the light of latest developments.*

Sources:
All Ministries, Civil Service Bureau, Aramco,
*Saudi Arabia: A Case Study in Development,*
McKinsey International, Inc.

# Monarchy

MORE than any other country in the modern world, Saudi Arabia is identified with her monarch. The King represents his people in a unique and individual way; he is their champion and they trust him. He speaks to them directly on all major matters which affect the welfare, honour and interests of the nation.

Kingship in the Arab lands has always been based on identity with the teaching of the Prophet and on prowess in war and peace. In addition, the people have expected their king to acquire wisdom, experience and the art of diplomacy.

Although the monarchy of Saudi Arabia is often described abroad as 'absolute', this is not accurate in the sense that Far Eastern monarchies were at one time absolute. No divinity has ever attached to Islamic kings. They are as their subjects are. Allah, alone, is God and under him all men are equal. One does not bow to an Arabian monarch.

The King's role is to lead his nation and keep in constant touch with the people. The legislative and executive power in Saudi Arabia is exercised by the Council of Ministers. When they draft a decree,

they submit it to the King for signature. He may return it for further consideration, but the whole active operation of the government machine is carried out by the Council.

The King either is or appoints the Prime Minister who chooses his colleagues. Their names are also submitted to the King who has a close working relationship with his Council. The Prime Minister has wide powers of supervision and control over the Ministries and departments, and he is responsible for directing the policy of the State. He also gets reports from the audit council and from the Grievance Bureau, a Saudi Arabian version of the Ombudsman.

The proof of the efficacy of any given form of government is the success it achieves. Saudi Arabia has greatly strengthened her international Arab and Islamic power and prestige. Beneficial agreements have been tenaciously negotiated with the foreign oil companies as the Saudi Government has sought a modern oil industry, maximising indigenous control and exploitation. The standard of living of Saudi Arabia's people has been improved at a rate which

no-one could have foreseen, and at the same time friendly relations with other powers in the West and in the East have been preserved and promoted. It is undeniably a success story.

Saudi Arabia has no intention of introducing Western-type parliamentary democracy. In this unique country the Qur'an appears a firmer basis for law, order and progress than the ballot box. Moreover there must be a wide degree of real democracy in a nation where the individual dignity of all men is recognized. The Head of State is available to anybody with a petition to present or a complaint to make, and this right is constantly exercised; the King is referred to by his given name. Ordinary citizens can and do have direct access to him on fixed days of the week. The King personally initiates the appropriate action or enquiry.

The monarchy of Saudi Arabia is refined by the Islamic concept of government which considers that "every shepherd is responsible for his flock" (as the Prophet said), and "were a sheep to fall from the bank of the Euphrates [the governor] will be responsible on the Day of Judgement for having failed to make

# Administration

a safe path for it." It reflects the tribal notion of administration exemplified by the proverb, "The master of the people is their servant".

## The House of Saud – the Royal Family of Saudi Arabia

When the late King Abdul Aziz ibn Saud by royal decree in September 1932 changed the name of his realm from "Hijaz and Najd and its Dependencies" to "The Kingdom of Saudi Arabia", not only did the new style express the unity of a greater part of the Arabian Peninsula than at any time since the Prophet Muhammad but also forever identified the new country with the family of its founder – the House of Saud.

Today, His Majesty King Fahd bin Abdul Aziz bin Abd ar-Rahman Al Faisal Al Saud, eighth son of the late King Abdul Aziz and fourth to succeed him, is ruler of the modern Islamic state of Saudi Arabia, in the government and administration of which other members of the large Royal Family also play an active and leading role.

Major posts, however, are often filled by Saudi citizens who are not connected to the Royal Family.

SAUDI ARABIA is an Islamic monarchy which has been developing from monarchical to ministerial rule. The duties of the King-Imam are defined in the Shari'ah law (religious Islamic law as recorded in the Qur'an and interpreted in the Hadith, the Prophet's sayings) which recognizes the Imam not as an absolute hereditary monarch but as one who reigns in order to rule for the public good.

The modern history of Saudi Arabia begins with the recapture of Riyadh by King Abdul Aziz ibn Abd ar-Rahman Al Faisal Al Saud in 1902. Other conquests followed and the Kingdom's international position was confirmed by a series of treaties, the most important of which was the Treaty of Jiddah signed in 1927, when Britain recognized the complete independence of the Kingdom in return for a pledge by King Abdul Aziz to abstain from attacking the Gulf Sheikhdoms. In 1932 the name Saudi Arabia was adopted.

The Royal Decrees, proclaimed in 1953 and 1958, which provided for a Council of Ministers and laid down its functions, may be regarded as the beginning of the "constitutional regime".

At the present time King Fahd heads

the Government as Prime Minister; the First Deputy Prime Minister is Crown Prince Abdullah bin Abdul Aziz, who also has charge of the National Guard, and the Second Deputy Prime Minister is Prince Sultan bin Abdul Aziz, also Defence Minister. The other members of the Council of Ministers – some of whom belong to the Royal Family – include the Ministers of Defence and Aviation, the Interior, Finance and National Economy, Foreign Affairs, Petroleum and Mineral Resources, Justice, Industry and Electricity, Planning, Agriculture and Water, Transport, Communications, Commerce, Higher Education, Education, Information, Health, Labour and Social Affairs, Pilgrimage and Waqfs, Public Works and Housing, and Municipal and Rural Affairs.

Ministers are responsible to the King. Almost all the apparatus of modern government – ministries, civil service, budgeting systems and so on – have been set up since 1955; in the early 1950s the Ministry of Finance was the only executive department of government. An independent judiciary and a modern judicial system were part of a reform programme begun in 1962, but the first

*There is the aspect of formal grandeur, exemplified by the Guest Palace in Jiddah* (far left), *and the Council of Ministers' offices, the Riassa Palace, in Riyadh* (left). *Yet an essential characteristic of kingly rule is that the monarch himself is available in person to any one of his subjects. This is a weekly fact of life in Saudi Arabia. The aggrieved citizen knows he can himself bring his plea to the King.*

Minister of Justice was not appointed until 1970.

Although there are no elections and no political parties, Saudi Arabia has its own form of Islamic democracy. All men are regarded as equal, and differences are minimized between the rich and the poor, the governors and the governed. Ministers and officials keep their doors open so that anyone with any business can call in, without prior appointment, and be offered refreshment in accordance with Arab customs. A morning visitor to a senior official may find himself waiting with a large number of other callers; and since most of the official's morning may be spent receiving visitors in this way, he often needs to return to his office in the evening to do uninterrupted work when the office is closed.

An element of decentralization was introduced in 1963 when the country was divided into four provinces: Western (Hijaz), Central (Najd), South Western (Asir) and Eastern Province (Hasa), each with an appointed governor, or Emir, who is charged with local administration, maintenance of order and implementation of Shari'ah judgements. Various ministries have field offices, and the Ministry of the Interior is responsible for appointing the Emirs, but Saudi Arabia has no effective local government as the term is understood in Western democracies. The municipalities are completely dependent on central Government for funds. The people expect the Government to provide whatever utilities and services are necessary, and the Government accepts an obligation to do so. The only form of local election is for council members, called al-Majlis al-Baladi, who have a purely advisory function, their advice being directed to the chief municipal executive. A new "district system" of local administration was approved in principle by Royal Decree in 1963.

In 1980, the Government appointed a new special nine-man committee to formalize the Kingdom's basic system of government and introduce a new Majlis Ashoura or consultative assembly of leading citizens. More decentralized local administration was also being studied. While the Islamic sharia or law is unequivocally the Kingdom's constitution, the committee was to describe the functions and elements of the modern Saudi government. King Abdul Aziz used an advisory Majlis Ashoura in the 1930s though few of its members

remain alive and it has long ceased to meet. The new Majlis was initially to be appointed, but it would represent another step in the evolution of Saudi government by widening the decision-making process. The local Majlis al-Baladi were expected to be strengthened, with more emphasis on local government.

Oil provides nearly all the Government's revenue, which in turn through contracts, salaries, loans and subsidies and gifts is the prime source of wealth in the economy. There is no income tax. Because of the heavy dependence on oil products, many of the Government's plans are aimed at diversification: by increasing farming and stimulating industry and mining.

The Civil Service Commission is responsible for staffing policies throughout the public service. Considerable efforts are being made in the direction of administrative innovation and reform, and impressive training schemes are being introduced to improve the structure and processes of public administration. The Institute of Public Administration, which was established in Riyadh by Royal Decree in 1961 as a semi-independent public agency, provides training and further education for civil servants, undertakes research, and assists government departments in re-organization and reform. It is probably the biggest and best equipped institute of its kind in the Middle East.

The Government's general objectives are to provide for national security and economic and social stability, and to raise the living standards of the people, while maintaining the religious and moral values for which the Kingdom, as the original homeland of Islam, is so well known.

The most difficult administrative problem is the shortage of manpower. Although increased effort is remedying this – including study of a possible wider working role for women beyond education and social services – it is unlikely that the Government will achieve its social and economic objectives without considerable continuing help from non-Saudis. Their numerical presence is being tightly controlled and it will be a matter of great interest to see how Saudi Arabia continues to develop towards objectives which anywhere else would be considered virtually irreconcilable.

*Statistical sources:* Ministry of Education and Ministry of Planning.

# Law

IN Saudi Arabia – uniquely in the modern world – Islamic law, in its Hanbali interpretation, still reigns virtually supreme. Article Six in the Fundamental Law of the Hijaz, 1926, unequivocally declares that "The law in the Kingdom of the Hijaz shall always conform to the Book of God, the Sunnah of the Prophet and the conduct of the Companions of the Prophet and of their Pious Followers." A year later King ibn Saud proposed that a code of Islamic law should be drawn up based not only on the doctrine of the Hanbali school but on that of whichever school seemed closest to the Qur'an and Sunnah (or practice of the Prophet) on the particular point concerned. The Hanbali *ulama* (scholars learned in the school of law named after the great jurist-theologian Ahmad ibn Hanbal, who died in 855 CE) persuaded him to abandon this project, and regulations issued in 1928 and 1930 made it obligatory on the *qadis*, or judges, to follow the recognized Hanbali texts. But in 1934 he affirmed his own policy, when he said: "We are seekers of the truth. We will accept what is sound in any school of thought or from any *alim* (learned Muslim scholar) ... We obey neither ibn Abd al-Wahhab (the founder of the Wahhabi school of thought) nor any other person unless what they said was clearly endorsed by the Book of God and the Sunnah of the Prophet. God made us – me, my fathers and ancestors – preachers and teachers according to the Qur'an and the Sunnah. So, whenever we find strong proof in any of the four schools, we will refer to it and be bound by it. Should we fail to find the evidence there, then we would resort to the teachings of Imam Ahmad ibn Hanbal".

Until about the middle of the last century, Islamic law (the Shari'ah or "path to a watering place") was dominant throughout the whole Muslim world. It was regarded as being firmly based on divine revelation, the only way in which man could distinguish between virtue and vice.

How was the divine will to be ascertained? First, from the Qur'an or "Book of God", which is regarded by orthodox Muslims as having been written from eternity in Arabic in heaven and revealed to Muhammad, as occasion demanded,

Modern and efficient administration and ministerial buildings are scattered throughout Riyadh and Jiddah and the towns of the Eastern Province. Frequently architects and designers have succeeded in combining the requirements of large official structures with a markedly Arabian flavour in the facades. Such is true, for example, of the Ministries of Agriculture (above) and Petroleum (below), both in Riyadh, and the new Jiddah airport (left).

by the archangel Gabriel. But there is comparatively little in the Qur'an which is of direct legal significance; so the second of the *usul al-fiqh* (or sources of the divine law as put together and systematized by the jurist-theologians of Islam) was the Sunnah or practice of Muhammad, equally inspired in content although not in form, and derived from a mass of Traditions (*ahadith*) as to what he had said, done or allowed to be done. Even this, however, was not enough. In very early days a judge or jurist would, where necessary, fall back on his own opinion (*ra'y*) of what was consonant with the spirit of the faith. But the view soon gained ground that this was far too fallible and subjective a source for a divine law: too fallible, so *ijma* or the consensus of the Muslim community (in practice, that of its jurists) came to be accepted as another reliable indication of the divine will; too subjective, so the "opinion" of an individual judge or jurist was replaced by *qiyas*, or the science of analogical deductions from one of the primary sources.

In early days, any qualified jurist was regarded as entitled to exercise *ijtihad*: that is, to go back to the authoritative sources of the law and deduce from them the solution to a particular problem. But soon the jurist-theologians began to draw together in schools, based in some cases primarily on a geographical area, and in others on their allegiance to some outstanding lawyer or theologian. With the crystallization of these schools, most Muslims came to regard the "door of *ijtihad*" as having been virtually closed, and all future lawyers as mere *muqallids* (men bound to accept as authoritative the views of the great scholars of the past). With the passage of time, moreover, the number of law schools in orthodox or Sunni Islam became limited to four: the Hanafis, Malakis, Shafi'is and Hanbalis. The Hanbali school relied on traditional rather than "speculative" material.

There were, however, a very limited number of Muslim jurists who not only proclaimed that the "door of *ijtihad*" had never been closed, but that they were themselves *mujtahids*, or men who had the right to exercise the faculty of *ijtihad*. Hence the suggestion made by King ibn Saud about following the doctrine of whichever school seemed closest to the Qur'an and Sunnah on any particular point. The opposition of the Hanbali *ulama* was not only to such

freedom of choice but to the very idea of any official compilation of the divine law. As a result, the law in Saudi Arabia is still derived principally from some six Hanbali texts, although some *qadis* exercise a certain amount of discretion.

The degree of legal orthodoxy which still prevails in Saudi Arabia contrasts with the course of development, since the middle of the last century, in the greater part of the Muslim world, where the Shari'ah has been progressively displaced by codes of commercial, criminal and even civil law which are largely of Western inspiration, and the Shari'ah, as such, has been chiefly confined to the law of personal status (marriage, divorce, succession, etc). Even in this sphere, moreover, the Islamic law has often been reduced to a codified form, during the last half century, by legislation based on a process of selection and reinterpretation. As a result, Saudi Arabia is virtually the only country today in which the criminal law of Islam is still in full force – characterized first by the treatment of homicide and wounding primarily as civil wrongs which involve blood-money or some other form of compensation; then by the imposition of certain very severe penalties for a few precisely defined crimes such as theft, brigandage, illicit sex relations and the consumption of alcohol (provided the offence can be proved by the oral testimony of the requisite number of unimpeachable, adult, male witnesses); and by discretionary punishments in all other cases. This is why one sometimes still hears of an adulterer being stoned to death, or a thief having his right hand amputated.

Throughout the Muslim world, however, a number of other courts, such as those of the local governor, the police and the inspector of markets, have always exercised jurisdiction alongside that of the *qadis*, together with a Court of Complaints presided over by the Caliph himself or some powerful official appointed by him, which acted, *inter alia*, as an unofficial court of appeal. And none of these other courts were, in practice, as strictly bound by the Shari'ah as were those of the *qadis*.

It was inherent in the theory of Islamic jurisprudence that there was exceedingly little scope for State legislation. According to a commonly accepted classification, all human actions were subsumed under one of five categories: what God had positively commanded, had recom-

mended, had left legally indifferent, had reprobated or had actually forbidden. So it was only in the middle category (things left legally indifferent) that there was, in theory, any scope for human legislation. For the rest, the Shari'ah was regarded as a divinely given blueprint by which all Muslims should try to abide.

In Saudi Arabia much of this concept still survives. Only comparatively minor concessions have been made to the exigencies of modern life – although it is true that, alongside the Shari'ah, there now stand an ever increasing number of administrative regulations promulgated by the Government. These certainly have the force of law; but they are normally termed either *nizam* (regulation) or *marsum* (royal decree) rather than *qanun* (which is the normal term for legislation throughout the Middle East). Such royal decrees have provided for a hierarchy of courts – Summary Courts, High Courts and a "Commission of Judicial Supervision". Summary Courts are of two types, one of which deals with Beduin affairs and the other with minor criminal and financial cases in urban areas. High Courts consist of three or four judges and try the more serious criminal and financial cases, together with matters of personal status or family law. In the more remote districts, local governors, sometimes assisted by a *qadi*, deal with crimes, civil litigation, tribal customs and mediation. The Office of the Chief *Qadi* and the Commission of Judicial Supervision have now been replaced by a Minister of Justice and a Supreme Judicial Council. The Supreme Judicial Council, which consists of twenty members chosen from the leading jurists and *ulama*, has the function, *inter alia*, of issuing *fatawa* or opinions on points of law and religion, and thus of adapting the law as traditionally accepted to the changing needs of contemporary life. But the ultimate responsibility for promulgating and implementing legislation remains with the Council of Ministers and with the King himself whose decrees have the force of law, who endorses the regulations formulated by the Council of Ministers and by whom sentences of execution or amputation must normally be confirmed.

From the first, King Abdul Aziz had himself acted both as chief executive and chief judge, to whom litigants might always appeal. But in 1954 a Board of Complaints (*Diwan al-Mazalim*) was set up, to which all complaints could be submitted for investigation and – with royal approval – final resolution. The Board also deals with administrative problems, questions of governmental corruption, disputes about taxation and matters which concern foreign nationals and their investments in Saudi Arabia.

One of the earliest and most important innovations was the establishment of a Council of Commerce in Jiddah in 1926 and the promulgation of a commercial code, or Regulations on Commerce, in 1931. In 1954 the Council was replaced by a Ministry of Commerce, and "Chambers of Commerce" were set up in Jiddah, Yanbu and Dammam to administer the Regulations (which are based on the Ottoman Commercial Code of 1850, but with all references to interest expunged). A number of concessions to modern life are being quietly introduced. Banks, for example, are now allowed to charge a "commission" (rather than "interest") on loans; and this is a matter of considerable importance, since people were apt previously to be charged a ruinous rate of interest in transactions which were completely illicit. Until recently, again, insurance contracts were allowed only in regard to maritime commerce; but this concession is now being extended to all forms of property, although not to life insurance.

There has been a spate of recent legislation. The General Personnel Regulation of 1957 was replaced in 1970 by the Disciplinary Code, which covers the behaviour, administrative negligence or defaults of civil servants, and the power of a Disciplinary Council – but with the proviso that any act which constitutes a crime or civil wrong still falls within the competence of the Shari'ah Courts. The Work and Workmen's Regulation of 1970 deals with labour disputes, injuries, dismissals, minimum wages and maximum hours of work; obliges all employers to enlist at least seventy-five per cent of their workmen from among Saudi nationals and to pay Saudis at least fifty-one per cent of the total sum expended on wages; and makes an employer responsible for any prohibited item, such as alcohol, brought to work by one of his employees. But administrative penalties which may be imposed under this law do not exclude the jurisdiction of the *qadis* in regard to the punishment of crimes or the computation of blood-money under the Shari'ah. Similarly, the Regulation on Motor Vehicles leaves

it to the police to investigate accidents and to determine questions of guilt, but reserves the allocation of blood-money to the *qadis*. The Regulation on Investing Foreign Capital, 1957, provides that at least fifty-one per cent of the controlling interest in an investment company must be owned by Saudi nationals, who must also make up three-quarters of the total number of employees and be paid no less than forty-five per cent of the total salaries paid by the company; the Regulation on Companies, 1965, established a special Committee for the Resolution of Disputes; and the Regulation to Control Commercial Fraud, 1961, lays down a variety of penalties.

Only in 1936 was the importation of slaves largely prohibited in Saudi Arabia, and not until 1962 was the status of slavery itself abolished. The theoretical implications of the abolition of slavery are of great significance, for Saudi Arabia has in this case demonstrated conclusively that it is both able, and at times willing, to abrogate by statute law what many would regard as a basic right under the Shari'ah – and to do so in deference to political pressure and the weight of contemporary world opinion.

Particular interest attaches to Royal Decree No 1135, by which the late King ibn Saud ratified the oil concession first granted to the Standard Oil Company of California and subsequently inherited by the Arabian American Oil Company (Aramco). This concession, while conforming to what has become a comparatively standard type of agreement in such cases, is *sui generis* in terms of the Shari'ah, which lays down in minute detail the conditions for a series of named contracts, rather than enumerating principles which would constitute a general "law of contract". Different parts of the concession would normally be classified under the Shari'ah as *ihya al-mawat* (cultivation of undeveloped land), *iqta* (grant or concession), *ijarah* (lease) and a form of *sharikah* (partnership); but it includes specific provisions which might strictly be held to invalidate each of these contracts or dispositions in their classical form. Yet this concession was certainly regarded as valid and binding by the King; and the Arbitration Agreement of 1955 expressly states that both the Government and the Company "respect all the obligations which they have undertaken" and "have never entertained the thought that they would not

be bound by the agreements they have made and now make with one another." There is, moreover, excellent authority in both the Qur'an, and in those traditions which are generally accepted by Muslims as authentic, for the proposition that Muslims are bound by their contractual stipulations – a principle wide enough to cover any contract which the exigencies of modern life may require. This principle is reinforced, in Hanbali teaching (which Saudi Arabia adopted), by the welfare (*maslaha*) of the individual and community.

In 1952, a Royal Decree promulgated new Regulations for the "Organization of Administrative Functions in the Shari'ah Court System". These provide for the *qadi*, as soon as a suit is brought before him, to fix a day for the plaintiff to be heard and to notify the defendant accordingly, and for the appropriate forms to be signed, writs of summons issued and files prepared. If two litigants appear and request an immediate hearing this request should be granted whenever circumstances permit; but in all other cases the *qadi* should study the case on the day before it is heard and the "special police post assigned to the court building, or nearby" ensure that the defendant is not only duly summoned but even, in some cases, brought to court by force (since all claims must be raised in the town in which the defendant is resident, provided this is within the Kingdom). Following the classical pattern, the *qadi* must ask the plaintiff to provide evidence for his claim and then ask the defendant to answer it, promptly if possible, or after a delay adequate to enable him to consult documents, accounts, etc, where this is necessary. Special provisions are included for those cases in which either party fails to appear; everyone, without restriction, is given the right to appoint a suitably qualified legal representative; and litigation must be conducted in public "except in circumstances in which the court considers it in the interests of morals for it to be in secret". Documents issued by registrars are to be refused by the court only when something in them is "contrary to the Shari'ah", and it is significant that documentary evidence appears to be freely admitted.

One of the major functions of the new Judicial Council is to resolve any conflict between the Qur'an and Sunnah on the one hand and the demands of modernization on the other.

## Defending the Country

Saudi Arabia's vast size and scattered centres require formidable defense – a sizeable army, an Air Force with manpower about one third that of the army, and a small navy. Internationally published reference sources list sophisticated aircraft, including Northrop F-5E fighter bombers, Lightnings (*right*) – to be superseded during the early 1980s by F-15s – and Strikemasters (*inset, left*); military ''hardware'' including various SAM missile launchers, and AML-60s and AML-90s; and for the Navy, fast attack craft, minesweepers and corvettes. Paramilitary forces include the highly trained and well-

manned National Guard, of which an officer is pictured in ceremonial dress (*far left*) and men in equestrian training (*overleaf*). *Below left*: Air Force cadets are put through basic training.

Source: *The Military Balance*, London, published annually by the International Institute for Strategic Studies; and other published reference works.

# World Affairs

AS the world's largest oil exporter, Saudi Arabia's most valuable contribution to international stability lies in its relatively restraining influence on the price of oil and continuing high output which has generated a secondary major contribution: responsible management of the vast cash surpluses it earns and cannot yet spend at home. The Saudi Government differs from some other OPEC members in fearing the effects of excessive and erratic oil prices on the world economy. The Saudis are acutely aware that extreme over-pricing or under-supply could easily create profound world recession, instability and disarray. Apart from shattering OPEC unity in the scramble for diminished markets as well as further destabilizing the tense international environment, such a recession would severely damage the Kingdom's investments abroad and its desire for orderly industrialization and development in co-operation with the West. Within OPEC, Saudi Arabia is the main sponsor of a long term strategy designed to stabilize the oil market with regular incremental price increases.

Saudi Arabia has remained unswervingly committed to the Arab cause in the continuing crisis over Israel, not hesitating to use its considerable economic authority to instil in the Western powers the need for an even-handed approach. It has also worked for a concerted and realistic Arab, and Islamic, policy, and is a major financial supporter of the frontline Arab states and the PLO: Despite its friendship for Egyptian President Sadat, the Kingdom immediately joined the rest of the Arab world in rejecting his peace treaty with Israel, realising it could not lead to real settlement. The treaty was backed by the United States, in other respects probably the most special of the Kingdom's many Western friends.

In 1981, Saudi Arabia hosted the historic, 38-nation, third Islamic summit in Ta'if, crowning its leading position in the burgeoning movement which had been founded largely at King Faisal's instigation eleven years beforehand. During the unifying "summit of Palestine and Jerusalem", the Heads of State prayed together before the holy Ka'bah

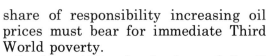

in Makkah watched, via the media, by millions of Arab, African and Asian Muslims around the world.

In many respects, Saudi Arabia has become the trustee of the Third World. Saudi aid is generously distributed through bilateral, Arab multilateral, and international institutions. Emphasis is placed on the needs of, first the Islamic world, then the Arab world and finally the rest of the Third World. For, beyond a natural Islamic propensity to share its wealth, the Kingdom is aware of the

share of responsibility increasing oil prices must bear for immediate Third World poverty.

In May 1981, the leaders of Saudi Arabia, Kuwait, Qatar, Oman, the United Arab Emirates and Bahrain met in Abu Dhabi to form the Gulf Co-operation Council. With headquarters established in Riyadh, the GCC's purposes were to foster the unity of the region, encourage a common stance towards world issues, shield the region from big power conflicts, and promote co-

*HRH Crown Prince Fahd (as he was at that time) presides at a session of the Third Islamic Summit Conference (the "Makkah Summit"), held at the Conference Centre in Ta'if (left), under the flags of the thirty-eight participating nations. King Khalid and Crown Prince Fahd (right) shared the tasks of greeting the Heads of State and delegates attending the Conference. The Conference in session (bottom left).*

ordination for comprehensive development. It promises to become a major force for regional security and stability.

In under a decade, Riyadh has firmly taken its place as one of the handful of top capitals of the world – as witnessed by an annual stream of heads of state and senior officials from Western, Arab, Islamic and developing countries in search of consultation and co-operation. The Saudi rulers, led by King Fahd and his predecessors, have in turn made their presence felt abroad.

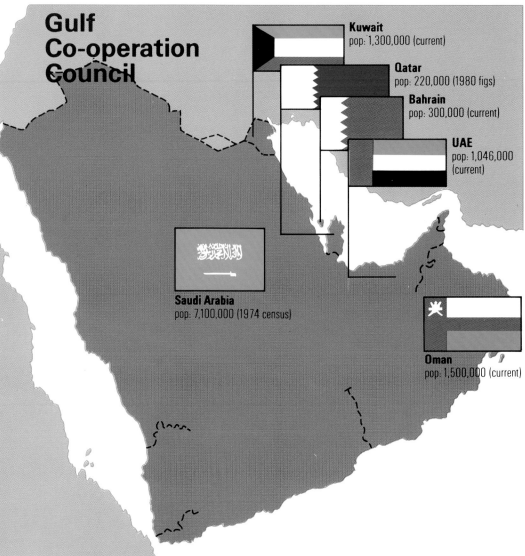

**Gulf Co-operation Council**

**Kuwait**
pop: 1,300,000 (current)

**Qatar**
pop: 220,000 (1980 figs)

**Bahrain**
pop: 300,000 (current)

**UAE**
pop: 1,046,000 (current)

**Saudi Arabia**
pop: 7,100,000 (1974 census)

**Oman**
pop: 1,500,000 (current)

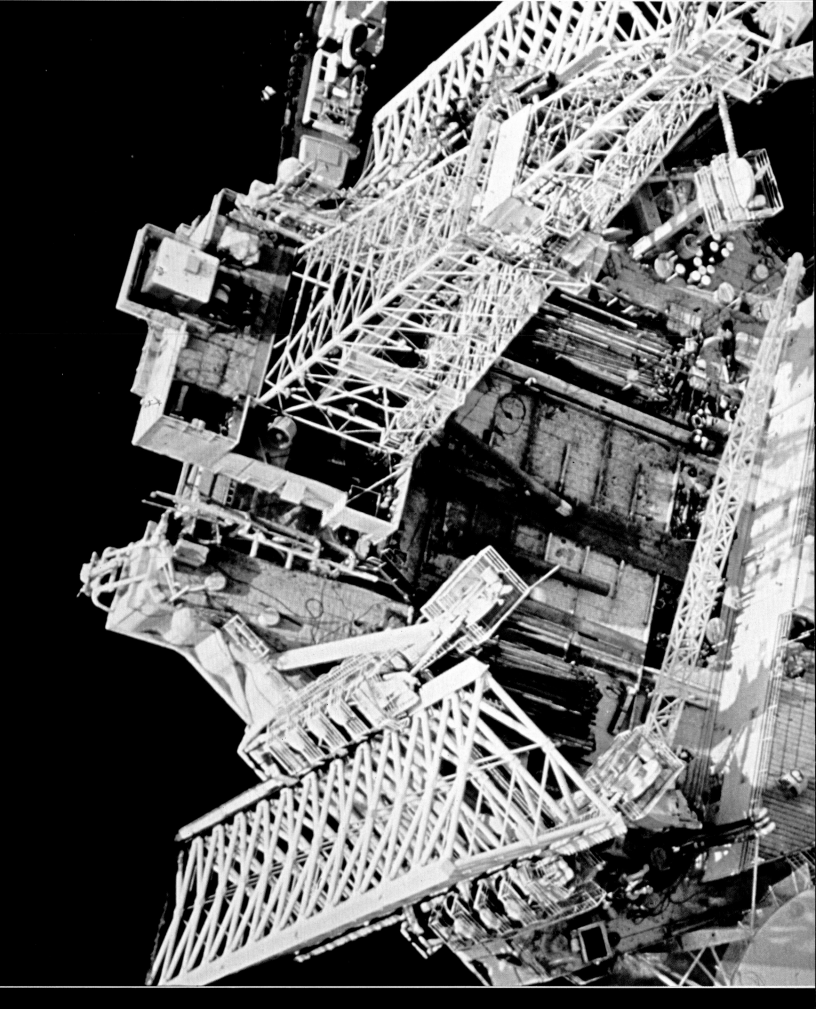

# 8
# Industry and Development

*Saudi Arabia came to riches through the long, hard school of poverty. There was to be no place for profligacy. Rather, the bounty of oil and mineral resource was to be made to provide, for generations to come, the infrastructure of modern statehood; and to fund a free economic system where human enterprise, working within a total plan, would ensure self-generating growth.*

*The boom of the world's most plentiful capital of mineral energy in the form of oil has turned Saudi Arabia from one of the poorest countries in the world to the richest of all, in terms of reserves, in scarcely more than a single generation. Some oil is obtained offshore (left).*

# Introduction

THE economic situation of Saudi Arabia in the last quarter of the twentieth century is unprecedented in the history of the world. This is a country whose sparse population had, historically, been subjected to a harsh, if ennobling, poverty, that came into riches beyond the range of dreams.

The Kingdom indeed proved to be blessed with the largest oil reserves of any country in the world; but it can certainly take credit for the skilful exploitation of these reserves and the sensible husbanding of the wealth that results. Saudi Arabia, by 1977, was already standing second only to West Germany in monetary reserves: each year was bringing substantial increases in the funds available for spending or invested against future needs.

Such a situation does not represent, as might be thought, an economic paradise, and indeed it presents responsibilities and challenges which, in their way, are only a little less frustrating than poverty. The persistent danger is that of destabilising the balance of traditional Saudi life, which in its intricate patterns of family and society must always be a delicate and subtle complex, by the sudden and overwhelming change that the availability of very substantial funds can mean. The late King Faisal largely separated oil from politics, leaving the petroleum industry to form its own markets and decisions on economic grounds. King Khalid's Government has refrained from exploiting the threat of the "oil weapon" as much as possible, concentrating instead on trying responsibly to help maintain a stable but fair world oil market. It could so easily have curtailed the flow of oil, but this would have resulted in seriously disturbing the vital market with devastating repercussions abroad and the build-up of different pressures at home.

And so Saudi Arabia has accepted the fact of its wealth, with a courage and determination to make use of it to the maximum advantage of the nation both internally and abroad, and to use the surplus with traditional Islamic generosity among poorer nations.

In 1973, when the Organisation of Petroleum Exporting Countries (OPEC) first took control of oil policy, and allowed the vital commodity to begin rising to its natural market price,

Western economies were already entering a spiral of inflation and recession. OPEC came in for much ill-judged criticism; in fact, increased petroleum costs were only one element in the inflationary spiral. Saudi Arabia has consistently appreciated the need for a stable Western economy. The economy in turn, however, learnt through the latter 1970s – which saw more substantial price increases – to value more realistically the worth of its vital, often wasted, energy supplies.

For the Kingdom openly accepts its dependence, for the coming period of history, on the skills and products that Western economies can offer. It has opened its arms to Western participation: first and foremost, of course, in its historic relationship through Aramco with the U.S., but also with Britain, France, West Germany, Japan and other major industrialized countries, in an immense range of new enterprises and products, from defence and telecommunications to every kind of manufacturing plant, agricultural aid and irrigation technique, at the same time welcoming the skills and instruction that new techniques require. Many developing countries and their people – Arab, Muslim, or otherwise – have also participated vigorously in the Kingdom's growth.

Simultaneously, the Kingdom has sought to secure its future – a future which will stretch indefinitely beyond the period of history in which petroleum and petroleum products are likely to be flowing and producing massive income – by responsibly investing its surplus income abroad. In 1981, for example, $10 billion was invested with the International Monetary Fund.

The Saudi Arabian Monetary Agency (SAMA) has a team of advisers, which include international bankers, and a list of accredited money brokers with whom it is prepared to deal, which includes all the leading European and American banks. A strong vein of conservatism runs through its national investment policy, and the precise areas where Saudi investment is concentrated are not in the main public, nor are the volumes. The major investor is generally considered to be the United States; American dollars allow for a high level of liquidity in the opportunities available for the purchase of corporate stocks and

bonds, and especially government paper.

The Euromarkets of offshore currencies entered through European financial centres like London and Zurich unquestionably handled much of the surplus flow, channelling it to governments, corporations and Third World borrowers. London is the home of the Saudi International Bank, created by SAMA (fifty per cent share) in partnership with Saudi and leading international banks as a Saudi window onto these markets – a Saudi-oriented corporate specialist, which will help the Kingdom's future banking expertise. But SIB sees little of SAMA's pressing surplus investments.

These investments found themselves increasingly diversified to strong European countries like West Germany, as well as Japan. But in the early 1980s, despite more direct corporate lending and investment, SAMA was increasingly trapped for new outlets, especially as it cautiously declined the risks of reaction abroad from investing more heavily, and so more prominently, directly into assets. The Kingdom, however, encouraged new international agreements among Arab and Islamic countries to protect and guarantee foreign investments. Unlike Kuwait, the Kingdom's surplus investment philosophy intended the money to be used before long for development at home, not as a profit-making "pension fund" for future work-free generations. On 19 November 1979, SAMA's banking department's balance sheet total was SR 186 billion, SR 22 billion down on the previous December, after transfers to cover development costs higher even than the fantastic oil earnings.

Private fortunes too are inevitably being made in Saudi Arabia today. Some of this wealth is invested at home; the rest, both of necessity and the desire for breadth of security, finds its way abroad. Property has remained an obvious attraction whether in Europe's cities, on the Mediterranean, or among the great developing lands of the United States. But increasingly bold and imaginative Saudi businessmen had reportedly found the world an oyster of exciting, fruitful opportunities, whether in film-making and sporting enterprises, or in factories, banks and mines.

Development aid is certainly a major outlet for the Saudi Government's

# Development

*Joint Commission Central Press Headquarters in Yanbu.*

HAVING too much money may sound like an enviable problem, but, for Saudi Arabia, it was a real one with political and economic consequences. The country's immense oil revenues made it possible, in a way which is perhaps historically unique, for the Government to plan virtually any developments, including a total transformation of the economic and industrial base, without financial constraint. Theoretically everything can be done at once.

But, in practice, everything could not be done at once. Pumping huge sums of money into a relatively undeveloped economy causes inflation, social upheaval and innumerable bottlenecks.

Opposite political pressures quickly arise, as they have in Saudi Arabia. On the one hand, there are impatient young Saudis who complain that the Government is moving too slowly. On the other hand, older and more cautious people are now asking for a slowdown, for a system of priorities, and for greater care in protecting a social structure which is inevitably being shaken by the speed of change.

Rapid development continues to be the Government's declared aim, entailing considerable expenditure. But while the Second Plan called for appropriations nine times larger than the First Plan it cost considerably more than expected. And the Third Plan only called for half as much again of its predecessor's cost. The money was still to come from oil revenue, foreign investments if needed, and from taxes on foreign economic activity in Saudi Arabia. It was still expected to leave a considerable reserve balance. But by the early 1980s, the real possibility of lower oil production loomed, a decrease that could follow declining, recession-hit and more conservation-conscious markets abroad. For Saudi Arabia had always been producing more than it otherwise might have done under its policy to stabilise the price of oil and to help the economies of the West. As Sheikh Ahmad Zaki Yamani, the Saudi Minister of Petroleum and Mineral Resources, long ago put it, "We know that if your economy falls, we fall with you."

In the early years of the 1975–80 Plan it soon became apparent that the Government could not immediately disburse as much money as had been hoped; Mini-

wealth. According to the World Bank, in 1979, it gives as much as 3.15 per cent of its Gross National Product to needy countries. The Kingdom has its own Saudi Fund for Development and is a major contributor to many Arab, regional and international development agencies like the OPEC Special Fund, the Arab Fund for Economic and Social Development or the Islamic Development Bank. Broadly speaking, priority is given successively to Islamic, Arab and then other Third World needy with special emphasis on the least developed countries. Internationally, Saudi Arabia has grown, with its wealth, to play a major role in financial affairs; it is actively engaged through such institutions as the International Monetary Fund in discussions and moves on the future of the world economy and its monetary system.

It was at home, however, that the new wealth was concentrated – with the Saudi people themselves. In a decade their country and their living standards changed as never elsewhere before. Roads, ports, telephones, schools, houses and hospitals – a complete physical infrastructure – were built in record time, much in the 1975–80 Five Year Plan which foreign cynics hailed as impossible when it began.

Modern farms and capital-intensive factories appeared as aquifers were tapped, desalination plants built, elec-tricity supplied and housing improved. With the infrastructure came a rush of consumer imports from cars to canned foods in new modern supermarkets. For the government spending passed through the economy to private Saudi hands, as workers, businessmen, and civil servants became the beneficiaries of new kinds of cheap loans and welfare.

But with the wealth came responsibility too, the responsibility of productive Saudi citizenship, of learning new skills and applying them with the tools of modern life that the Government provides. As Dr Ghazi Al Gosaibi, the Minister of Industry and Electricity, said, "We are making it clear from the very beginning that being a Saudi only entitles you to prove yourself. It does not entitle you to become the boss, or to run things, or to assume positions for which you are not qualified." For the base was being laid for a future beyond the revenue from crude oil, and the Third Five-Year Plan, which began in 1980, aimed to focus on the Kingdom's productive and human infrastructure, its manpower, government efficiency, farms, factories and petro-chemical plants.

(see section 11)

*Pipelines now run 750 miles across Arabia from the Gulf to the Red Sea.*

stries were congratulated for spending as much as possible and creating the capacity to project, design, monitor and assess new work. And as the money passed through the economy it fuelled bottlenecks at the Ministries, the ports, the hotels and for houses. Inflation soared as the new money chased goods and services the economy could not supply, or even import and distribute quickly enough.

By 1978, however, the frustrated queues of ships waiting outside the ports of Jubayl and Dammam had disappeared as great efforts created new berths and more than adequate capacity. Inflation levelled out as the Ministry of Finance and National Economy sharply but effectively applied the monetary brakes; contractors waited for payment as spending Ministries found their money delayed; delayed too were compensation payments for land expropriated by the Government for development work; the doors of the Real Estate Development Fund closed for nine months to citizens seeking to take its soft loans and fulfil its motto of "a new home for every Saudi". Thenceforth control of the vicious inflation became the paramount fiscal aim of Sheikh Muhammed Aba Al Khail, the Minister of Finance. But the Government also shielded its people from the inflation as well as unnecessary poverty with controls on prices and rents, subsidies on basic foodstuffs, increased consumer protection with quality standards, increased wages, and capital assistance for homes, businesses and industry. By standard statistical measures of per capita economic growth, total GDP per capita rose almost five per cent per annum during the Second Plan.

With recession and economic slowdown throughout in the West, Saudi Arabia increasingly became a focal point for international exporters of goods and services. It continued to be one of the largest centres of new design and building. Demand for new equipment, construction materials, electrical generators, factory plant, or arms, made it a key international market from suppliers all over the world. Similarly with consumer goods, whether for cameras or cakes, the Kingdom could choose from the best in an atmosphere of intense competition, which forced generous prices on the suppliers. Beforehand there had been

*Aramco's LPG refinery at Yanbu,
the new industrial city on the Red Sea.*

suspicions in the Government that many more unscrupulous foreign contractors and suppliers had not been giving of their best, or at least not without considerable profiteering. That changed under the stimulus of competition and particularly as Saudi skills at negotiating and assessing values improved. On several occasions construction bids were simply cancelled on major jobs and new ones called in search of a fairer price.

With the introduction of the Third Five Year Development Plan in 1980 (*see* The Future), the thrust of Saudi development shifted from basic infrastructural development of the cities, roads, ports and telephones towards the longer term development of its productive and human resources. The planners well realized the difficulty of the task and made considerable allowance for changes based on closer monitoring of performance. For while foreign designers and labourers can be temporarily imported to build highways, with the consequent social stresses of a massively increased foreign population, it is much harder to create a productive economy based on a Saudi workforce. Whereas in the Second Plan, supply bottlenecks, principally undercapacity at the ports, had been the major problem, manpower was expected to prove difficult in the Third, especially as the rise in foreign workers was to be levelled off. It was hoped that, numerically, labourers released from the declining construction and rural sectors would supply industrial and urban demand. Capital-intensive agricultural and industrial technology would save labour; women would work more widely. By 1985 the workforce was estimated to increase production by almost thirty per cent.

The shortage of water remained a limiting factor. Irrigation has consumed, in recent years, about seventy-five per cent of the available water supply. The growing demands of industry and the cities cannot be met from local sources.

Even in the Eastern Province, where water has not hitherto been a problem, shortages could soon be felt, because this is also the region in which most of the country's oil and gas is situated, which means that industrial demand is growing very fast. The Kingdom's desalinated water programme would ease this, however, as a National Water Policy was also forged to help harness the vast supplies

## *Future growth depends on an increasingly Saudi labour-force.*

of ancient water in aquifers under the Kingdom's eastern half.

Industrial development requires large and continuous amounts of energy. During the foreseeable future, oil and natural gas will provide most of this energy, and Saudi Arabia is, of course, uniquely well endowed. The reserves should last for many decades. But alternative sources of energy are being actively explored. For example, joint venture research and development work in solar energy.

The most acute and frustrating shortage, however, was of men. At managerial and professional level the need was expected to double between 1975 and 1980. Every trainable Saudi Arabian could be absorbed and there would still be a serious deficiency. The education and training programmes, which were already very large, were hugely expanded. But there is a limit to what can be done. Money alone cannot provide teachers and train officers as rapidly as it can supply equipment. The teachers have to be taught. Some 54,000 more professional people were seen as needed in 1975, and of these almost two-thirds would become teachers. In addition, there would need to be another 170,000 trained civil servants.

At the same time, the demand for production and service workers, and for labourers both skilled and unskilled, was huge. The vocational and craft training centres which are being planned cannot hope to provide more than a fraction of them. Already twenty per cent of the country's work force come from abroad; by 1980 the proportion was expected to be larger – perhaps thirty-five per cent – consisting of at least 800,000 people.

This influx of manpower created its own requirements and challenges. For instance, they have needed housing. Over thirty new towns and seventy-five new municipalities were planned. The volume of construction was to grow at

*The heavy and hydrocarbons industry of the future are based at Jubayl, rising under the control of a Royal Commission from a tiny fishing village to become a mainstay of the Kingdom's industrial future.*

an average rate of sixty per cent a year – on top of a very high existing base-level. Vast amounts of government money would be involved, but again money alone is not enough. Sufficient materials and specialized equipment – not only for houses, but also for hospitals, schools, power stations, airports and so on – were sometimes not available within the time envisaged. But most targets in the late 1970s were being met.

Although the Saudi Arabian Government is hardly short of revenue, foreign investment in most of these development projects is welcomed. Partnership between Saudi businessmen and foreign or international companies is considered more advantageous than if Saudi Arabia just bought the machinery, the patents and the personnel required. Partnership guarantees a continuing interest, through which not only supplies of capital but supplies of experienced and talented people are most likely to be found.

Amid all this expansion, the social and religious values of Islam remain the permanent guideline: and these, in turn, have economic implications. For a Muslim, it is a duty to give alms, and not demeaning to ask for, and to receive,

them. This principle, rather than any socialist philosophy, is the foundation of Saudi Arabia's welfare state. Free education and free medical services, pensions and social insurance of every kind, are being provided and expanded as fast as the problems of construction and personnel will allow. In addition, a wide range of subsidies are being built into the economy – subsidies for farmers, subsidies against the rising cost of materials, subsidies on imported food, subsidies for housing. The Government, however, strongly believes that while the poor should be protected and basic opportunities provided, subsidies should not be allowed to get out of hand.

Such are the economic challenges caused by sudden and enormous prosperity. But King Faisal passionately believed that the sheer speed of development would enable Saudi Arabia to avoid many of the strains and the social disintegration which other countries of the modern world have had to endure. So too have his half-brothers, King Khalid and King Fahd, whose regimes have seen a measure of decentralization to ease the processes of development. It is a fascinating, unprecedented experiment.

# Gross Domestic Product by Economic Activity

AT 1974 PRICES
IN MILLION RIYALS

| | 1972/73 | 1973/74 | 1974/75 | 1975/76 | 1976/77 | 1977/78 | 1978/79 |
|---|---|---|---|---|---|---|---|
| **INDUSTRIES & OTHER PRODUCERS EXCEPT PRODUCERS OF GOVERNMENT SERVICES:** | | | | | | | |
| AGRICULTURE, FORESTRY & FISHING | 1,138·7 | 1,242·4 | 1,392·1 | 1,586·3 | 1,810·3 | 2,255·0 | 2,706·0 |
| MINING & QUARRYING: | | | | | | | |
| Crude petroleum & natural gas | 26,284·4 | 79,720·3 | 104,696·1 | 109,559·8 | 128,465·8 | 126,156·0 | 132,118·0 |
| Other | 90·4 | 135·9 | 247·5 | 677·1 | 1,260·3 | 1,025·0 | 1,227·0 |
| MANUFACTURING: | | | | | | | |
| Petroleum refining | 1,810·8 | 5,126·4 | 5,765·8 | 5,962·0 | 6,221·2 | 5,908·0 | 6,104·0 |
| Other | 617·1 | 729·9 | 931·2 | 1,191·1 | 1,494·2 | 4,066·0 | 5,187·0 |
| ELECTRICITY, GAS & WATER | 319·1 | 366·6 | 317·7 | 390·7 | 549·7 | 204·0 | 248·0 |
| CONSTRUCTION | 1,808·9 | 2,717·6 | 4,949·2 | 13,524·8 | 25,206·6 | 31,959·0 | 37,798·0 |
| WHOLESALE & RETAIL TRADE, RESTAURANTS AND HOTELS | 1,553·5 | 2,385·9 | 3,044·9 | 4,939·9 | 7,951·6 | 11,049·0 | 13,912·0 |
| TRANSPORT, STORAGE & COMMUNICATION | 2,121·3 | 2,745·7 | 3,945·7 | 5,853·8 | 8,661·7 | 9,960·0 | 14,045·0 |
| FINANCE, INSURANCE, REAL ESTATE & BUSINESS SERVICES: | | | | | | | |
| Ownership of dwellings | 1,000·3 | 1,300·0 | 2,000·0 | 3,000·0 | 4,500·0 | 7,632·0 | 8,412·0 |
| Other | 522·5 | 664·5 | 1,107·4 | 1,654·6 | 2,508·2 | 5,072·0 | 6,102·0 |
| COMMUNITY, SOCIAL & PERSONAL SERVICES | 338·9 | 397·6 | 522·8 | 711·9 | 918·4 | 3,293·0 | 4,163·0 |
| LESS IMPUTED BANK SERVICE CHARGES | −51·0 | −56·1 | −76·6 | −95·8 | −124·5 | −1,561·0 | −2,432·0 |
| **SUB–TOTAL** | **37,554·5** | **97,476·1** | **128,843·0** | **148,956·2** | **189,423·5** | **207,018·0** | **229,590·0** |
| **PRODUCERS OF GOVERNMENT SERVICES:** | | | | | | | |
| PUBLIC ADMINISTRATION & DEFENCE | 1,362·6 | 1,554·5 | 2,689·3 | 4,207·6 | 5,881·1 | 9,204·0 | 10,515·0 |
| OTHER SERVICES | 1,170·5 | 1,383·5 | 2,301·4 | 4,063·6 | 5,031·7 | 5,942·0 | 6,907·0 |
| **SUB–TOTAL** | **2,533·1** | **2,938·0** | **4,990·7** | **8,271·2** | **10,612·8** | **15,146·0** | **17,422·0** |
| **GDP IN PRODUCER'S VALUES** | **40,087·6** | **100,414·1** | **133,834·5** | **157,227·4** | **200,036·3** | **222,164·0** | **247,012·0** |
| IMPORT DUTIES | 463·5 | 550·5 | 375·8 | 633·4 | 715·4 | 1,583·0 | 1,400·0 |
| **GDP IN PURCHASER'S VALUES** | **40,551·1** | **100,964·6** | **134,210·3** | **157,860·8** | **200,751·7** | **223,747·0** | **248,412·0** |

## The Money Story

After the Second World War, Saudi Arabia survived on a subsistence economy with almost no infrastructure. The oil income started from $10 million in 1365/66 AH (1946 CE). It reached the level of SR 790 ($212) million in 1952. The Government Budget for the last fiscal year of King Abdul Aziz's reign 1371/72 (1952/53 CE) allowed for expenditure of SR 758 ($205) million. The country's GDP is roughly estimated to have been around SR 4,000 million in 1372 (1953 CE) and imports amounted to SR 435 million in that year. That was the year of SAMA's start. Its first six-monthly balance sheet for the period ending 30 Jumad Thani 1372 (16 March 1953) listed total assets and liabilities of SR 47.5 ($12.67) million.

In those days, Saudi Arabia had a coin-operated silver standard. The country's monetary system consisted of Saudi silver Riyals and cupro-nickel coins. A number of foreign currencies circulated alongside these, particularly the British gold sovereign. The Saudi silver Riyal was, however, the most popular coin and constituted the backbone of the country's currency system.

The country had no paper currency of its own. However, some paper notes of foreign origin circulated during the pilgrimage season. The banking system was in its infancy; the volume of deposits was very small and the role of cheques was negligible.

One of SAMA's first tasks was to complete the country's own monetary system. In 1953 SAMA issued Saudi Arabia's first gold coin to replace the British sovereign. This was followed in 1957 by a new gold sovereign of the same size and weight but of different design. Next it introduced decimal coinage in December 1959 when the Riyal was stipulated to be equal to 20 qirshes instead of 22 qirshes and each qirsh was made equal to 5 halalahs. The 1, 2 and 4 qirsh coins were replaced in 1392 AH (1972 CE) by new cupro-nickel coins of the denominations of 5, 10, 25 and 50 halalahs. This completed the decimal coinage system.

An experiment with paper currency was made with the issuance of Pilgrim Receipts on 18 Zul Qa'dah 1372 (July 23, 1953). These Pilgrim Receipts started with the 10-Riyal denomination but were followed by five and one Riyal denominations. The Pilgrim Receipts became generally accepted throughout the Kingdom and virtually enjoyed the status of paper currency thus paving the way for the issue of official paper currency in Muharram 1381 (June 1961) after the 1377 Charter had removed the constraint against issue of paper currency imposed on SAMA by the 1371 Charter. With the issue of paper currency the gold and silver coins were demonetized by Royal Decree No. 6 dated 1 Rajab 1379 (31 December 1959).

In the mid-1950s, a few years after the establishment of SAMA, the country passed through financial difficulties which brought about depreciation in the free market rate of the Riyal, depletion in the country's foreign exchange reserves to the extremely low level of RLs 10.21 ($2.72) million in January 1958 and imposition of exchange controls. But the Government's determined implementation of the Stabilization Programme improved the country's financial and economic position and led to an increase in SAMA's foreign exchange reserves and strengthening of the Riyal. This enabled the Government to abolish all exchange controls and to stabilize the exchange rate of the Riyal

The new Charter (Rajab 1379) made SAMA responsible for all the normal functions of a central bank including issue of currency, stabilization of the internal and external value of the Saudi Riyal, management of the country's monetary reserves, handling of Government receipts and payments, and regu-

---

## IMF

Saudi Arabia joined the International Monetary Fund in 1957. Its small annual quota was increased rapidly through successive quota reviews from SDR 10 million at first to SDR 1,040 million after the seventh general review in 1980. But 1981 was the year when its estimated general reserves of $110 billion truly made their mark in the fund. (SDR – Special Drawing Right – is a unit of currency unique to the IMF).

In that year the Fund's board approved a special increase in the Kingdom's quota which almost doubled again to SDR 2,100 million with its share of total rising from 1.74 per cent to 3.5 per cent. This increase in percentage quota with attendant voting rights put the Kingdom among the top handful of Fund members and well ahead of several Western industrial states. At the same time an agreement was made whereby the Kingdom would make available SDR 8,000 million (or just under $10,000 million) to the Fund for its vital programme of lending to troubled member economies, especially those of the developing world. The agreement called for money to become available to the IMF in equal tranches over the next two years; half as much again might also be made available in the third year, subject to the Kingdom's balance of payments and reserve position. Such sums as were drawn down by the IMF

would be paid back in four equal instalments beginning at the end of the fourth year and ending by the seventh, thereby giving the loans average lives of five and a half years. Interest was to be paid on the basis of the weighted average of returns on government securities in the five currencies making up the IMF's SDR which, since the 1980 agreement reducing the number of currencies involved, comprised the US dollar (by far the heaviest in the basket), the West German mark, the Japanese yen, the British pound and the French franc.

The agreements were seen in international financial circles as tremendously important in supplying the Fund with much needed liquidity for its important work. At the same time, the Kingdom was diversifying its foreign reserves at good rates of return, with security, but also assisting in "recycling" its petrodollars especially to those developing countries most hurt by oil price increases and most in need of immediate cash. On its own, the Kingdom would have had difficulty in building the new structures to channel the money itself.

Now, with the deputing of Saudi Arabian Monetary Agency personnel to participate in courses organised by the IMF, twenty-five years after it first joined the Fund, ties between the Kingdom and the IMF continue to strengthen.

---

lation of commercial banks.

Saudi Arabia considered it necessary to sever the link between the Riyal and the Dollar as of 15 March 1975. Since then the policy has been to stabilize the exchange rate of the Riyal with respect to the SDR basket of currencies with a band of 7.25 per cent on either side of the SDR/Riyal parity of Rls 4.28255 per SDR. The exchange rate of the Riyal has been changed several times since then to maintain a stable value in relation to the SDR basket of currencies but as the SDR basket has itself weakened, the Riyal has appreciated against the SDR.

Saudi Arabia's exchange reserves have continually strengthened the external position of the Riyal to make it one of the world's strongest currencies.

The phenomenal growth in the role of SAMA as Government's fiscal agent may be seen from the rise in the Government expenditure budget from Rls 758 million in 1371/72 (1951–52 CE) to Rls 111.4 billion in 1397/98 (1977–78 CE), a growth of 147 times in twenty-six years.

Far left, *special bank branches allow women to engage in business.* Below, *motifs on Jiddah bank.* Right, *bank sky-scrapers dominate Jiddah.*

## Budget Government Expenditure
IN MILLION RIYALS

**Note:** Foreign Aid has gone into Council of Ministers figures.

| | FISCAL YEARS 1974/75 | 1975/76 | 1976/77 | 1977/78 | 1978/79 | 1979/80 | 1980/81 |
|---|---|---|---|---|---|---|---|
| COUNCIL OF MINISTERS | 5,620·6 | 10,330·1 | 9,092·5 | 11,432·8 | 13,546·4 | 27,659·6 | 39,101·9 |
| INFORMATION | 321·8 | 802·6 | 1,164·7 | 1,356·7 | 1,136·3 | 1,054·8 | 1,442·6 |
| FOREIGN AFFAIRS | 221·5 | 327·2 | 351·5 | 373·3 | 450·4 | 542·4 | 736·3 |
| DEFENCE & AVIATION | 8,813·3 | 23,723·7 | 31,906·4 | 31,601·9 | 35,202·7 | 47,060·4 | 59,366·0 |
| INTERIOR | 6,601·5 | 19,278·9 | 5,853·6 | 7,985·3 | 9,029·9 | 9,838·9 | 12,963·2 |
| LABOUR & SOCIAL AFFAIRS | 1,406·6 | 3,891·9 | 3,693·1 | 4,421·6 | 3,289·9 | 4,182·2 | 2,732·4 |
| HEALTH | 1,163·0 | 3,197·4 | 2,972·7 | 3,384·1 | 4,040·5 | 4,177·0 | 5,656·4 |
| EDUCATION | 3,781·2 | 12,973·9 | 14,029·8 | 15,167·2 | 15,221·7 | 16,401·6 | 21,485·3 |
| COMMUNICATIONS | 4,558·2 | 11,564·6 | 16,567·8 | 8,541·9 | 8,346·2 | 10,778·7 | 16,088·5 |
| FINANCE & NATIONAL ECONOMY | 2,052·3 | 7,431·5 | 4,372·6 | 4,162·1 | 3,862·0 | 8,435·7 | 11,420·8 |
| PETROLEUM & MINERAL RESOURCES | 211·6 | 401·4 | 429·1 | 587·0 | 622·5 | 999·5 | 1,224·5 |
| COMMERCE & INDUSTRY | 164·3 | 841·8 | 1,430·9 | 856·1 | 1,379·9 | 1,506·4 | 1,658·1 |
| AGRICULTURE & WATER RESOURCES | 1,303·2 | 2,178·4 | 2,336·0 | 2,187·9 | 2,940·0 | 4,169·2 | 4,160·6 |
| PILGRIMAGE & ENDOWMENTS | 243·8 | 455·3 | 557·2 | 1,028·6 | 1,113·3 | 1,102·4 | 1,307·8 |
| JUSTICE & RELIGIOUS AFFAIRS | 204·5 | 353·8 | 419·1 | 556·7 | 675·5 | 814·0 | 1,089·4 |
| FOREIGN AID | 4,758·0 | 4,658·1 | 2,967·3 | — | — | — | — |
| SUBSIDIES | 1,317·6 | 6,924·4 | 6,246·4 | 19,190·6 | 31,638·3 | 23,029·3 | 32,975·9 |
| PUBLIC INVESTMENT FUND | 3,000·0 | 1,600·0 | 1,600·0 | 1,600·0 | 4,000·0 | 4,250·0 | 7,500·0 |
| LESS EXPECTED SAVING | — | — | 20,361·1 | 22,853·5 | 18,676·3 | 20,258·6 | — |
| **TOTAL EXPENDITURE** | **45,743·0** | **110,935·0** | **110,935·0** | **111,400·0** | **130,000·0** | **160,000·0** | **245,000·0** |

# Agriculture & Irrigation

THE HIGHWAY runs east of Kharj into the typically barren Najdi landscape of sandy, parched soil highlighted by a few dull-green shrubs. The occasional small roadside wheat or tomato plot carefully tended by groups of small farmers barely hints at the agriculturalists' claim that only water and their skills stand between the aridity and a great splash of green.

But fifty miles out of Kharj the horizon lights up to the right as one of the Kingdom's new modern large-scale farms comes into view. Two 50-metre sprinklers stand in a haze of spray on the radii of their great 52-hectare circles of green forage and wheat. A third, motionless and freshly installed, stands amid a flattened circle of virtual dust to prove the point.

Saudi Arabia is characterized by the vastness of its land area, which is more than 900,000 square miles, over 1.5 per cent of the world land mass. Under 0.2 per cent is cultivated and the total area utilized for agriculture and forests is less than three per cent. Huge oil revenues give the country a high income *per capita* rate, but the traditional agricultural sector is still dominant in terms of the numbers employed within it.

The tenure of agricultural land in the Kingdom is unlike that of other Middle Eastern countries. There is no concentration of ownership by a few rich individuals and the cultivated land is remarkably evenly distributed. Owner-occupied agricultural holdings make up the bulk of the cultivated areas. By the mid-1970s, 600,000 hectares were under cultivation. An estimated 200,000 million hectares of livestock grazing land exists but only a twentieth has been described as being of high quality.

During the Second Plan period, the agricultural sector only grew some five per cent per annum – a fifth of the rate of the total Saudi non-oil economy's growth. Farmers were attracted to the new wealth of the cities, creating labour shortages in traditional agricultural areas like date production. Machines were hard to introduce because most farms are small – 6.7 hectares average in 1976 – and generally not sufficiently co-operative. A few remote areas suffered from lack of infrastructure. These problems were to be tackled with more co-operatives and more rural roads.

Traditional flood irrigation is wasteful of precious water and increases the poisonous salinity of otherwise fertile soils – with sufficient water and the Saudi sun they can be up to five times as productive as Europe. Subsidies and investment assistance did not always produce significant improvements, especially with livestock and crops competing with subsidized imports. Fishing resources too were barely exploited along the 1,000 mile Red Sea and 350 mile Gulf coastlines. The annual catch by some 4,400 fishermen on 1,400-odd small boats was estimated at 16,000 tonnes during the late 1970s. The UN's Food and Agriculture Organization, however, estimated the potential annual catch to be as high as 3–500,000 tonnes.

Insufficient emphasis was placed on the vital agricultural sector during the first two plans, government officials concluded. Significant progress, however, had been made and would definitely continue in the Kingdom's search for prudent levels of agricultural self-sufficiency, increasing welfare for its rural people and optimum use of its water, land and marine resources. Skill levels would improve while the environment would be protected – al-Sada and Dalghin in Asir and Abu Hadah, for example, were made protected areas; there was substantial reafforestation and a number of national parks were created.

Farmers still comprise a quarter of the Kingdom's workforce. In the latter half of the 1970s it took fewer of them to produce more than ever before. Productivity increased by eight per cent, and modern large-scale farming techniques were introduced by investors attracted by subsidies and investment incentives.

By 1979, twelve new dairies – like the one near Kharj – were established, including one of the earliest, owned by King Khalid himself. He was also involved in modern production of camel's milk. From negligible levels, fresh milk and laban output (as well, later, as some cheese, cream, butter and ice-cream) increased to 20,000 tonnes a year. During

## Irrigation

Fresh water remains the scarcest essential.
Determined to become self-supporting in
foodstuffs, Saudi Arabia makes careful use
of its underground and rain water for
irrigation.

*Examples of irri-
gation are seen in the
dam in highland
Abha* (above), *the
massive Jizan Dam*
(far left) *and com-
plexes such as those
at Haradh* (left),
*and in Qasim* (right),
*where hot artesian
water is tapped.
Some eighteen lesser
dams have been built
to contain floodwater*.

*Horticulture has been highly developed in experimental farms* (right and above), *adding to the accumulated experience of skilled farming in the areas* (below and opposite) *naturally endowed with adequate rainfall.*

1979 another sixteen dairies were already being built. Most of the dairies drew heavily on foreign expertise. Their cows were flown in – at the Government's expense – from Australia, Europe and North America.

The dairies, required by their loan agreements to farm as well despite subsidized feed, were among the first modern farms to benefit from extraordinarily high-priced incentive purchasing by the Government's Grain Silos and Flour Mills Organization. Wheat output doubled in several years and would continue to soar as farmers, traditional as well as new, reacted to the opportunity. Dates, a traditional crop, had already been benefiting from a similar scheme with effective results, and wider use of "output subsidies" was being considered.

Another, earlier success had been the introduction of intensive poultry and egg farming. By 1980, Saudi chickens and eggs were supplying an estimated quarter and half of their soaring domestic markets. With new wealth and a growing population, including foreigners, food demand continued to rise sharply, especially for poultry, eggs, vegetables and fruit, as well as meat. Sheep imports grew dramatically; beef was introduced and would be locally produced. As diets changed, demand for dates, rice, flour and melons was expected to taper.

Vegetable crops were becoming very popular among farmers increasingly connected to urban markets by improved roads. The Kingdom also has up to nine million, or a tenth of the world's, mature

date palms. The Government was improving its supply of better seeds which had already brought significantly higher yields for wheat and barley as against sorghum, millet and corn. The tomato and water-melon crops were also producing large tonnages as were onions and citrus fruits.

New research and new techniques would substantially improve Saudi farming's yields. Pest control, water efficiency, salinity control and full-time training for 4,000 farmers would all help. At Jizan, in the Kingdom's verdant southwestern corner unique for its considerable natural rainfall, the Al Hakmah research station worked in dam-water irrigated fields more reminiscent of Europe than the Najd. The station extension programmes – among many

around the Kingdom – had begun to encourage the precise and extremely efficient drip-feed irrigation among nearby farmers who were eager to learn. The Eastern Province's Al Hasa demonstration farm had turned wasteland into cropland with new drainage systems. Work continued at eleven other research centres and experimental farms in the Kingdom.

At sea, the newly-created Saudi Fish joint stock Company would begin to exploit, and then process and market, the abundant resources with new boats and modern techniques. The Marine Resources Research Centre in Jiddah had studied these resources closely with foreign help as well as investigating the possibilities of intensive fish farming in the Kingdom. These were found to be

excellent and were being taken up by businessmen.

Government assistance to farmers would total SR 7.5 billion in the first half of the 1980s in its drive behind the agricultural effort. A third would go on the animal feed and output subsidies, the rest on cheap money for new farms and equipment. More too would be spent on the Government's work which would include creating new farmable land, as well as poultry and dairy farmer organizations. Saudi farming's efficiency and market would be closely monitored.

The most binding constraint on Saudi agriculture is imposed by water (*See also* Geography and Climate). The general availability of water in areas of cultivable soil is insufficient almost everywhere in the Kingdom: but studies conducted by

the Ministry of Agriculture and Water have revealed that underground water resources are much greater than was believed ten years ago. Comparative studies of known water sources with recent national water consumption rates demonstrate that they should be sufficient for tens or even hundreds of years. Surface water is intermittent and primarily available in the south-western highlands and coastal areas, brackish water is abundant and sea-water is available for desalination in unlimited quantities.

It has been found that the eastern, northern and central areas of the Kingdom are compiled of sedimentary rocks containing water-bearing formations which vary in quality and quantity. Such sedimentary deposits cover the

*Healthy flocks of sheep for breeding purposes have been reared under scientific care at Haradh (above).*

eastern two-thirds of the country. Most of these deposits are represented by sandstone or limestone, which hold a considerable amount of ground water.

These aquifers contain water more than thirty thousand years old. Some formations are near the surface but some are very deep, so diving and pumping equipment are necessary to extract the water. Some of these formations are not rechargeable, so water resources, like oil resources, are diminishing. According to studies made by consultants, twenty-eight important sedimentary aquifers have been discovered. Artesian water,

once tapped, reaches the surface under its own pressure, often at a high temperature, from the heat of the earth's core.

As for surface water, Saudi Arabia is the largest country in the world without rivers. The annual rainfall does not exceed 100 mm, although the south-western parts of the country are affected by monsoons and the annual rainfall average in these areas might reach 500 mm. In general, rainfall is sporadic and variable. There can be periods of drought of up to seven years, great humidity, high evaporation, strong wind effects and rapid run-off floods.

The accumulation of salts in the soil is one of the permanent problems facing irrigated agriculture. All surface water

contains some soluble salts in negligible amounts, but after several years of irrigation a harmful accumulation appears. Salts found in irrigation water remain in the soil, while water itself is lost by evaporation and drainage. Irrigation water is used in Saudi Arabia with a salt content ranging from one thousand to more than four thousand parts per million (ppm). Generally 3,150 ppm is considered the maximum for the safe watering of any plant; so salinity is a severe problem.

Irrigation agriculture has been and will continue to be by far the largest user of water. The demands made by agriculture on water supplies reflect crop needs and also determine minimum production and maximum cost levels.

The depth of ground water in the Kingdom varies from a few feet to three thousand feet. It is estimated, however, that there is enough water, in rainfall and below ground, for the area of cultivated land to double in the short run.

The main means of combating the constraint imposed by scarcity of water are by dams, wells, water-towers, draining and long-distance piping. Forty-one dams are already built, of which the largest, across the Wadi Jizan in the South-Western Tihama region, provides irrigation for 6,000 hectares. The greatest of the irrigation and drainage schemes – to rid the soil of its salinity – is at Hasa. The reclamation of land has led to a marked rise in the number of sheep raised, to which the Faisal Model Scheme bears striking witness. Here, a total of 3,600 hectares have been reclaimed, and the sheep population reached 33,000. The Faisal Model Scheme was converted into a private commercial enterprise after failing to settle Bedu.

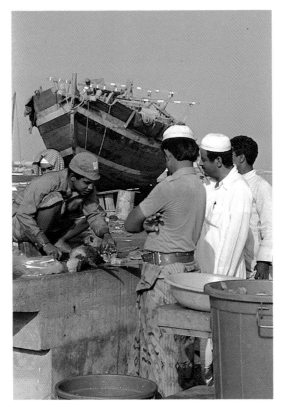

The final protection against lack of water is the sea. And the Government is immersed in an extensive desalination program. It includes the world's largest water pipeline from Jubayl to Riyadh which can be used to supply rural areas – half of whose people and livestock will receive ready access to water by 1985. Meanwhile a National Water Plan was to be established and enforced to co-ordinate water use and sharpen public awareness. And for the distant future, one of King Faisal's sons, Prince Muhammad, was privately developing the possibility of towing ice-bergs to the Kingdom from the Antarctic.

The leaders of the country are committed to the processes of agricultural development. They recognize its connection with the maintenance of political stability.

*Statistical sources:* Ministry of Agriculture & Water and Ministry of Planning.

*The sea is an untapped resource with a potential catch of half a million tonnes.*

## Fruit, poultry and honey

Figs (*top left*), grapes (*middle left*) and pimentoes (*bottom left*) speak of diversity of fruit production. Contrary to popular belief, much of the soil of Saudi Arabia is cultivable. Only the sand desert will grow nothing. The great expanses of powdery loess "desert" would bloom if water could reach it. Where this has been possible, vivid patches of green enliven the dun of the landscape. Meanwhile, more specialist areas of food production are being exploited. Saudi Arabia is already a major exporter of fruit to neighbouring countries, and egg farms are run on scientific methods (*right, top and middle*), providing a protein diet for people who, in earlier generations, had depended largely on dates, rice and sorghum. Bee culture (*bottom right*) has recently been added to the country's indigenous industries.

Other successful crops of fruit include water-melon, squash and tomatoes. The development of cash crops has been greatly stimulated by the expansion not only of the water supply (usually from underground), but also of the road system. Many small trucking enterprises have sprung up, linking producers with their markets in other parts of the country.

Local production of such foods is swiftly changing dietary habits. Dates are seldom, today, a staple; although they remain an important supplementary food. At the same time, the reclamation of the desert and the marking out of new smallholdings act as a spur to settlement.

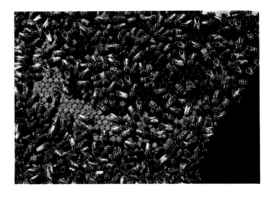

# Communications

THE romantic view that travel and communications in Saudi Arabia depend on the camel, the caravan and the dhow, has long been belied by reality. For more than a generation Saudis have enjoyed most Western means of communication, from a complex modern road network to sophisticated telecommunications. The Ministry of Communications and the Ministry of Telegraphs, Posts and Telephones have become two of the most active and important Ministries in the Kingdom. This importance was reflected in the "Physical infra-structure development" section of the 1395 AH (1975 CE) Five Year Plan and its successor. International and inter-city transportation networks were developed in anticipation of increased passenger and goods traffic; so were the telecommunications and postal services. Old roads, airports, railways and ports were expanded and improved, and new ones were to be built. Telephones were to expand to a capacity of 1,177,000 lines as well as 16,000 mobile telephones. The realization of these ambitious plans necessitated complex planning, energetic recruiting of manpower, and very considerable budgetary allocations from the Government.

As the map on p. 150 shows there was already a substantial road network in the Kingdom which only first gained paved roads three decades ago. This was to be significantly extended in the 1970s, when the overall length of paved road in the Kingdom tripled and the rural network grew fivefold. The Kingdom was linked with its neighbours, Jordan, Yemen, Kuwait, Qatar and UAE. Rural roads were to be expanded to facilitate agricultural, mineral and industrial development. By 1405 AH, the Saudi road network would include 10,000 miles of highway and considerably more again of earth-surfaced rural road which was to connect a further 4,600 villages. Moreover "back-up" services are as important as the actual construction processes, so laboratory testing of materials, road research, maintenance teams and improved safety measures had to be provided. Licensed vehicles increased from 40,000 in 1970 to 800,000 in 1978. (*See also* Construction.)

As the demand increased for imported capital and consumer goods to support the development of the economy, the major ports of Jiddah and Dammam expanded at a remarkable rate, as did the lesser ports of Yanbu, Jubayl and Jizan. More berths were constructed, and the amount of cargo handled per berth increased. Specialized industrial facilities were set up at Jizan, Yanbu and Jubayl, and at the same time minor ports were improved for small boats and fishermen. Improved training of port personnel was in hand, as were improved technical and maintenance facilities.

Great distances and the difficult terrain of much of Saudi Arabia has made aviation a vital element in the transport network. Saudia, the national airline, has become the largest Middle Eastern airline, serving twenty national and thirty-eight international airports regularly. A fleet of ten advanced Tri-Stars, ten Boeing 707s, three DC-8s, two Apache 235s, two Cessna 421-Bs, two Beechcrafts, three Fokker F-27s, and four Grumman G11s was operating by 1978. The same year saw the number of passenger journeys rise to 6,400,000 – compared with one million in 1973. But the fleet was to expand rapidly, including a large order for new European Airbuses, and would carry up to fifteen million passengers annually by the mid-1980s.

The airline and the Presidency of Civil Aviation sought to "Saudize" their operations as rapidly as possible. With the exception of one tragic incident at Riyadh airport in 1980, they have maintained their traditionally excellent air safety record.

In 1981, Jiddah's vast new international airport became operational. Larger than Kennedy, Newark and O'Hare airports combined, it could well handle the annual flood of pilgrims bound for Makkah. A few years later, Riyadh's new airport would be operational. Wholly modern flight handling methods had been introduced at the major domestic airports several of which were to be expanded or replaced.

The Saudi Government Railroad Organization runs and operates the 350-mile line from Dammam through Hofuf to Riyadh as well as a short line to Dammam port. Long-distance freight and passenger traffic increased by fifty per cent in the latter half of the 1970s when a "dry port" of customs and warehousing was

*The airports of Jiddah* (top) *and Dhahran* (right) *are triumphs of architectural caprice. A new one is planned for Riyadh* (above).

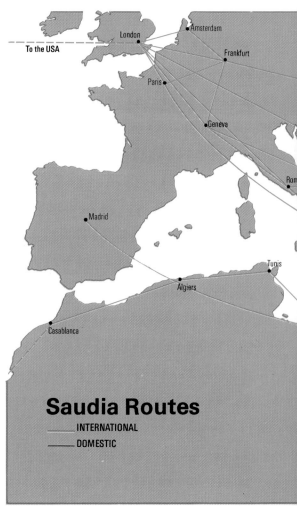

**Saudia Routes**

—— INTERNATIONAL

—— DOMESTIC

148

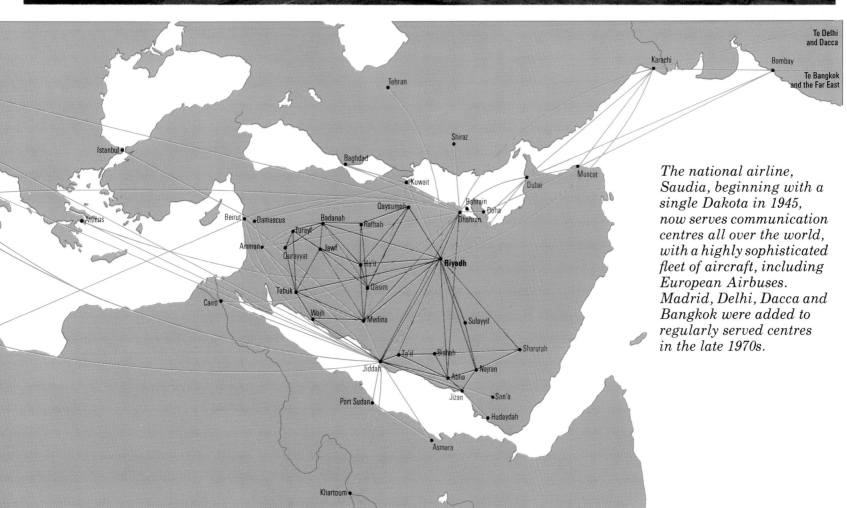

*The national airline, Saudia, beginning with a single Dakota in 1945, now serves communication centres all over the world, with a highly sophisticated fleet of aircraft, including European Airbuses. Madrid, Delhi, Dacca and Bangkok were added to regularly served centres in the late 1970s.*

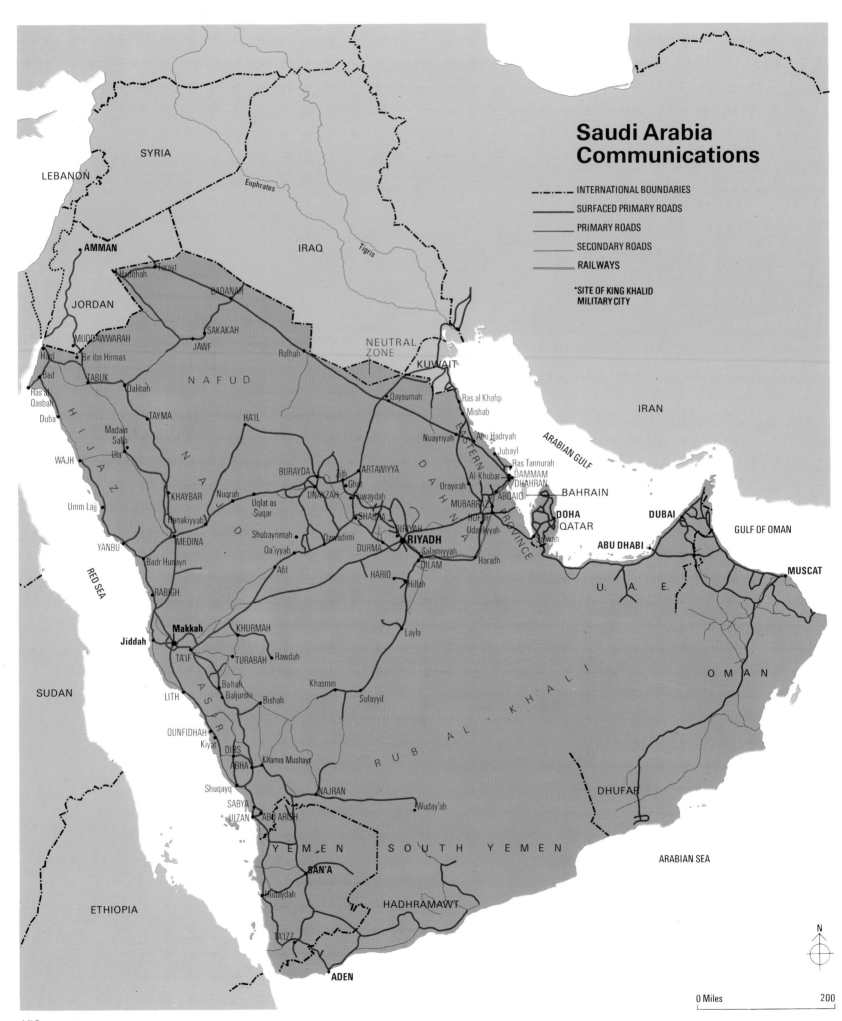

# Saudi Arabia Communications

- ·—·· INTERNATIONAL BOUNDARIES
- ——— SURFACED PRIMARY ROADS
- ——— PRIMARY ROADS
- ——— SECONDARY ROADS
- ——— RAILWAYS

*SITE OF KING KHALID
MILITARY CITY

LEBANON

SYRIA

*Euphrates*

IRAQ

*Tigris*

AMMAN

Hadithah · Turayf

JORDAN

BADANAH

MUDAWWARAH

SAKAKAH

Haql

Bir ibn Hirmas

JAWF

Rafhah

Bad

TABUK

Qalibah

Daysumah

NEUTRAL
ZONE

KUWAIT

Ras al Khafgi

Ras al
Qasbah

Mishab

IRAN

Duba

TAYMA

HA'IL

Nuayriyah

Abu Hadryah

ARABIAN GULF

Madain
Salih

Jubayl

Ula

Ras Tannurah

WAJH

BURAYDA

Zilfi

ARTAWIYYA

Al-Khubar

DAMMAM

Umm Lajj

KHAYBAR

Nuqrah

UNAYZAH

Ghat

Huwaydah

Urayrah

DHAHRAN

ABQAIQ

BAHRAIN

Hanakiyyah

Uqlat as
-Suqar

MUBARRAZ

HOFUF

DOHA

DUBAI

MEDINA

Shubayrimah

SHAQRA

DIRIYAH

QATAR

Udariyyah

GULF OF OMAN

YANBU

Qa'iyyah

Dawadimi

RIYADH

Salwah

ABU DHABI

Badr Hunayn

Afif

DURMA

Salamiyyah

U.   A.   E.

MUSCAT

RABIGH

HARIQ

DILAM

Haradh

Makkah

KHURMAH

Hillah

Jiddah

Layla

O  M  A  N

TA'IF

TURABAH

Rawdah

RED SEA

Bahah

Khasmin

Baljurshi

LITH

Bishah

Sulayyil

R  U  B     A  L     K  H  A  L  I

SUDAN

QUNFIDHAH

Kiyat

DIRS

Khamis Mushayt

ABHA

DHUFAR

Shuqayq

NAJRAN

SABYA

Wuday'ah

JIZAN

ABU ARISH

ARABIAN SEA

Y  E  M  E  N

S  O  U  T  H     Y  E  M  E  N

ETHIOPIA

SAN'A

Hudaydah

HADHRAMAWT

TA'IZZ

N

ADEN

0 Miles    200

built in Riyadh to ease pressure on Dammam. The Arabian climate and landscape is good for railways with long, flat stretches, but its drifting sands are a challenge to maintenance. New track and rolling stock were to be added to the line. The Government, however, would also study significant new elements to a possible national rail network. It might recommission with Syria and Jordan the historic Hijaz pilgrim line from Damascus to Medina which could connect the Kingdom's railways to Europe's network through Turkey. A possible Jiddah–Riyadh line could be connected to Medina, and a rapid transit line to Makkah from Jiddah was thought useful.

Wireless telegraph stations were established in Makkah, Ta'if, Jiddah and Riyadh long ago, in the reign of King Abdul Aziz. Telephone systems followed and, in 1956, modern radio stations were set up. The Ministry of Communications (PTT) embarked upon large scale projects, both to develop the services, and to modernize the entire telecommunications system.

In 1974, the most modern means of long-distance communication was installed. Portable earth stations were established first at Riyadh, and later at Jiddah, working with Indian and Atlantic Ocean satellites and using Rome as the gateway. Standard earth stations were then built at Riyadh and Ta'if. Telephone, telegraph, and telex links spread nationally and internationally. The nation's telephone microwave network was connected to Sudan and would be expanded domestically and to the UAE, Qatar, Kuwait, Yemen, Jordan and Egypt. Telex would have more lines; telegraph would receive modern radio links to remote towns. Saudi Arabia's telecommunications organization was to be scrutinized for efficiency and possible sale to the public. Training would include 2,400 graduates from expanding Saudi institutes; a third would be built.

Postal services have made considerable progress: a twenty-four hour service for inland mail was being widely established. Some facilities were still antiquated and there was a shortage of

*The twisting highway up to Abha is a monument to modern road-building.*

trained manpower. But sorting and delivery schedules improved the inland mail, and by the end of 1977 big city postal services, both for internal and foreign mail, had become dependable. New post office buildings and equipment were being set up, and mobile facilities used. Recruiting methods, qualifications and pay scales were being studied, reviewed and improved. There are postal training courses in secondary schools. The National Computer Centre was being used to improve statistical and accounting methods. Specialized financial sections dealt with foreign post. Plans aimed for "a prompt service of unquestionable reliability." The sophisticated changes which were planned would swiftly transform the whole of the Kingdom's communications system.

*Statistical sources:* Ministry of Posts, Telephones & Telegraphs and Ministry of Planning.

151

## Ports

Over seventy million tons of shipping docks annually at Saudi Arabia's major ports, of which the foremost is Jiddah (*far left*). The immense inflow of goods led to acute congestion, especially at Jiddah, where ships were obliged to wait many weeks to unload. But Jiddah has expanded enormously since the days of only a couple of generations ago when its principal traffic was shiploads of pilgrims bound for Makkah, and from 1977 all congestion was eliminated. Further north on the Red Sea coast, Yanbu (*above left*) was designated to become the country's second port, above all to relieve Jiddah. On the Gulf, Dammam and Jubayl (*below left*) have been built to cope with rapidly increasing traffic, though the main load of shipped oil takes place by the pipeline off Ras Tannurah. At the same time facilities were not forgotten for small boats and fishermen (*above*).

# Manufacturing

*Until 1980 Saudi wealth had been built on revenues from the sale of a non-renewable asset; hence the growing preoccupation and determination to build up the non-oil sector of the economy. Capital-intensive manufacturing became a priority of the Third Plan.*

## Television

It was the late King Faisal who recognized television as a means of bringing to people in their homes a widening of knowledge and a more vivid sense of the unity and achievement of their own country. In a land where the public cinema was disallowed, the decision to create a national television network came as a surprise to some. A sophisticated service steadily developed, linked by Telstar to international networks for programmes and news from abroad, and bringing a familiarity with the affairs and leadership of the homeland among the people which would have been otherwise impossible.

*Various indigenous programmes are produced in sophisticated studios* (below) *and production centres* (left) *now transmitted from the Television Tower* (far left) *at Riyadh's Ministry of Information.*

INDUSTRY, especially hydrocarbon-based, is destined to become a major source of Saudi Arabia's future income, diversified away from almost total dependence on the export of crude oil.

Several government agencies are at work behind the Kingdom's industrial effort. But it is firm policy that Saudi manufacturing should be profitable in its own right and private individuals play a central role both as industrialists and as future investors in the hydrocarbon and other heavy industry being founded by the Government.

On the private side, the Second Plan period saw considerable new manufacturing activity, especially for construction materials in its middle years. The Government's semi-autonomous Saudi Industrial Development Fund (SIDF) provides viable new factories or extensions with cheap money up to half the start-up cost to Saudi industrialists or Saudi-foreign joint ventures with licences from the Ministry of Industry and Electricity. The Ministry, with SIDF assistance, monitors industry closely, and licences and loans are curtailed if particular areas appear to have sufficient or surplus capacity. It also provides and expands the industrial estates in most cities and towns, where manufacturers gain cheap land, water and electricity as well as other necessary services.

By 1981, SIDF had financed over 600 new factories, many on these estates, in its first six years. Its capital had been increased to over SR 7 billion, and planners hoped it would lend a total of SR 10 billion during the second plan for a further 14 million square metres of industrial estate created by expansion at Riyadh, Jiddah, Dammam, Qasim, Hofuf and Makkah and new construction in Medina and Khamis Mushayt in the Asir. Manufacturing variety was enormous, although much of the SIDF's lending had gone to the construction supply industry for the construction boom of the late 1970s including block crushers Kingdom-wide, asphalt plants, aluminium door and window frame manufacturing, pipe plants, and new or expanded cement plants in Jiddah, Riyadh, two in the Dammam area including one to supply Bahrain as well, the Southern province, and, it was expected, near Kuwait. Foodstuffs processing, whether soft drink manufacturing and bottling, fruit juices, vegetable oils (through a joint stock company) or cakes and sweets, was a major area. A perfume factory was built; Jiddah received a carpet factory. Industrialists began to build plastics products factories too in anticipation of the downstream petrochemicals industry which would supply the raw material. Virtually all appropriate areas of light and even heavier manufacturing were begun during the Second Plan and it was thought that future opportunities would include everything from metal products, including pipes and tanks, based on Jubayl's new steel industry, car parts, animal feed concentrates or an agro-industry for packaging and even processing of Saudi farm produce. Saudi manufacturing, however, was constrained by the smallish size of the Saudi market and by the relative shortage of Saudi labour – most of the 40,000 new industrial jobs went to foreign workers imported from the Far East, Pakistan and India, and Yemen and Arab countries with Western expertise. Co-operation among the Gulf states was expected to increase, partly through private initiative and partly through the Doha-based Gulf Organization for Industrial Consulting which had begun studies of possible factories to supply all Gulf countries, for example, with a light bulb factory. Many industrialists wanted tariff barriers to protect them against cheap imports, but govern-

ment policy on viable manufacturing kept barriers to twenty per cent or less, and this was not expected to change. The Government would continue to encourage foreign manufacturing participation by licensing joint ventures and allowing them to benefit from the SIDF's soft loans and generous tax holidays for the foreign partner's profits. As manufacturing had been a relatively new Saudi endeavour, there was a shortage of management and technical expertise, but like the supply of necessary infrastructure, this would become increasingly available.

By the end of the Second Plan the semi-autonomous Government's Grain Silos and Flour Mills Organization had grain silos with a capacity of 320,000 tons per year, flour mills for 449,000 tons per year, and could produce 300 tons per day of animal feed concentrates. Smaller complexes than those in Jiddah, Riyadh and Dammam, would be built in Khamis Mushayt and Jizan, and grain storage capacity would be increased to give the Kingdom capacity for a six month stock of wheat and to produce all its flour requirements.

During the Second Plan the Ministry of Industrial Studies and Design Centre was transformed into the Saudi Consulting House which, after a generous capital send-off, and with foreign expert advice, was to become a major Saudi centre for consulting, in market research and eventually engineering studies. It began to operate on a private basis, competing against foreign and domestic firms, although it was anyway awarded government research contracts. For example, it was to investigate the effect of government basic food subsidies on the consumer, and also the effectiveness of industrial and other joint ventures in transfering technology into Saudi minds

*The solemn purpose of the country has been to provide an infrastructure that will outlast its age of plenty. Industries firmly based on indigenous resources include an aluminium plant at al-Khubar (above), while a Saudi Mercedes factory (top) shows another aspect of the manufacturing sector. Massive development has changed the face of the cities, none more so than Jiddah (left), though quieter, more ancient skills such as wood-carving (right) remain in vogue, and highly sought after.*

and hands.

Saudi heavy and hydrocarbons industry of the future, however, was to be based in the new industrial cities of Jubayl on the Gulf and Yanbu on the Red Sea being established by a special Royal Commission. They were tremendous jobs, master-designed and managed with assistance from the American firms Parsons and Daniels. The desert was levelled and infrastructure installed; complete suburbs were designed and to be built with a wide array of international and Saudi contractors on projects expected to last over two decades.

Jubayl, ultimately, would be a city of 370,000, and Yanbu, 150,000, each with ports, airports and mammoth world-scale petrochemical plants.

In Jubayl, the Third Plan would see the completion of the Saudi Arabian Basic Industries Corporation (SABIC) basic steel industry in co-operation with Korf Shahl of West Germany. This would include an 850,000 tons per year direct-reduction type basic steel plant, fuelled by Aramco's gas gathering system (*see* Petroleum Development), linked to an 800,000 tons per year steel-rolling mill. Jiddah's steel-rolling mill would be in-

creased to 150,000 tons per year. SABIC, however, dropped plans for a Saudi aluminium smelter in 1980 in deference to one in Bahrain which would be sufficient for Gulf demand. This move was considered a major point of Gulf co-operation.

After years of discussion and negotiation, two of every three export industries originally scheduled for Jubayl were cancelled to ensure the survivors' viability and success. The early 1980s saw the completion of final agreements for most of SABIC's petrochemical projects with foreign partners, attracted by profits and

157

*By the mid-1970s, Saudi Arabia was producing no more than 50,000 tons of its own iron and steel. SABIC now has an annual production capacity of more than 2,000,000 tons.*

especially the incentive of direct oil supply agreements proportional to their investment. In Yanbu, projects would include an ethane-fed joint venture with Mobil to produce ethylene, ethylene glycol and low and high density polyethylene. Jubayl would have a similar 500,000 tons per year ethane "cracker" jointly shared by a SABIC joint venture with the Dow chemical company and a large Mitsibishi-led 54-Company Japanese consortium, the Saudi Petrochemicals Development Corporation (SPDC); originally both were to have their own crackers but SABIC decided to reduce output but still feed plants for polyethylene production.

Saudi Pecten, a joint venture with Shell Oil would transform salt, benzine (from the Petromin-Shell International refinery in Jubayl) and ethane into ethylene styrene, ethylene dichloride and crude industrial ethanol and soda. Another SABIC joint venture with a Japanese consortium, led by C. Itoh, Saudi Methanol, would produce six hundred thousand tons per year of methanol by a process of extraction from methane gas. At the same time similar plant with two American companies Celanese Chemical Company and Texas Eastern, would produce 650 thousand tons per year. Another SABIC joint venture with the Taiwan Fertilizers Company would transform methane into 500 thousand tons of urea per year. Exxon was to take ethylene to produce 260,000 tons per year of low density polyethylene, whose hard raw pellets are used for a wide variety of malleable plastics such as films, moulded products and synthetic fibres.

By 1990 it has been estimated that the Kingdom's petrochemical plants will earn it three billion dollars a year, admittedly small by crude oil earning, but nevertheless significant. The downstream plants not only allow the Kingdom to add value to its crude oil exports but create the opportunities to train a Saudi workforce for the future. The planned projects will give the Kingdom a modest share of international petrochemical markets (two to eight per cent for various types), and, by the end of the 1970s, early fears of overcapacity on the markets implying little room for the new Saudi output began to appear unfounded. It is also stated Saudi oil sales policy to link sales of crude oil with sales of its petrochemicals and other products if necessary.

# Mining

HALFWAY to Sudan from Jiddah, the Atlantis II hot brine deep, one of many along the Red Sea rift, could prove an exciting source of mineral wealth as the world's first ocean-bed mine.

Thick mud on the seabed 2,000 metres down was found to contain seventeen metallic elements when brought up from the 29 million-year-old rift in the earth's mantle. They include gold, silver, mercury, iron, copper and zinc. The Saudi-Sudanese Commission for the Development of Red Sea Resources considered a mine feasible. Its work, contracted largely to international specialists, was generating new patents and techniques at the forefront of world research on ocean floor mining, which in most of the ocean's rifts is complicated by legal problems of ownership. Atlantis II, deep in the Red Sea's relatively young and narrow rift – still widening at an estimated 2.5 centimetres a year – is wholly within the two countries' territorial waters.

During the early 1980s, the Commission expected to establish a pilot plant at Yanbu to process the mineral-bearing muds which would be piped or barged to it from a mining rig.

By then, however, the first mine in the Kingdom's new mining era was to be nearing production. Appropriately it was to be Ma'had Dhahab – "cradle of gold" in Arabic – the Arabian Shield's most historic of mines. The existence of ancient mineworkings had always hinted that Saudi Arabia would prove to be rich in much more than oil. Geologists had discovered it because of ancient tailings and workings like others which litter the Shield.

Ma'had was to produce annually some 2–3 tons of gold, 5–7 tons of silver, 1,000 tons of copper and 2,500 tons of zinc for a standard 50:50 joint venture between the Government's Petromin and the London-based Consolidated Goldfields.

But while Goldfields, Ma'had Dhahab was the most advanced prospect, six other international mining companies had specific exploration licences to investigate deposits largely discovered by the Government's uniquely intense geological effort to chart its mineral resources and, ultimately, found a mining industry.

Gold at Jabal Guyan and nickel-iron,

## *Ancient mineworkings had always hinted that Saudi Arabia would prove rich in much more than oil.*

possibly cobalt, nearby at Wadi Qatan in Najran on the Yemeni border were being prospected by a Saudi-American joint venture, the Arabian Shield Development Company. Its American-Palestinian President, Hatem el Khalidi, had been prospecting the rugged terrain since the early 1960s. Khalidi, encouraged and assisted by a Saudi government loan, was expected to prove adequate deposits for a highly profitable mine.

British Steel continue to investigate iron ore deposits at Wadi Sawwawin in the North-West on behalf of the Government to see if both mining and elaborate ore-processing were justified. The iron would supply the Kingdom's new direct-reduction steel mill at Jubayl. Minerals policy is to relate closely to industrial needs while mapping resources and investigating the more promising of over 700 mineral occurrences. Other commercially promising deposits were copper at Nuqrah and phosphates at West Thanayat. Uranium reserves were being discovered and water resources maps completed on various scales.

By 1980, seventy-six quarry lease permits had been issued for such building materials as marble, granite, clay and limestone. Nine quarries opened and others were being encouraged by model quarries and ornamental stone cutting and polishing plans.

*Quarrying at Ma'had Dhahab, the Arabian Shield's most historic mine.*

# Construction

NEW construction, often on a massive scale, has taken place in Saudi Arabia, drawing contractors from around the world and creating a new domestic industry. In terms of amenities and standards the Kingdom has been transformed into a modern society as the work has taken place.

In the 1980s, the furious pace of building was expected to slow down once the final elements of essential infrastructure had been built when more emphasis would go to maintenance. But the Saudi urban and rural landscapes would still see yet more roads, hospitals, housing

*The complex of Conference Palace and mosque (Qasr Al-Mu'tamarat) has given Riyadh one of its most beautiful architectural sites. Sulaymaniyya's "Grand Festivals Palace" (left) remarkably reproduces a traditional palace.*

KEEP
CLEAR

## Construction

The massive building programme has inspired the international community of architects and designers to stretch their skills and imaginations. All government projects are put out to international tender. British, American, Japanese, German, Lebanese, French, Italian and Egyptian architects have all been successfully at work. More recently, indigenous Saudi Arabian architects have played a part. New wealth spreading among the population has inspired originality in home building.

*Given Saudi Arabia's low rainfall, ferro-concrete has become the most-used construction medium. Though concrete absorbs rather than reflects heat, internal air-conditioning is de rigueur. Concrete has a plasticity which allows for imaginative design. Grand modern hotels took advantage of this to provide the conference centres and international meeting places of Arabia. Left: the site of the Holiday Inn, Jiddah, seen from across the water. Below: the Al Hada Sheraton in Taif. Pictures of buildings in Jiddah (right) and the interior of the royal pavilion at its new airport (below right) show the concern to incorporate traditional motifs in new design.*

*The top of the water tower in Riyadh (top right) affords a splendid panorama of the city and its environs. The striking sports city in Dammam (above), completed in 1979, contains three swimming pools and a multi-purpose gymnasium. A new hotel (left) encloses an elegant stairway. It is the cleanliness of the atmosphere and the strong light that have stimulated architects and designers into attempting forceful new ideas – both in detail and on the grand scale – in new townships and universities.*

*The furious pace of building in the 1970s, when the time from idea to completion on many projects was perhaps the lowest in the world, has changed the face of Arabia's cities. Cityscapes, whether in Jiddah (above), or Dammam (below), have been transformed by the most modern of building techniques.*

or sewage treatment plants.

The Bahrain causeway, for example, was expected to be built by the mid-1980s, crowning a decade of massive road building with thousands upon thousands of miles of inter-city highway where before there was little. Still more roads extended the cities which spread for miles beyond traditional limits. Large numbers of cars arrived to use them. Many of the Kingdom's new generation of roads were outstanding construction feats, like the twisting drive up Ta'if's escarpment or down from Abha towards Jizan. Dozens of flyovers in Jiddah and Riyadh

as well as thousands of elegant new villas and homes built with the help of cheap government loans. Cityscapes were transformed with new building, whether the dozens of grand new ministries or government buildings in Riyadh or the tall office-blocks of downtown Jiddah. In the towns and villages of the country, new buildings went up, matched, less visibly, by sewage systems, electricity and water – all extended in the cities. A modern telecommunications network efficiently connected the Kingdom nationwide. Thousands of new hospital beds, among the most sophisticated in the world, marked the Government and the private sector's determination to serve Saudi citizens. Schools similarly blossomed to cater for the Saudi youth. Grand modern hotels, perhaps even too many, were built in the cities and towns, whose industrial estates saw the rise of modern, capital-intensive Saudi manufacturing. Above all, work continues in Jubayl on the Gulf and Yanbu on the Red Sea to found new cities from scratch to cater for the Kingdom's modern petrochemical refining and steel industry of the future.

It is firm government policy that local contractors should be preferred where possible, but Saudi Arabia's larger projects turned it into an international construction forum drawing keen competition from America, Europe and the Far East for the work. South Korean contractors particularly prevailed for basic building work as they and other Asians, like the Filippinos, outpriced Western builders but maintained equally high standards. But American, British, French, German, Italian, Greek, and especially Saudi firms won considerable work. Design – much of it unique in imagination and scope – similarly brought all nationalities, though Saudis themselves took an increasing role.

The Kingdom witnessed the most modern of building techniques with much use of precast elements and shortened the time from idea to completion on many projects to among the lowest in the world. Jeddah boasts the world's largest pre-engineered panel manufacturing plant – a Saudi operation building houses, schools and office blocks from scratch, exporting building systems worldwide.

sought to ease the traffic flow, several running for miles above the urban streets.

In Riyadh, another world scale construction job would put the academic core into Riyadh University's new campus. Nearby an entirely new suburb was being built to house diplomats from Jiddah. Jiddah's University too would see new buildings and, among much other university work, the University of Petroleum and Minerals in Dhahran is an architectural triumph for the Islamic "mood" of the Saudi building boom.

New ports or massive expansions at Jiddah, Jizan, Yanbu and Jubayl paved the way for soaring imports and construction. Even Riyadh received a "dry port", to store and customs-clear cargo brought by train from Dammam. Jiddah's new international airport, together with its award-wining *hajj* terminal, a vast stunning white fibreglass "tent", opened in 1981. It was one of the most modern airports in the world. Properly equipped aircraft could land entirely on automatic pilot. New airports at Riyadh and Dhahran would open soon after.

New housing included the mammoth rush housing schemes of the three cities

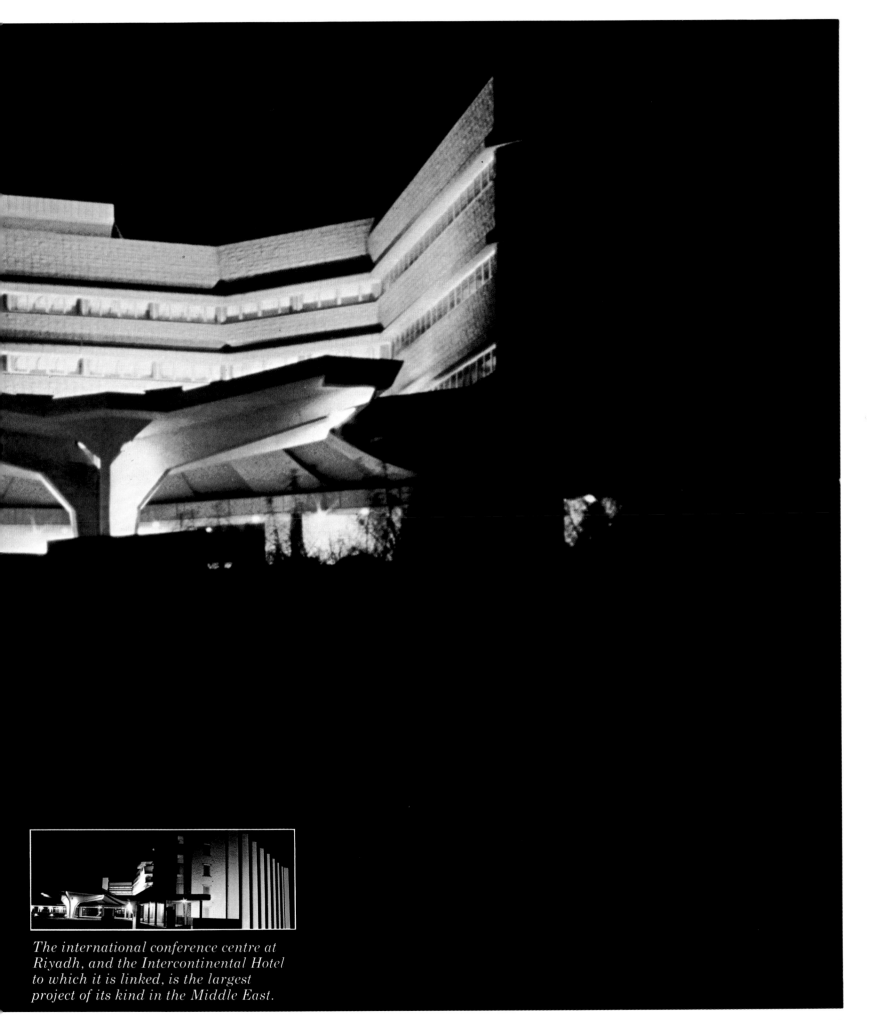

*The international conference centre at Riyadh, and the Intercontinental Hotel to which it is linked, is the largest project of its kind in the Middle East.*

# Petroleum-Discovery & Development

THE founder of the modern Saudi State, King Abdul Aziz ibn Abd ar-Rahman Al Saud, opened the door to the development of Saudi Arabia's vast hydrocarbon resources in 1933 when he granted a concession to the Standard Oil Company of California (Socal) to explore for oil in the Kingdom. Socal formed an operating company (California Arabian Standard Oil Company), of which Texaco bought a half share in 1937.

The story of the discovery of oil in Arabia is remarkable. Socal was one of the largest oil producers in the United States, but by 1930 its exploration in eighteen foreign countries had produced nothing substantial. Meanwhile, an enterprising New Zealander, Major Frank Holmes, went to Bahrain in the early 1920s to assist in developing water resources, although his principal interest was in the possibility of oil. In 1922 he crossed over to the Arabian mainland and negotiated with Abdul Aziz Al Saud for a concession covering more than 30,000 square miles in the eastern Hasa Province. It was granted in 1923 and, in 1925, Holmes succeeded in obtaining an oil concession for Bahrain.

These concessions were taken in the name of the Eastern and General Syndicate, a British group with which Holmes was associated and which, although not made up of oil operators, hoped to interest British companies who were. In this effort it was unsuccessful. The concession in Hasa was allowed to lapse for want of £1,000 to keep it in operation. Gulf Oil Corporation took up the option in Bahrain, but because of their oil interests in Iraq, assigned it to Socal in 1928.

With Socal established in Bahrain, it it was only a matter of time before American geologists were on their way to Jiddah, to the King of Saudi Arabia. By the end of 1933, eight American oilmen were working in the Dammam area. It was Well No 7 that turned the company's fortunes in 1938. Drilled to 4,727 feet, it encountered large quantities of oil in what is now called the Arab Zone.

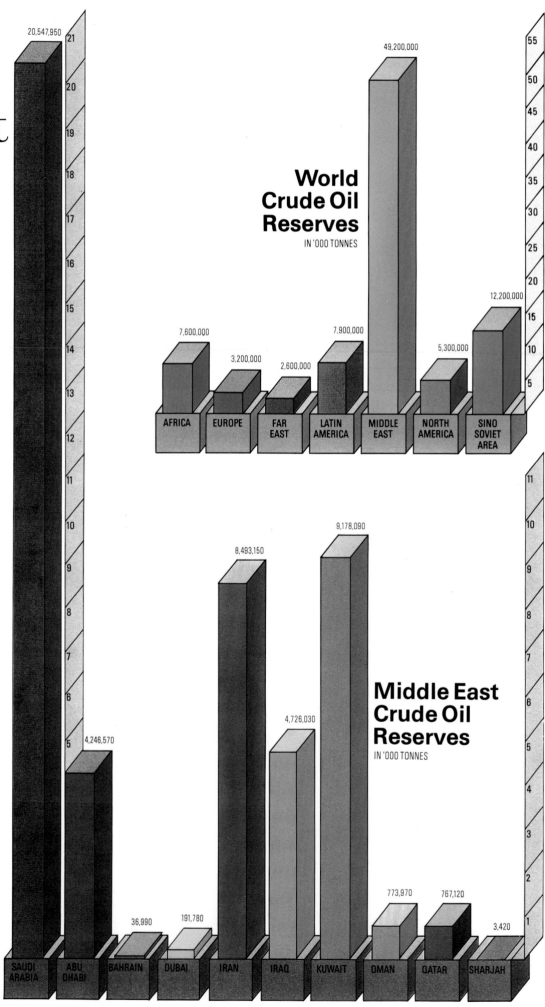

**World Crude Oil Reserves**
IN '000 TONNES

- AFRICA 7,600,000
- EUROPE 3,200,000
- FAR EAST 2,600,000
- LATIN AMERICA 7,900,000
- MIDDLE EAST 49,200,000
- NORTH AMERICA 5,300,000
- SINO SOVIET AREA 12,200,000

**Middle East Crude Oil Reserves**
IN '000 TONNES

- SAUDI ARABIA 20,547,950
- ABU DHABI 4,246,570
- BAHRAIN 36,990
- DUBAI 191,780
- IRAN 8,493,150
- IRAQ 4,726,030
- KUWAIT 9,178,090
- OMAN 773,970
- QATAR 767,120
- SHARJAH 3,420

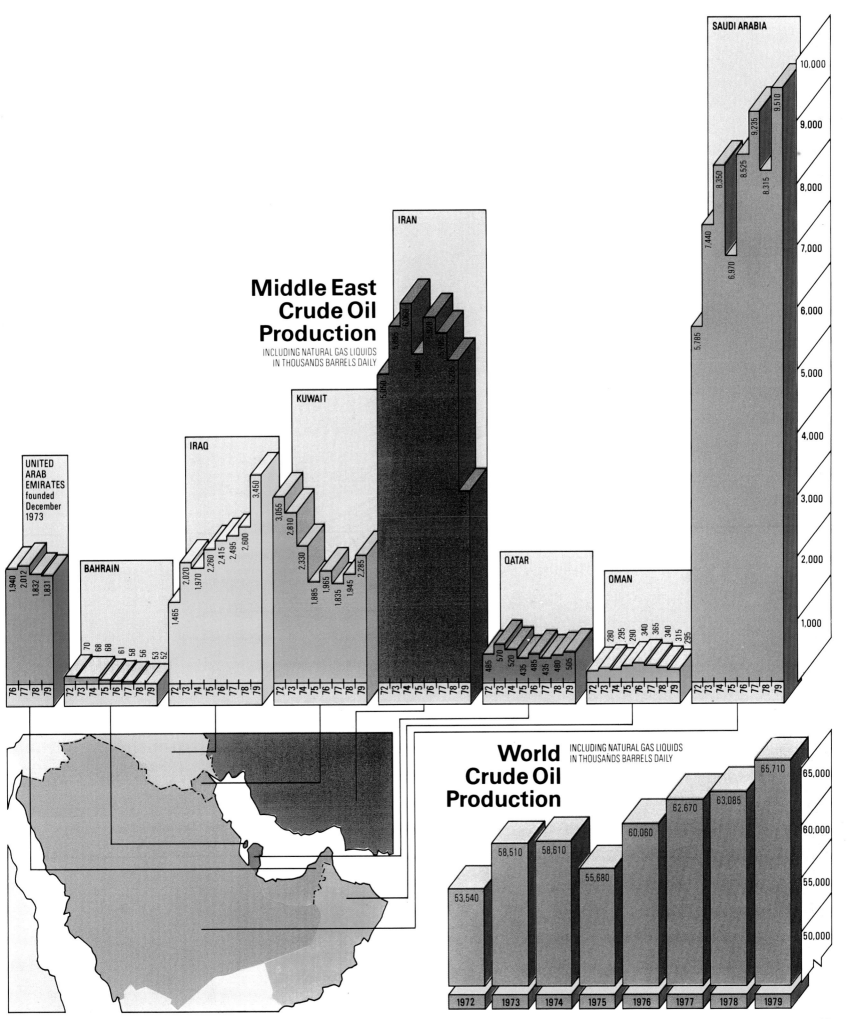

# Middle East Crude Oil Production

INCLUDING NATURAL GAS LIQUIDS
IN THOUSANDS BARRELS DAILY

**UNITED ARAB EMIRATES** founded December 1973

1.940 2.012 1.832 1.831
76 77 78 79

**BAHRAIN**

70 68 68 61 58 56 53 52
72 73 74 75 76 77 78 79

**IRAQ**

1,465 2,020 1,970 2,260 2,415 2,495 2,600 3,450
72 73 74 75 76 77 78 79

**KUWAIT**

3,055 2,810 2,330 1,885 1,965 1,835 1,945 2,285
72 73 74 75 76 77 78 79

**IRAN**

5,050 5,895 6,060 5,385 5,900 5,705 5,265 3,175
72 73 74 75 76 77 78 79

**QATAR**

485 570 520 435 485 435 480 505
72 73 74 75 76 77 78 79

**OMAN**

280 295 290 340 365 340 315 295
72 73 74 75 76 77 78 79

**SAUDI ARABIA**

5,785 7,440 8,350 6,970 8,525 9,235 8,315 9,510
72 73 74 75 76 77 78 79

10,000
9,000
8,000
7,000
6,000
5,000
4,000
3,000
2,000
1,000

# World Crude Oil Production

INCLUDING NATURAL GAS LIQUIDS
IN THOUSANDS BARRELS DAILY

53,540 58,510 58,610 55,680 60,060 62,670 63,085 65,710
1972 1973 1974 1975 1976 1977 1978 1979

65,000
60,000
55,000
50,000

## Probability of
## Oil Occurrence

FAVOURABLE

POSSIBLE

The first tanker was loaded on 1 May 1939.

In 1944 the Company's name was changed to Arabian American Oil Company (Aramco), by which it is known today. Mobil (formerly Socony-Vacuum Oil Company) and Exxon (formerly Standard Oil Company of New Jersey) obtained shares in 1948, and ownership of Aramco was divided on the basis of thirty per cent each for Socal, Texaco and Exxon, with ten per cent for Mobil.

The discovery and development of Saudi Arabia's oil fields began slowly, affected by transportation difficulties and material shortages resulting from the Second World War. Activity resumed in a limited way in the autumn of 1943 when plans were announced for a 50,000 barrels a day refinery at Ras Tannurah. With the ending of hostilities, Aramco's crude oil production jumped from an average 20,000 barrels a day before 1944 to 500,000 barrels daily by the end of 1949. By 1974, Aramco was producing 8,209,706 barrels of oil per day; its refinery at Ras Tannurah was turning out 482,411 barrels a day of products for marketing in Saudi Arabia and abroad.

Aramco accounted for ninety-seven per cent of Saudi Arabia's production,

but it was not the only oil company operating in the Kingdom. The Getty Oil Company was assigned a concession in Saudi Arabia's undivided share of the Neutral Zone in 1949 and, in co-operation with Aminoil (the American company carrying Kuwait's fifty per cent interest in the Neutral Zone), discovered oil in what is called the Wafrah field in 1953. The Japanese-owned Arabian Oil Company was assigned a concession by both Saudi Arabia and Kuwait to explore the offshore area of the Neutral Zone in 1958, and discovered oil in the Khafji field in 1960. By the start of 1980, Saudi Arabia's estimated crude oil reserves stood at 167 billion barrels, about a quarter of total known world reserves. Production remained high as the Kingdom sought a balanced international oil market and averaged 9.5 million barrels per day over the year. It is the world's second largest crude oil producer, topped only by the Soviet Union. The USA lies third. Of the 62.5 million barrels produced worldwide each day in 1979, about fifteen per cent came from the Kingdom. And since about eighty-three per cent of this was exported, Saudi Arabia was the world's biggest exporter.

The following illustrations give an

indication of the magnitude and importance of Saudi Arabia as a world energy supplier. Currently, Saudi Arabia's rate of liquid hydrocarbon production is running at about one-tenth of all primary energy consumed in the non-communist world (including coal, oil, lignite, peat, gas, hydro-electric energy, geothermal energy, and nuclear energy). It could generate all the electricity produced in the whole of South America and Western Europe combined.

Since Saudi Arabia and other members of the Organization of Petroleum Exporting Countries combined to take the power of oil-pricing decisions away from the multinational oil companies in the early 1970s, much has changed in the Kingdom's oil scene. As OPEC's largest producer it has remained a moderating force while oil prices multiplied many times with OPEC spurred by the international markets pushing them up erratically but many times above the artificial low levels set by the multinationals. But Saudi Arabia, when necessary, has maintained high output levels to prevent disarray in the Western economies and has sought to introduce stabilising pricing formulas for gradual, predictable rises.

At home, the Government was gradu-

170

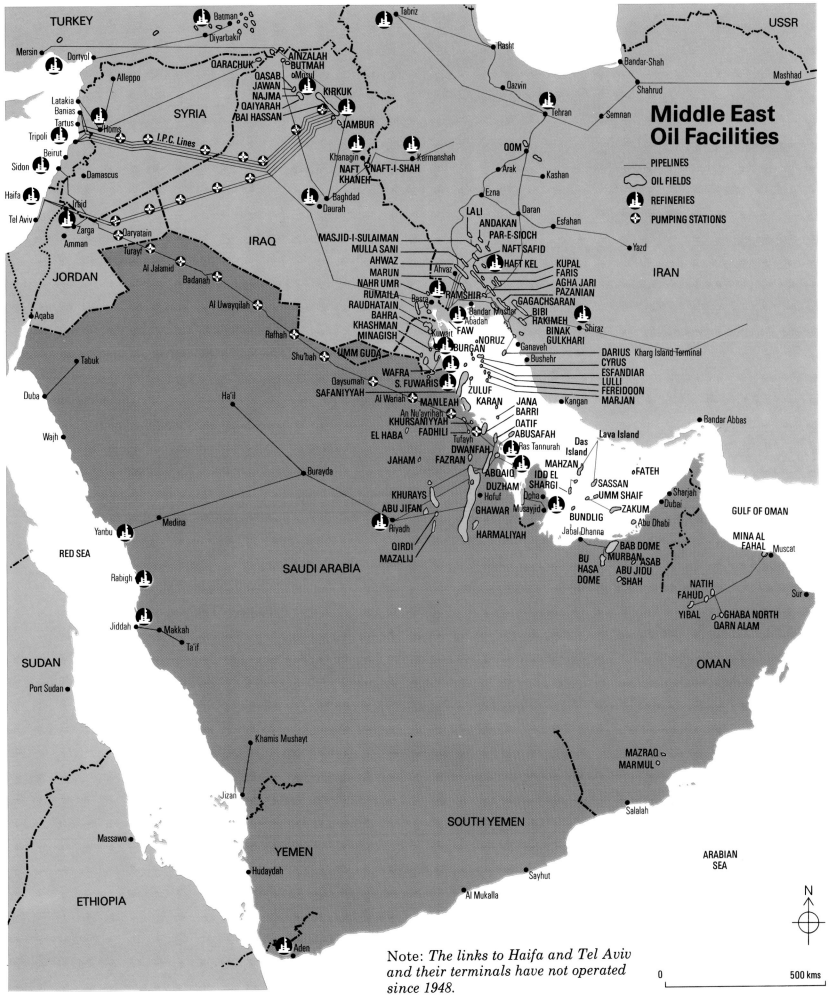

# Middle East Oil Facilities

PIPELINES
OIL FIELDS
REFINERIES
PUMPING STATIONS

Note: *The links to Haifa and Tel Aviv and their terminals have not operated since 1948.*

0                    500 kms

ally taking control of its vital oil sector in partnership with foreign expertise and developing it to ensure its maximum contribution to the Kingdom's longterm future. For it was well appreciated that the petroleum resources were not infinite.

In 1962 the Saudi Arabian Government established the General Petroleum and Mineral Organization (Petromin) to develop the Kingdom's oil and mineral resources and to establish related industries. Petromin is an autonomous government agency, working in conjunction with the Ministry of Petroleum and Mineral Resources. It entered into a joint venture with the Italian state oil company AGIP, and with Philips Saudi Arabia to explore for oil in the Rub al-Khali and Hasa areas. Under an agreement with Tenneco – the American oil exploration company from Tennessee – it has been exploring for oil offshore along Saudi Arabia's Red Sea coast.

In addition, Petromin has established joint venture organizations. Argas (Arabian Geophysical and Surveying Company) and carries out aeromagnetic, geodetic and seismic surveys for local and foreign oil companies. The Arabian Drilling Company drills, and performs well work-overs, on the same basis. In 1967, Petromin Marketing assumed control of Aramco's Kingdom-wide marketing network for the distribution and sale of refined products, and has since expanded and modernized it. The Petromin Tankers and Mineral Shipping Company (Petroship) has purchased a number of oil tankers to haul crude oil from Ras Tannurah to the Jiddah refinery, one of a growing number under Petromin's wing (*see* below). In the future, Petroship might grow to handle Saudi hydrocarbons and petrochemical exports.

For, above all, Petromin began to establish direct crude oil export contracts with usually government-backed consumers. These bypass the multinational oil companies which traditionally handled international oil flows. By the early 1980s direct oil deals accounted for over two million barrels of oil per day. Petromin too would handle "incentive" oil contracts awarded to international companies investing in the Kingdom's downstream hydrocarbons industry of the future. The Saudi Arabian Basic Industries Corporation is forging ahead with this in the new industrial cities of Jubayl and Yanbu. (*See* Industry). Petromin is also behind huge increases in

172

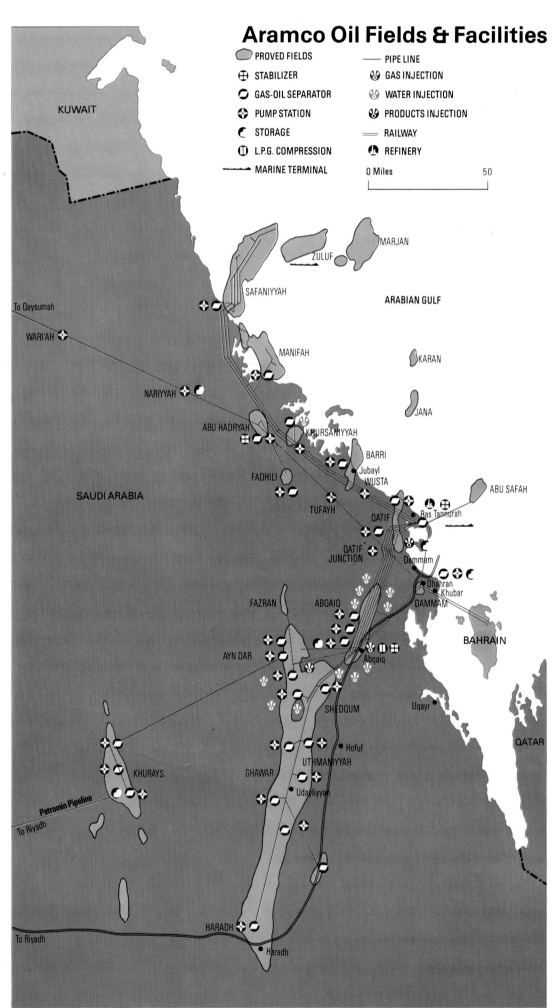

**Aramco Oil Fields & Facilities**

PROVED FIELDS
STABILIZER
GAS-OIL SEPARATOR
PUMP STATION
STORAGE
L.P.G. COMPRESSION
MARINE TERMINAL

PIPE LINE
GAS INJECTION
WATER INJECTION
PRODUCTS INJECTION
RAILWAY
REFINERY

0 Miles        50

refining capacity for soaring domestic consumption as well as export. (*See* Refining). And it will operate the new east-west crude oil and gas pipeline from the oilfields to Yanbu on the Red Sea. (*See* Pipelines).

To support large-scale industrialisation and to conserve resources, a massive gas-gathering system was being established in the Eastern Province oilfields. The system (*see* chart) developed by Aramco, allows Saudi Arabia to use much of the gas produced in association with crude oil. As most Saudi gas is associated, with an average gas-oil ratio of 500 standard cubic feet per barrel of oil produced, its output is essentially related to the output of crude oil. So plans for gas exploitation have evolved with plans for increasing crude production as well as limitations on cost. Later, the system may be expanded to draw gas from distant and offshore gas-oil separation plants. But initially three gathering centres and three plants further downstream will yield up to 3.4 billion cubic feet of associated gas per day. They will transform this into up to 4,000 tonnes a day of sulphur which is to be exported manufactured into sulphuric acid, and up to two billion cubic metres a year of fuel gas, mostly methane. Some of the methane will be feedstock for methanol and urea petrochemical plants, some will be reinjected into the oilfields to maintain pressure, the rest will fuel the industrial complexes of Jubayl and Yanbu, major seawater desalination and power plants around the country and thermal heating. A pipeline connects one centre, Shedgum, with Yanbu. Beyond this, three further plants transform the remaining natural gas liquids into up to 0.37 billion cubic metres a year of ethane and 375,000 barrels per day of liquid petroleum gas. The ethane provides feedstock and fuel requirements for SABIC's ethylene petrochemical complexes. Most of the liquid petroleum gas is sold abroad, much of it to Japan, and exports were beginning to rise in the early 1980s. Saudi Arabia was taking its place, albeit less eminently than with crude oil, in the international gas markets, and replacing with gas sales the wasteful flares which once marked the oilfields of the East. Under Saudi supervision, Aramco has ensured that these fields are carefully nurtured to maximise their output, for example maintaining balanced production of different types of crude. Facilities were also being expanded to increase

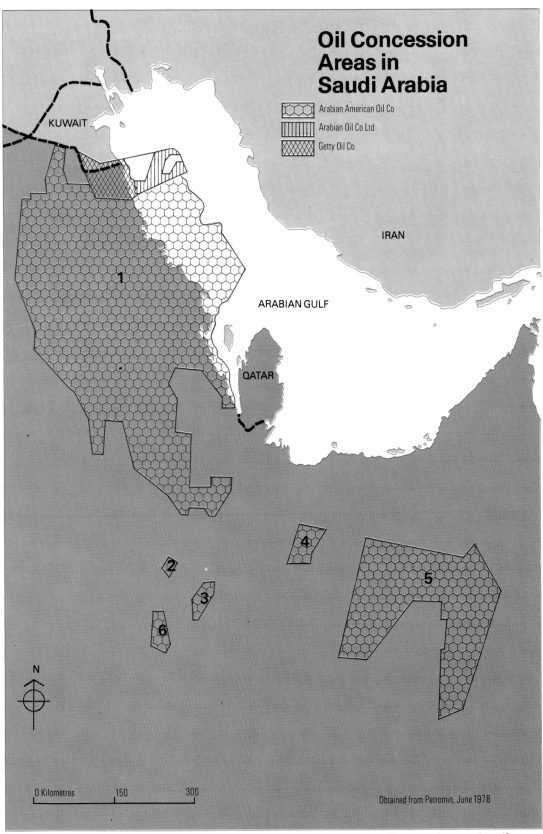

**Oil Concession Areas in Saudi Arabia**

Arabian American Oil Co
Arabian Oil Co Ltd
Getty Oil Co

KUWAIT

IRAN

ARABIAN GULF

QATAR

N

0 Kilometres    150    300

Obtained from Petromin, June 1978

sustainable Saudi productive capacity to up to twelve million barrels per day in the mid 1980s.

In the late 1950s, two Saudi officials joined Aramco's Board of Directors, and this number was later increased to three. In 1968, the Kingdom's interest turned to participation and ownership as well as management. In 1972, the Saudi Government acquired a twenty-five per cent interest in Aramco's crude oil concession rights. On 5 June 1974 this share was increased to sixty per cent. Negotiations were then initiated to bring the Government's participation up to one hundred per cent while preserving the role of the American companies in providing expertise. The financial takeover was completed in 1980, by which time Saudi oil officials had long been respon-

## Exploration

Continued exploration for oil and gas proceeds not because any greater production is required, but to establish as precisely as possible the extent of the country's reserves. Proved oil reserves already make Saudi Arabia a substantially richer country than any other. The presence of oil is calculated in the first instance by trough-like geological "structures", but to strike an oil seam usually involves an extensive phase of trial and error. By the end of the 1970s, over forty fields had been discovered in Saudi Arabia, of which nearly half lay either wholly or partly under the sea. Under half had been put into production. The Ghawar field was the world's largest field onshore, and Safaniyyah the largest off-shore. There were also seven commercial fields in the Neutral Zone which Saudi Arabia shares with Kuwait.

*While heavy drilling materials must be dragged across the surface of the desert by specially designed vehicles* (left and above), *camps are supplied by air-drop from helicopters* (above, right). *Rock depths can be calculated either by drilling, or seismically by blast* (right). *A gusher may produce black oil, or* (far right), *gas.*

## Extraction

Oil from an underground reservoir rises to the surface as a result of an injection of gas. The oil mixed with gas then proceeds to the Gas-Oil Separation Plant (GOSP). The gas is then re-cycled back into the gas injection plant, below ground, to force more oil upwards. The unstabilized oil then proceeds to the crude oil stabilizer, and, as a stabilized oil, it is pumped either aboard tankers, or in pipelines across the desert. Alternatively, stabilized oil may go to the refinery – in Aramco's case to the refinery at Ras Tannurah. The great size of Saudi Arabia's oil resources, the ruggedly hostile nature of the terrain, the distances over which the oil must be transported before it can be loaded on to tankers, and the vast infrastructure of men and organization required to get the oil out, called for the most modern petroleum technology, much of which has been developed in Saudi Arabia. Aramco has been a leading innovator in improving water and gas injection techniques to maintain oil-field pressure, so that production levels can be sustained. It also helped to develop the low-pressure, off-the-road sand tyre now commonly used in desert exploration.

## Refining

The heart of the oil refinery at Ras Tannurah (*left*), is the bubble car or fractionating column of the crude distillation unit. Into the bottom of the car is fed the heated crude oil, which is flashed into vapours. Crude oil is a mixture of different types of hydrocarbons, all having different boiling points. The vapours of the heavier hydrocarbons condense at a higher temperature near the bottom of the fractionating column. Those of the lighter hydrocarbons, such as kerosene and gasoline, bubble up through a series of trays until they condense at the relatively low temperatures at the top. Thus, a process of distillation separates the crude oil into various "fractions". Each fraction in turn must be refined before it is ready for the market. Fuel oil accounts for about half the production of the Ras Tannurah refinery, which refines more than 500,000 barrels of crude oil daily.

It was first and for many years the only refinery, later joined by smaller export ones operated by Getty Oil and the Arabian Oil Company (now 80,000 barrels per day combined). Refineries for domestic use were built by Petromin in Jiddah and Riyadh. Jiddah refinery's capacity was increased to 100,000 barrels per day in the second plan, though plans for still further expansion were halted. In the early 1980s, expansion at Riyadh will give it a capacity of 120,000 barrels per day. But this will not meet soaring domestic demand and construction began in Yanbu for a 170,000 barrels per day refinery. Jiddah's capacity was to be expanded to a

further 250,000 barrels per day in 1985. Petromin, however, has joined foreign companies to build massive new export refineries of 250,000 barrels per day each with Shell in Jubayl, Mobil in Yanbu and Petrola in Rabigh. They were to be completed in 1984, and other projects were being considered to increase the Kingdom's value-added earnings on its oil. Saudi lubricating oil plants were also to increase. Jiddah lube oil blending plant was to become more efficient in producing both Petromin oils and others using the special additives of foreign companies. A grease plant was to be built in Jiddah as were new lube oil blending plants in Jubayl and Riyadh. Others were to be studied both for export and domestic use.

## Pipelines

Conceived in the mid-1970s, the 750-mile Petroline pipeline began pumping oil and gas across Arabia in the early 1980s. It is a stategically vital alternative to the tanker route through the straits of Hormuz and saves 3,550 miles sailing round the peninsula for supplies to the new industrial city of Yanbu. The initial flow of 1.85 million barrels per day on the six-day journey was expected to be increased to 2.4 million barrels per day and possily more in future years. It might also connect with shuttling tankers to Egypt's Sumed pipeline from the Red Sea to the Mediterranean. The 48-inch steel line has eleven pump stations from Abqaiq and Ain Dar to Yanbu each with uniquely strategic turbines that can be powered on natural gas, NGL, diesel fuel or even crude oil right out of the buried line. Alongside Petromin's Petroline, Aramco built an NGL line to carry the petrochemical feedstocks to Jubayl. At Yanbu, two very large crude Carrier oil tankers can be simultaneously loaded in thirty-six hours; eleven tanks store one million barrels of crude each. The entire system is operated from a computerized control room in Yanbu where refineries and petrochemical plants will eventually process much of the flow.

sible for all aspects of the Kingdom's oil policy. Agreements were to be forged specifying access to the Kingdom's crude oil for the multinational Aramco partners, who continued to supply expertise while Saudi Arabians prepared to take their place.

Saudi Arabia's leaders realized early that technicians and trained personnel would be needed. The College of Petroleum and Minerals was therefore established in 1963 in Dhahran (*see also* Education). From an initial enrolment of sixty-seven in 1964, the College's student body grew to about 1,500 in 1974–75, and was expected to reach the 3,000 level by 1985. In 1974 the College moved to a new campus with the most up-to-date classroom, laboratory and workshop facilities and a computer centre. In 1975 the College became a University, offering programmes for a Master's Degree in Industrial Management and Petroleum Engineering.

Saudi Arabia realized that its petroleum resources were not infinite. Part of the resulting industrialization effort was directed to developing petrochemical industries so as to maximise profits on each barrel of crude oil produced while importing new technologies into the

Kingdom. Hence Saudi Arabia also planned huge increases in its refining capacity (*see also* Development).

To support large-scale industrialization, a gas grid system was planned in the Eastern Province to provide methane and ethane gas. Under this plan, which was developed by Petromin, Aramco is to design, construct and operate a gas system enabling Saudi Arabia to utilize virtually all the gas produced in association with crude oil. Since almost all gas produced in the Kingdom is associated gas, its output levels are essentially a function of oil production. With an average gas-oil ratio of 500 standard cubic feet per barrel of oil produced, current gas output levels are over 3.5 billion cubic feet of gas daily, with gas reserves estimated at 85,000 billion cubic feet. Some of this gas is to be used for the industrial complexes planned for Jubayl on the Arabian Gulf and Yanbu on the Red Sea, with still more to be used for reinjection into oilfields and to desalinate large quantities of sea water in the country's major desalination plants at Jiddah, Al-Khubar, Yanbu and Jubayl. Several thousand megawatts of electric power is to be generated from gas, while the Saudi Cement Company plant at

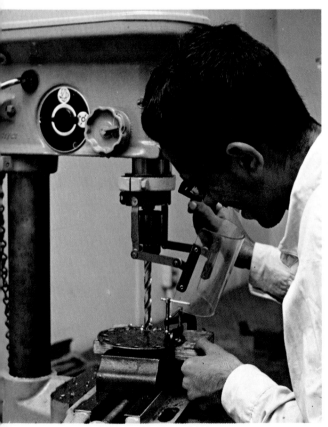

*Oil production requires shortwave radio transmission between staff* (top) *and a high technical precision* (above).

## *Aramco brings out over 95 per cent – the (Japanese) Arabian Oil Co. and Getty share the rest.*

Hofuf at present uses gas for thermal heating. At Abqaiq, gas is separated into methane, as feedstock for the Saudi Arabian Fertilizer Company and for use in the petrochemical industries, especially those at Dammam and Jubayl; and into natural gas liquids for the Aramco-owned Ras Tannurah refinery. Aramco itself owns two natural gas fields. Such gas as cannot be used locally is to be exported in the form of gas liquids.

Initial plans for gas exploitation have undergone certain changes since their instigation by Petromin in 1974, largely because the projections of long-term oil production levels are still to be finalized. Gas production from the northern off-shore fields of Safaniyeh, Marjan and Zuluf is to be postponed, whereas the project was initially set up to collect gas from all the Arabian oilfields.

For years, immense quantities of gas have been wasted. But with the completion of gas projects now in hand, Saudi Arabia is on its way to becoming one of the major natural gas liquid producers in the world.

*Statistical sources:* Petromin and Aramco.

## Principal Petroleum Products

**TOTAL 278,382,000**

| Product | Value |
|---|---|
| ASPHALT, JET FUEL & MISCELLANEOUS | 5,893,000 |
| KEROSENE | 9,855,000 |
| GASOLINE | 19,716,000 |
| DIESEL OIL | 34,963,000 |
| NAPHTHA | 48,285,000 |
| NATURAL GAS LIQUIDS | 64,876,000 |
| FUEL OIL | 94,794,000 |

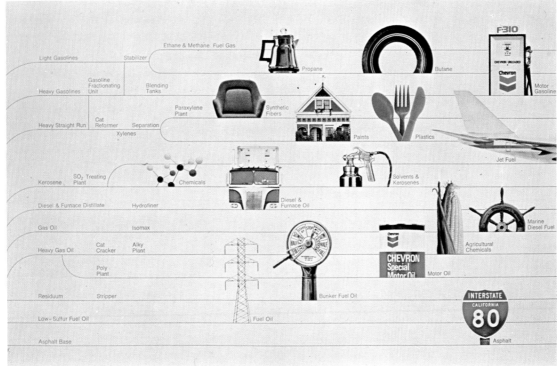

*Massive tankers plying the Gulf route (including the world's largest, such as Globtek II) are fed their crude oil by pipeline direct from the Saudi oil fields. The re-opened Suez canal shortened western routes but some tankers were too large.*

# 9 Youth

*The young of today grew up in a country which their grandfathers, at the same age, would hardly have recognized. This has been the continuing challenge: to provide the young with the opportunities to fulfil themselves and their country's needs, yet shielding them from disorientation through the onslaught of the meretricious from the outside world, and preserving in them the inheritance of wisdom.*

*At Dhahran's University of Petroleum and Minerals, devoted to the study of oil technology, young Saudi students take advantage of the best resources that the world can offer in that field upon which Saudi Arabia's economy chiefly rests. Built for over 3,000 students, it provides qualified engineers and managers in oil technology for the country.*

# Policy for Youth

THE youth of Saudi Arabia is growing up in a period of dramatic expansion. They are living at the centre of this drama: it is widely recognized that their innate abilities and talents should be as fully developed as possible. Luqman's proverb "A father's blows upon his son's back are like manure upon a field" could not be more outdated. Education is seen as the true means to build the personality of society's individual members, in order to enable them to continue developing their society. Education is free, but is regarded as imposing a debt on the student which he should repay by his service to the state.

In a Kingdom with a high level of illiteracy in the early 1960s a policy decision had to be made between opting for quality or opting for quantity of education. The urgent need for education led to the rapid expansion of primary and intermediate schooling. This emphasis resulted in a relatively small proportion of students passing on to secondary education. In the early and mid-1970s substantially fewer pupils who qualified for secondary education entered it. Many in fact joined the armed services, vocational schools or religious institutions where their education continued.

At the secondary stage the policy prevails of not allowing pupils to specialize too rigorously, but pupils can choose between the literary and scientific streams after the first year of the secondary stage.

Although many modern textbooks and syllabuses were initially imported from abroad, the aim of the Government has been to keep the study of Islamic beliefs as a basis of the educational system, so that new generations should not only achieve intellectual and practical skills, but should acquire them in the context of an awareness of their duties towards God and man.

Education is seen as a process which develops, controls and guides the life of a community towards its ideal, and awakens individual students to an awareness of their responsibilities towards their country. Different pupils with different aptitudes now have open to

them a wide range of establishments in which they can gain practical and theoretical learning: at the secondary level they can opt for the industrial education programme in technical institutes and the Higher Industrial Institute. At a higher level plans are being formulated

to increase the number of post-secondary polytechnics offering two to three years of technical training.

Commercial and administrative education has attracted far more pupils than was originally envisaged. Teacher training is being expanded at secondary level institutes, in particular through the establishment of a junior college system for teacher training.

Young people are being encouraged to participate actively not only in intellectual pursuits but also in community activities, such as those attached to Community Development Centres.

School health services are being massively expanded, with a particular emphasis on preventive medicine; and sports facilities are growing as well. During 1974 the General Presidency for Youth Welfare was formed to frame policies for youth welfare. Eight general objectives were formulated, and in achieving these objectives it was the policy to ensure that services were comprehensive, integrated and justly distributed, and that the services were in harmony with both the Islamic code for

rearing youth and modern knowledge of handling young people. A balanced education is looked for, such as will organize creative capabilities so that they both make an effective contribution to the nation's development, and support the family structure, by which great store is set in the Kingdom.

At the same time it is hoped to encourage young people to invest their free time in sporting and recreational activities that both enhance the enjoyment of living and improve physical fitness, so that the nation may raise the standard of excellence in sports to an international level.

The Supreme Council for Youth Welfare provides programmes of activities in cultural, scientific, athletic and social fields. There are fifty-three sports clubs officially registered and nine national societies covering the following sports: football, basketball, volleyball, bicycling, handball, table-tennis, swimming, weaponry, athletics, karate and judo. (*See also* Sport).

As part of the Third Five-Year Plan beginning in 1980, nearly twenty-five per cent of the Kingdom's resources was earmarked for education. There are bound to be problems; yet the frustration of youth which has been a feature of Western societies and which at times has erupted in anti-social ways is considered unlikely to appear since the roots of that frustration lie in lack of facilities, educational and recreational, and in lack of opportunities.

Saudi Arabia is committed to the provision of superb facilities; few countries have experienced such a proliferation of opportunities for young people, whether male or female, to fulfil themselves as individuals, and as members of a nation.

A policy for youth, in a country where family ties are so strong, must take account of parental attitudes. It is seen as important that parents are themselves involved in the education and wider social activities of the young, and that a living relationship exists between home and school. The "generation gap" so evident outside the Kingdom, and which one would expect to be caused by so rapid a growth of change, may well thus be avoided.

Both the young and the old are enjoined to bear in mind the Prophet's recommendation for the adult to forgive the young and for the young to respect the adult.

## Schools

- FOR BOYS
- FOR GIRLS

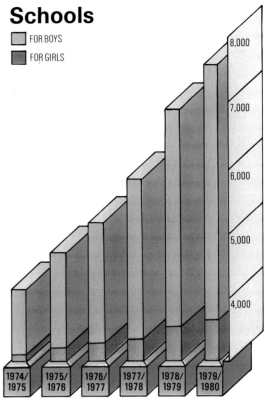

8,000
7,000
6,000
5,000
4,000

1974/1975 | 1975/1976 | 1976/1977 | 1977/1978 | 1978/1979 | 1979/1980

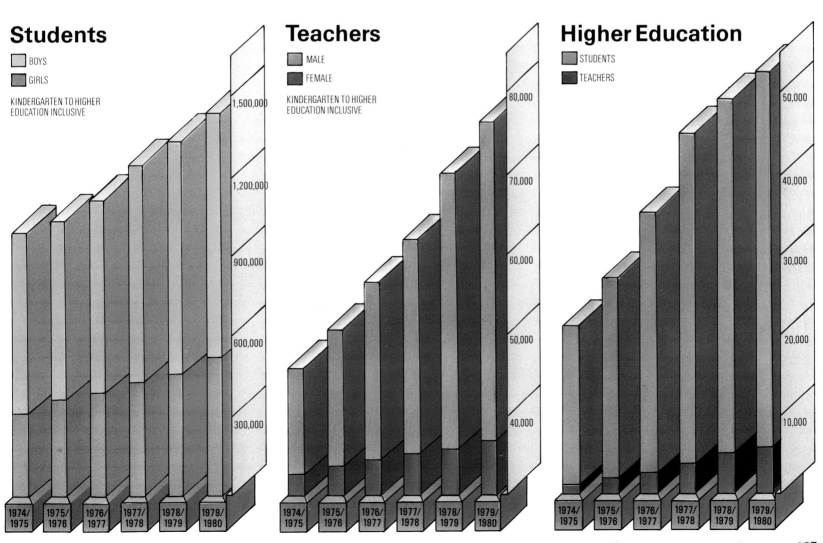

## Students

- BOYS
- GIRLS

KINDERGARTEN TO HIGHER
EDUCATION INCLUSIVE

1,500,000
1,200,000
900,000
600,000
300,000

1974/1975 | 1975/1976 | 1976/1977 | 1977/1978 | 1978/1979 | 1979/1980

## Teachers

- MALE
- FEMALE

KINDERGARTEN TO HIGHER
EDUCATION INCLUSIVE

80,000
70,000
60,000
50,000
40,000

1974/1975 | 1975/1976 | 1976/1977 | 1977/1978 | 1978/1979 | 1979/1980

## Higher Education

- STUDENTS
- TEACHERS

50,000
40,000
30,000
20,000
10,000

1974/1975 | 1975/1976 | 1976/1977 | 1977/1978 | 1978/1979 | 1979/1980

187

Pupils are happy amid the familiarity of local architecture, as in the south-western school (above), or being taught in the open air as (opposite) in the Eastern Province.

At Khaibar a modern school is tastefully decorated.

The principal boys' school at Ta'if is one of the most successful in the country.

# Boys' Schooling

BEFORE the establishment of a Department of Education in 1924 there were few schools, all of them private institutions in the Hijaz concentrating on Qur'anic instruction and the rudiments of reading and writing. In the early years of the Department, growth was hampered by lack of money. At the same time there were many who feared that a modern educational system would damage the fabric of a profoundly religious society. Expansion was therefore confined to the few large towns and it was only in 1954, when the Department became a Ministry, supported by increased funds and headed by HRH Prince Fahd ibn Abdul Aziz, that school education began to spread systematically throughout the Kingdom.

The Ministry of Education is not the sole agency concerned with boys' education. The Ministry of Defence and the Religious Colleges and Institutes Administration each account for approximately 1.5 per cent of the total enrolment of boys at school, while private schools take care of some 4.5 per cent. Education closely follows the pattern of other Arab countries, and consists of four stages: kindergarten (*rawdha*), primary (*ibtida'i*), intermediate (*mutawassit*) and secondary (*thanawi*). Government kindergartens are very few and most children start with primary school at the age of six. The primary stage lasts for six years at the end of which pupils take the Primary Certificate before entering the intermediate stage. Three years and another exam, the *Kafa'ah*, then another three years at secondary school and the Saudi Baccalaureat, the *tawjihiyyah* – key to the tertiary stage. After one year at secondary school there is a choice of streams, scientific (*ilmi*) or literary (*adabi*). Progression is rigidly controlled by end of year exams, which take place in May–June with re-sits in September or October.

At the post-intermediate level there are a number of schools attended by those not wishing to go to secondary school: among these are the vocational schools which are a vital source of

189

future Saudi technicians. The Royal Technical Institute in Riyadh takes graduates of the vocational secondary schools and gives them two years' higher technical training. The vocational secondary schools run by the Ministry of Education should not be confused with the vocational training centres run by the Ministry of Labour and Social Affairs, which take students of low educational level and turn them into craftsmen and artisans. By 1980 there were thirteen of these centres, and the Ministry of Labour plans several more.

The Special Education Department of the Ministry of Education also runs schools for the blind, the deaf and dumb and the mentally retarded. In the late 1970s the Ministry expressed interest in establishing a village for the handicapped near Riyadh, and this could be followed by similar villages in the Hijaz and the Eastern Province.

The steady progress in education can be measured by the increase in pupil/ student enrolment and teaching staff, and the growth of educational institutions. During the surge forward from the second half of the 1970s, enrolment was increasing by some seven per cent annually, and, at the beginning of the academic year AH 1400–01 (1980–81 CE), there were over one million pupils (thirty-four per cent girls) in the primary stage alone. The most dramatic increases have been in higher education with an increase in the five years to 1980 from 14,500 to over 46,000.

For administrative purposes the country is divided into zones. These vary enormously in size and importance – the Riyadh zone has more than 6,000 teachers, the rural Aflaj zone a mere 200 or so – but each one is a complete entity, with its own health unit, educational aids unit and so forth. The headmaster of each school reports to the zone director, who is in turn answerable to the Assistant Deputy Minister; the latter reports to the Deputy Minister for Educational and Administrative Affairs, who, under the Minister, is the *de facto* chief executive for most matters concerning boys' school education. Within the Ministry there are departments for primary, intermediate, secondary and technical education, each headed by a director-general. Attached to each department are a number of subject-specialized inspectors-general, who ensure that the centralized *curriculum* laid down by the Ministry is properly worked through in the schools. The inspectors-general are assisted by cadres of inspectors based in the larger towns.

The administration of school education is being decentralized with more authority given to each of the three main Zone offices – Central Zone in Riyadh; Eastern in Dammam; Western in Jiddah. There is therefore a great need to train and retrain large numbers of lower grade officials, many of whom may have had only a very basic education themselves. The Institutes of Public Admini-

*At Unayzah's secondary school, pupils display their work, including a maquette of a mosque. The teaching of English is imaginative* (below). Right, *Riyadh pupils observe the pull of surface tension.*

*As young minds are put in reach of knowledge,
the fever to learn grows. Scientific disciplines
carry the greatest allure – but not at the expense of
respect for the country's special role in Islam.*

stration located in Riyadh, Dammam and Jiddah, and the Ministry itself have arranged special courses and in-service training programmes to meet the needs of the employees.

In education particularly, the Saudi tradition of right of access at any level by members of the public militates against devolutionary procedures. But this time-consuming contact with members of the public is both an essential part of the Saudi democratic tradition and also a practical way for senior education officials to monitor the needs of the people and the public mood. Nevertheless the load of many officials is extremely heavy.

Formal centralization is most apparent in the financial and supply systems. The zone director has comparatively little say in financial matters, controls only a very small budget for local expenditure and is entirely dependent on the central authority for the supply of all equipment. And the rapid expansion of the system – at one time new schools were being completed at the rate of three a day – has placed an additional burden on the existing services.

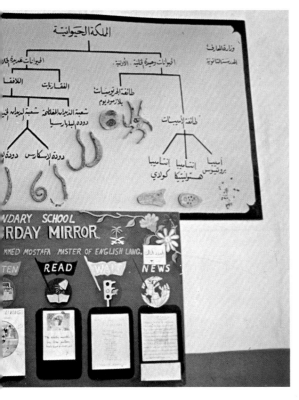

*The challenge of the expansion of education was not only of more schools, more teachers and more materials. It was how to bring in the new and modern methods without putting at risk all that was old and valued.*

As Saudi Arabia had no university of her own until 1957, many of the brightest students had to go to other Arab countries for their higher education. Because of this, *curricula* and materials were largely imported or adapted from those being used in the other Arab countries. But by the late 1960s and early 1970s much of the *curricula* of those countries had been renewed and the textbooks changed in order to keep abreast of more modern teaching techniques. At most levels Saudi Arabia was left with materials that were sadly outdated and which often reinforced the traditional rote methods of learning. The Ministry had the choice either of continuing to adapt foreign materials to the unique cultural, religious and social background of Saudi Arabia or of producing a *curriculum* and a set of materials specially designed for the Saudi situation. By and large the Ministry has opted for the latter, and most courses will be radically altered by early 1980. (*See also* Higher Education.)

*The spread of wealth throughout the population reaches boys in relatively remote Jizan, where well accoutred bicycles were the rage (far left). Playgrounds vary from the informal, in a Riyadh school (left), to the formal sportsground at Abha sports centre (above).*

The design for the new *curriculum* and the production of new materials are carried out under the auspices of the Ministry's *curriculum*, research and materials department by experts drawn from many quarters. And each year an ever-increasing number of Saudi experts return to the Kingdom, after completing their studies abroad, to take their place in the specialist departments.

In the early 1970s less than half the teachers in the Kingdom were Saudi, and four out of every five Saudi teachers were in primary schools. From 1975–80 the number of Saudi teachers increased by over fifty per cent, but at the same time the network of schools is expanding so rapidly that large numbers of expatriates, particularly at intermediate and secondary school levels and in mathematics, the sciences and English (the only foreign language taught in government schools), will be needed for many years to come. Most of the expatriates are Arabs; Egyptians, Jordanians and Palestinians predominate.

In the past the Ministry has relied on the universities – and in particular the colleges of education at Riyadh and Makkah – to provide teachers for intermediate and secondary schools, but graduates intending to devote a career to school teaching were at first too few.

To increase the number of teachers at intermediate and secondary levels, the Ministry went forward with several schemes designed to supplement the output of graduates. One of the most successful of these is the two-year programme at the Science and Mathematics Centre in Riyadh. Other such centres were then planned.

The educational planner in Saudi Arabia faces many challenges, but perhaps none is more daunting than that of finding a way of introducing modern educational materials, techniques and experience without disturbing the country's social and religious heritage.

*Statistical sources:* Ministry of Education and Ministry of Planning.

# Girls' Schooling

*The education of girls was championed by the late King Faisal's wife, and from a relatively late start education is now in reach of most of the population. A number of outstanding schools, like Dar el-Hanan School in Jiddah (pictured below and opposite) lead the way.*

SINCE the establishment of the first girls' school in Saudi Arabia in 1956 female education has become one of its fastest growing areas of social development. By 1980, some two decades since the foundation of the pioneering Dar el-Hanan Institute for orphans there were over 450,000 girls in full-time education, both at primary and secondary levels, many of whom will pursue careers closed to women only a generation previously.

Before 1960 girls' education was generally limited in scope and haphazard in organization, available only in the larger cities such as Jiddah, Makkah, Medina and Riyadh. As it was not socially acceptable for a girl to go out of the house on her own she would receive lessons from a private tutor or in a small group known as a *Kutab*.

Sufficiently wealthy families would employ for their daughters private teachers who lived with the family and in many cases acted not only as tutor and adviser, but also as nurse and companion to the children. Sometimes the tutor would be asked also to instruct the mother of the family in reading and writing.

The *Kutab* was the first method of group teaching for girls. A small number would attend classes given by a woman who had been fortunate enough herself to receive tuition from her father or a private tutor. This early form of education was religious rather than technical, but it was usual for pupils to learn to solve simple mathematical problems as well as read and memorize parts of the Qur'an.

In the late 1950s more organized teaching groups started to appear and private schools spread to other cities. The girls who learned at these schools or privately in their homes took the same exams and received the same certificate as boys, but mixed education has not been adopted in Saudi Arabia.

The history of the Dar el-Hanan Educational Institute for Girls gives an interesting example of the expansion of education in its early stages. Dar el-Hanan was founded in 1956 as a small home and school for orphans by H. M. Queen Iffat al Faisal, widow of the late

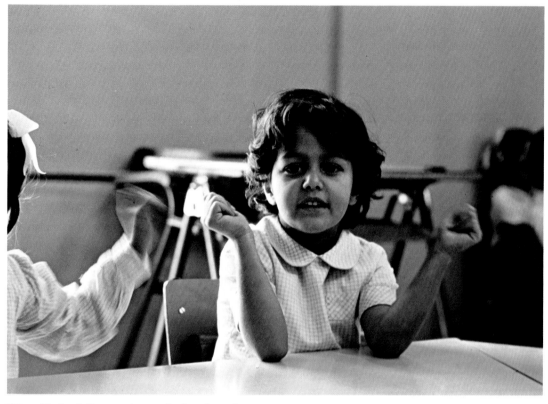

King Faisal. It was intended to be a home for needy girls, giving them an opportunity to learn and to acquire a better standard of living later on. In 1957 the Queen, realizing the pressing need for a girls' school, opened some classes at the upper nursery and primary education level, and thus the small institution started its work.

In 1959–60 the first group of girls studying at the school were able to present their primary school certificates. As the Saudi Government approved girls' education in the same year and opened some of the first state primary schools, the need then arose for intermediate (junior high) schools. In 1960 classes for teaching students at intermediate level were opened. In 1963 the first group of girls graduated from the intermediate school (the equivalent of the 9th grade in the American system). This brought Dar el-Hanan to its most challenging step – adding a secondary school (high school) for a small group of girls who wanted to further their studies. Despite the lack of qualified female teachers and equipment and a shortage of space, secondary stage classes were opened with eighteen girls in the first year (10th grade) and

nine girls in the second year (11th grade). The nine senior girls had already studied in other Arab cities such as Cairo, Beirut, or Damascus, or at home, and were now able to devote their attention to the sciences.

Intermediate education was taken over by the Government for the first year and the school followed the programme of the Ministry of Education with the help of a very small staff, most of whom were not adequately qualified. At the end of the school year 1964–65 the first group of secondary school pupils graduated from Dar el-Hanan, seven in sciences and one in arts subjects. They were the first group of girls to graduate from any regular school in the Kingdom. At that point the need for a better building was urgent and work started on the new school which now exists. By 1966, the year in which the school moved to its new location, the intake of students had risen to 620, rising further to 1,050 in 1973.

In 1969–1970 the General Presidency for Girls' Education opened a Teachers' Training College in Riyadh, relying on graduates from Dar el-Hanan and the Riyadh Secondary School for the re-

cruitment of their students. By that time a fully developed administrative staff had been established and girls were able to follow a well planned educational programme at all levels.

Dar el-Hanan will continue to forge ahead, opening up new lines of study and developing modern teaching techniques. These will be apparent, for example, in the learning of languages, where some schools are already making use of audio-visual 'language laboratory' methods to teach English and French. Those girls who are unable to move on to university but would like to work after completing their secondary education will be able to take one- or two-year courses in accountancy, arts and crafts, administration, child psychology or secretarial studies. Exchange schemes with schools or colleges abroad are under consideration.

Dar el-Hanan, although a typical Saudi Arabian girls' school in many ways, also exists to fill certain specialized functions. It provides a boarding school for girls whose parents do not live in Jiddah and for the daughters of those employed in the Foreign Service, who may already have started their education abroad. The institution has become an educational centre and laboratory for women's education in the Kingdom, with well-equipped laboratories, audio facilities and other modern aids. It already attracts women lecturers from a wide range of academic backgrounds and will always be an innovator in the academic world.

In 1960 the Government invested responsibility for girls' education in a group of religious leaders who formed what is now known as the General Presidency for Girls' Education. This body is effectively a Ministry but remains independent of the Ministry of Education. It is governed by a sheikh with the same powers, privileges and status as a Minister and an equal vote in the Council of Ministers.

Education for women is now available in every village, town and city. There are 800 communities with schools for girls, well over the target of 300 set by the five

year plan ending in 1975. School construction projects have so far provided the government school system with 1,500 elementary schools, 230 intermediate schools and 50 secondary schools, with more planned for the future.

In the elementary sector, nearly half the Saudi girls between the ages of six and twelve had school places in 1976, and elementary school enrolment had increased by nearly one hundred per cent by 1400 AH (1980), with a parallel reduction in overcrowding, and emphasis on school welfare facilities.

Intermediate education was brought to more small communities and rural areas and continued to absorb eighty per cent of elementary school leavers. At this level the average number of students per class fell to twenty-five by the end of the 1400 AH (1980) Five-Year Plan. (*See also* Boys' Schooling).

Half of those who complete the intermediary stage progress to secondary education; here, the average number of

*In the sharp and sunny winter air of the desert, the girls of a school at Hofuf, in the Eastern Province, take a break from their lessons* (left). *The curriculum at the Intermediate level invariably includes the study of the English language* (above).

*Following the precepts of the ancient Greeks, physical education is playing an increasing part* (opposite page). *Modern language-teaching devices* (left and below) *are inevitably bringing an unprecedented cultural diversity within reach of the next generation of Saudi womanhood.*

*The Prophet Muhammad is reported to have said, "To seek knowledge is obligatory on every Muslim, male and female." Basic education today is in reach of girls in every part of the Kingdom, and many go on to secondary schools.*

students per class was reduced to twenty-three by 1400 AH (1980).

One of the difficulties involved in the rapid expansion of education is the recruitment of enough people with sufficient academic qualifications willing to become teachers. In the initial years a considerable number of non-Saudi teaching staff had to be employed; during the next decade these are to be replaced gradually by local staff. Participation in teacher training programmes by students from rural areas is to be encouraged through the provision of housing and special financial incentives, and the course of study in the secondary level teacher training institute programme will be increased from two to three years.

In keeping with the emergence of the Kingdom as a developed nation, and with a changing attitude towards the role of women in society, school *curricula* have expanded to embrace sciences and languages as well as Islamic studies. Although some careers are still not considered suitable for Saudi females, there is a wide variety of occupations

taken up by western women for which technical training can be received. Enrolment in the four technical training centres in Riyadh, Jiddah, Makkah and Hasa doubled between 1975 and 1980 from 550 students to 1,200 and new departments were created to provide skills such as those taught at Dar el-Hanan.

As an alternative to technical training, girls also have the opportunity of continuing their academic studies at a university. At Riyadh University undergraduates may study at home and take their degrees in Arts or Social Science subjects without compulsory regular attendance. There is also a School of Medicine and a teacher training college in the capital. Abdul Aziz University in Jiddah offers arts and science courses and the university of the same name in Makkah has degree courses in Arts, Education or Social Sciences as well as Shari'ah (Islamic law).

Social services required by school education are also being expanded. Medical laboratories and dental and ophthalmic clinics are to be established

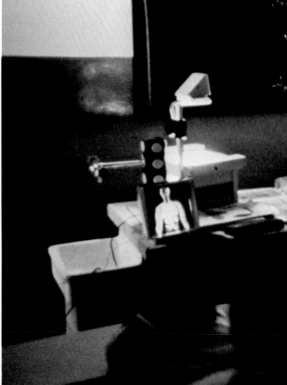

*The present nucleus of school health units with around forty-four doctors and medical specialists is being added to and all remote schools will enjoy visiting medical services.*

in school health units at Dammam, Jiddah and Riyadh.

To attract staff, housing will be provided for them and for students at intermediate and secondary schools and institutes that serve rural areas. The enlargement of bus fleets and replacement of outdated vehicles will also make school transport more efficient.

With a large proportion of older women still unable to read or write, an extensive adult literacy campaign is being conducted. Ninety-nine schools have been built to carry out adult literacy programmes and the present enrolment of some 29,000 women was increased to 383,000 in 1399–1400 AH (1979–1980 CE), producing a total of 89,000 graduates during this period. The current syllabus is to be modified to make the basic subject material more relevant to women's needs and in co-operation with the Ministry of Information programme material to supplement and reinforce classroom work will be transmitted by radio and television. Short-term training courses for literacy teachers and supervisors are to be organized to improve the effectiveness of the current literacy programme.

These different branches of female education together make up a vigorous programme of learning for the young Saudi woman. The Kingdom is by now well on the way to providing universal state education at primary level, and when this has spread to higher levels future generations will enjoy social, academic and professional opportunities which could not have been envisaged only twenty years ago.

*Statistical sources:* Ministry of Education and Ministry of Planning.

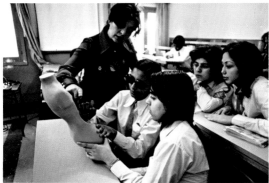

A study of medical science – and hence of anatomy and associated subjects – is considered a natural extension of girls' education for brighter pupils. A number of Saudi girls have gone on to qualify as doctors. While modesty in public remains the accepted conduct for women of all ages, increasing educational and social participation is widening the opportunities for women in careers such as teaching and medicine.

# Higher Education

THE rapid advance of Saudi Arabia is seen at its most startling in the field of education and, in particular, education at the university and post-school technical level.

*The Educational Policy in the Saudi Arabian Kingdom*, published in 1970, laid out on its first page a statement about the nature of educational policy. It gave as the basis of educational policy to meet the "duty of acquainting the individual with his God and religion and adjusting his conduct in accordance with the teaching of religion, the fulfilment of the need of society and in achievement of the nation's objectives."

Higher education is thus not beset by the confusion of intent that is encountered so widely in Western European countries concerning the ends of education, nor, so far, by problems of student politics. Indeed politics at university are not permitted; the authorities' attitude is that, all education being free, the student owes it to the State, in return, not to attack the State.

Thus by Western standards higher education in Saudi Arabia is determinedly paternalistic at all levels. The political and religious authorities keep a careful watch on the Universities and the administrators keep a careful watch on the students. Thus, "Any regular student whose attendance at the lectures, exercises and practical work in each of the prescribed courses is less than seventy-five per cent may be prevented by the faculty board from presenting himself for the examination. In this case the student is considered as having failed in all subjects." (*General Rules for Students* from the University of Riyadh Calendar).

In a country where primary education began only in the late 1930s, and where a serious secondary educational programme was only conceived in 1953, it is natural that Higher Education was at first given a lower priority than general education. But with the programme of general education increasing at an accelerating pace, King Faisal directed that special attention should be given to education at university level.

The ideals set by King Faisal are continuing with his successor King Khalid, in the conviction that the benefits of modern industry and technology can be transferred from the West without importing the disadvantages. By the late 1970s higher education was receiving a higher proportion of the education budget than previously, and at a time when the overall education budget was growing at an unprecedented rate. In 1954–55 the education budget was 15 million riyals: by 1980 it was 15 billion riyals. In the year 1980 the number of College students was 45,000 (men, women and external students), These figures represent an advance that is perhaps without precedent in the world.

The goals for development laid down at the beginning of the Second Five Year Plan once more put "maintaining the religious and moral values of Islam" above "developing human resources". This very close relation between religion and education, while

not posing problems at primary or secondary level, could be expected in the longer run to pose some problems at the level of higher education. Understandably, higher education in the present phase is very largely orientated towards the acquisition of technical and professional skills, rather than to purely academic intellectual development in philosophy, politics or the arts. The pure academic in a non-scientific subject is likely to find himself at the country's main non-secular university—the Islamic University of Medina which was founded in 1961 and had 4,000 students in 1980. Here the teachers speak Arabic only, and the University serves as a centre of Islamic studies for foreign students.

The aim presented in the Five Year Plan was to provide the nation with 25,000 university graduates by 1980. The main secular institutions of higher education are Riyadh University, in the capital itself, Abdul Aziz University, with faculties at Jiddah and Makkah, the Imam Muhammad bin Saud University, also at Riyadh, the University of Petroleum and Minerals, at Dhahran, and King Faisal University at Dammam

*At Riyadh's Abdul Aziz Technical Institute, over 1,000 boys receive a broad grounding in the basic sciences, which can lead directly to jobs in industry or to further education either at Saudi universities or abroad.*

201

and Hofuf. In 1975 the Ministry of Higher Education was established, which is now in charge of all policies concerning scholarships awarded to Saudi students for study abroad, universities, and all other aspects of higher education. Within the universities policy is controlled by University Boards headed by the Minister of Higher Education.

Riyadh University was the first university to be established in the Kingdom

Media and Sociology; and in 1958 a Faculty of Science was opened with Departments of Physics, Mathematics, Chemistry, Botany, Zoology and Geology. The Faculties of Pharmacy and Commerce were opened in 1959, followed by a Faculty of Engineering in 1962, a Faculty of Agriculture in 1965 and the Faculty of Medicine (1969/70). Latterly, Faculties of Dentistry and Nursing have been added, and a Faculty of Education centred at Abha.

to train as teachers.

Riyadh University is particularly advanced in its Faculties of Medicine and of Engineering. In these faculties the system, based on that used in Egypt, of lectures given to large numbers of pupils, is giving way to a system of more individualized instruction. This is partly due to the determination that these faculties should refuse to lower their high entrance standards; consequently classes are smaller. To enter, all students

versity to be established in the Kingdom of Saudi Arabia. It started in 1957–1958 with the Faculty of Arts. In its first year it had twenty-one pupils and nine teachers. By 1964 there were 1,032 students; by 1974 this had increased to almost 6,000 students, and 300 lecturers and professors and by 1980 to over 14,000 students, making it then the largest university in the Kingdom. The Faculty of Arts included Departments of Arabic language, English language, History and Geography and, more recently, of Mass

Courses of study for a first degree last three years in all faculties except those of Pharmacy and Medicine (four) and Engineering (five) and in most of the first year are treated as an intermediate stage between secondary and university education, and are occupied with studies of a general nature.

The University also includes a Faculty of Education (1967) offering a four-year course, and an Advanced Training Centre. This centre provides a one-year course for university graduates wishing

must have achieved a grade of at least seventy-five per cent in their baccalaureat examination, taken when they are eighteen years old (*tawjihiyyah*). By 1985 Riyadh University, which hitherto has had different faculties operating from a number of buildings in different suburbs of Riyadh, with no single focal point, will have been moved out of the suburbs to a desert site on the edge of the city at Diriyah. Work was well advanced in 1980 on the massive project, estimated to cost $1.5 billion. The campus is to accommodate 19,000 students, all in residence, together with housing for all faculty.

Teaching materials were initially imported from abroad, and were often outdated, but latterly a greater allocation of resources is resulting in the most modern techniques being made available and adapted for specifically Saudi use by the Research and Materials Department of the Ministry of Education. Thus, for example, the Faculty of

The number of staff was increased from 1,400 in 1975–76 to 2,300 in 1980, aiming at a staff student ratio of 1:10. Over the same period the total enrolment was increased from 5,600 students in 1974–75 to 14,000 in 1980. The criteria for admission would remain the grades achieved in the secondary school certificate. One quarter of incoming students were to be allocated to the Faculty of Education.

At the same time other faculties at

it would play in building the country, decided to found a university in the Western Province of the Kingdom in the thriving Red Sea port and commercial centre.

The University developed so rapidly that its founders petitioned the government to take it over, and this took place in 1971. At the same time, the Government gave the University administrative jurisdiction over two institutions in Makkah formerly administered by the Ministry of Education: the College of Education, and the College of the Shari'ah (Islamic Law), which were incorporated as faculties of the University. Both faculties concentrate on

*Saudi students of technology – both in Riyadh (as here), and elsewhere – have the advantage of the finest equipment available.*

Medicine at Riyadh has made a long-term agreement with London University under which the latter is providing technical advice and teaching staff. In view of the eventual relocation of the University near Diriyah, development of facilities in Riyadh was restricted to renovation work, with overcrowding both in classrooms and in the administrative quarters of the University. The University has also suffered from shortages of Saudi teachers, and of suitably qualified university administrators.

Riyadh will follow the lead of the Faculty of Education in switching from the system of yearly examinations with all its attendant traumas, to an American-style credit system, allowing continuous evaluation of student progress. The Faculty of Education is planning to establish a Short-Course Centre on specialized topics.

King Abdul Aziz University was started in Jiddah in 1967 when a number of Saudi businessmen, convinced of the need for higher education and the part

the preparation of qualified teachers, the latter specializing in the training of judges. Courses are four years long and one of the admission requirements, as in Riyadh University, is that "students must undertake to teach, after graduation, for a period equivalent to the time spent at the faculty at government expense".

There are three faculties in Jiddah, namely those of Economics and Administration (opened 1968–69), of Arts (opened 1969–70), and of Science (opened 1975),

and Institutes of Marine Sciences, and Applied Geology and Mineralogy have been opened recently.

The University has also built two new campuses within close proximity, one for men and one for women. Women were first admitted in 1969. Today it competes with Riyadh as the largest university in the Kingdom.

The double campus highlights the problems in higher education for women. Paragraph 153 of the 1970 *Educational Policy* document reads:
"The object of educating a woman is to bring her up in a sound Islamic way so that she can fulfil her role in life as a successful housewife, ideal wife and good mother, and to prepare her for other activities that suit her nature such as teaching, nursing and medicine."

Paragraph 155 reads "Co-education is prohibited in all stages of education with the exception of nurseries and kindergarten."

In a country where the veil is still worn and women are not expected to speak to men other than of their own family, the number of women entering higher education is still low. The Saudi Government only approved education for women in 1959–60; but within sixteen years over half the Saudi girls between the ages of six and twelve had school places, and this soon brought increased pressure for places at universities.

At King Abdul Aziz University the rule until the mid-1970s was that: "Female students can use the Central Library on Thursday evenings under the supervision of female tutors." (*Admission Guidebook*, page 26). Recently Aramco have helped to finance a new library specially for women. "Realizing the special position of women," continues the *Guidebook*, "the University began in 1971–72 to use a closed circuit television system to broadcast a number of lectures, and when broadcast live this system enables female students to take part in the question and answer interchange in the lectures."

The problem with this television learning is that it is impossible to apply to practical subjects (such as dissection in the Medical College for Women at Riyadh).

The alternative is for equal but

*With three major comprehensive universities and three specialized universities, Saudi Arabia is now able to provide places for its most able youngsters.*

separate facilities. While expensive, it is the probable development, and the first university where women will have equal facilities may well be King Abdul Aziz University where the new female campus is planned. But women are also allowed affiliation to Riyadh University, and the King Faisal University in Dammam.

Apart from the system of affiliation to male universities, women have their own institutes of further education. In 1970 the Girls' College of Education in Riyadh opened with a four-year undergraduate *curriculum*. By 1975 there were 1,147 students, and their number had been increased by over 300 per cent by 1980; over the same period the number of staff was increased from 115 to 364.

The Riyadh College programme includes seven major fields of study, and it was planned to increase this to ten fields by promoting existing minor divisions in history, mathematics and biology to major subjects.

In 1975–76 a two-year Master's Degree programme was introduced. At the same time a model school was launched to provide students with opportunities for practical application of teaching methods and educational aids.

In 1974, although not anticipated in the first development plan, a second College of Education was opened in Jiddah. It was planned to expand the Jiddah College along the same lines as the Riyadh College, with a structure of ten departments and a staff increased from sixty-four to 289 catering for 2,895 students.

The new development plan aims "to provide female students with a sound education that will prepare them for participation in the social, economic and cultural growth of the Kingdom".

It is also planned that a new College of Arts should be established in Riyadh. This college is to commence enrolment in 1978–79, and by 1980 had forty teachers and twenty-six administrative staff.

The University of Petroleum and Minerals (UPM) is situated at Dhahran in the Eastern Province. It was founded as a College in 1963 with under one hundred students; by 1974 it had increased its intake of students to 1,500, and in 1975 was raised to university status. Its intake then was rapidly increasing.

The University is an autonomous institution, with the Minister of Higher

Education as Chairman of its board. Degrees at the Bachelor and Masters level are offered in Engineering (Civil, Mechanical, Electrical, Chemical, Petroleum, Architectural and Systems) in the Sciences (Mathematical, Geological, Physics and Chemistry) and in Industrial

*In one of Saudi Arabia's oldest colleges of further education, the Abdul Aziz (or Royal) Technical Institute at Riyadh (above), a mature social life among students has evolved – including amateur theatricals. Far left, students on the stage of the Institute's theatre rehearse a skit depicting what occurs when Government inspectors arrive at a remote desert community to persuade an elderly "youth" to attend literacy classes.*

Management. While "in principle Arabic is the language of Education in all its items and stages", here all teaching is in English.

The number of instructors in 1974-75 was 166. Although this exceeded the number foreseen in the first development plan, it was in fact sixty-nine fewer than were needed to cope with the increased student intake, and by 1980 the number of instructors had increased to 350, and students to over 3000.

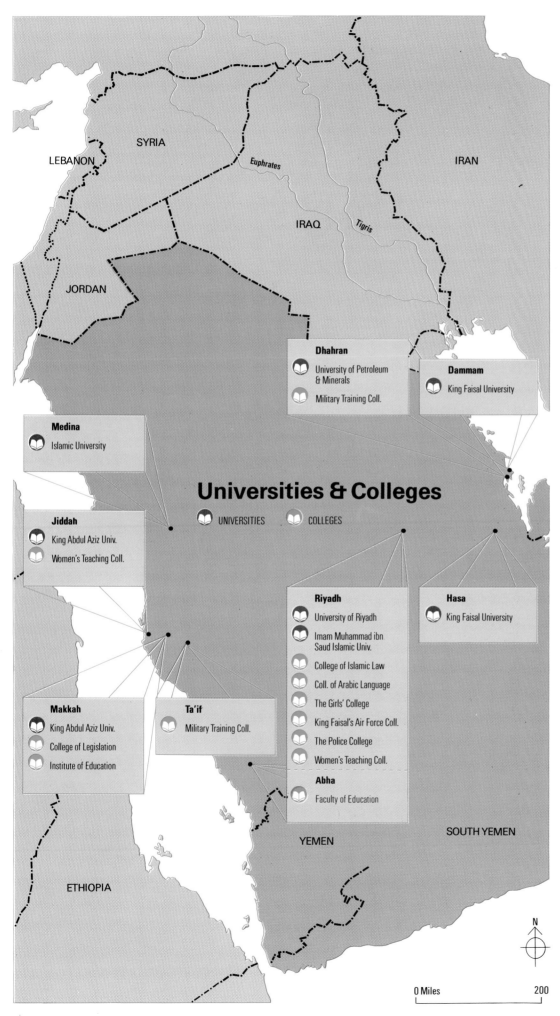

**Universities & Colleges**

📖 UNIVERSITIES  📖 COLLEGES

**Medina**
📖 Islamic University

**Jiddah**
📖 King Abdul Aziz Univ.
📖 Women's Teaching Coll.

**Makkah**
📖 King Abdul Aziz Univ.
📖 College of Legislation
📖 Institute of Education

**Ta'if**
📖 Military Training Coll.

**Dhahran**
📖 University of Petroleum & Minerals
📖 Military Training Coll.

**Dammam**
📖 King Faisal University

**Riyadh**
📖 University of Riyadh
📖 Imam Muhammad ibn Saud Islamic Univ.
📖 College of Islamic Law
📖 Coll. of Arabic Language
📖 The Girls' College
📖 King Faisal's Air Force Coll.
📖 The Police College
📖 Women's Teaching Coll.

**Abha**
📖 Faculty of Education

**Hasa**
📖 King Faisal University

SYRIA

LEBANON

IRAN

Euphrates

IRAQ

Tigris

JORDAN

YEMEN

SOUTH YEMEN

ETHIOPIA

N

0 Miles     200

The continued development of the University into a Technical University of excellent international standard preparing students with the high degree of expertise necessary to fulfil the professional and managerial needs of the petroleum and minerals industry, will be achieved by expansion. A graduate school, a Research Institute and a College of Industrial Management have been added to the UPM programme. It is set fair to becoming a magnet for students from abroad seeking high training in petroleum technology and allied fields.

The King Faisal University opened the Faculties of Medicine, of Architecture and of Agriculture in 1975–76 with campuses both at Dammam and Hofuf (Hasa).

Campus life for students in Saudi Arabia has its own special air of seriousness and commitment to learning. The pace of learning is certainly quickening, yet an atmosphere of conservatism prevails. Increasingly, of course, professors are drawn from Saudi Arabia itself. But the faculties attract staff from a very wide range of countries indeed. Professors and lecturers at the University of Petroleum and Minerals, for example, were drawn from Egypt, Jordan, Iraq, Syria, Canada, Pakistan, Morocco, France, Holland, Great Britain and the United States. While this remarkable eclecticism brings to university life a wide range of influences, and consequent stimulation, one result is that universities themselves are only slowly developing their own distinct characteristics and traditions.

Energy and enthusiasm for education prevail everywhere. And the restlessness and rebelliousness that appear so often elsewhere to be a characteristic of youth have so far been harnessed by the sheer excitement of the acquisition of wider and new skills.

Technical training plays a major part in the structure of further education in the Kingdom. There are, for example, the technical school at Hofuf, and the vocational Higher Technical Institute, known as the Royal Technical Institute, in Riyadh. Schools have been opened kingdom-wide which all who have finished primary or intermediate school may enter for specialized training. In preparation for this manual work is taught for two periods weekly in primary and intermediate schools while several inter-

207

mediate schools provide workshop experience. Instructors from abroad, particularly from France, Germany and Italy, serve on the staff of the major centres of vocational training.

At the Royal Technical Institute (Riyadh) and Hofuf Technical Training School particular emphasis is put on automotive, electro-, machine tool and metal mechanics. The Hofuf school was launched in AH 1386 (1966 CE) with an initial enrolment of seventeen students. By 1980, the student body already numbered over 1000. Other vocational schools were established in Jiddah and Medina. Plans have been set in motion for the establishment of vocational schools in Abha, Ta'if, and Unayzah. At the same time two technical institutes are planned for Jiddah and Dammam with a maximum capacity of 1,220 students.

King Faisal himself, at the time, gave his personal endorsement to this area of endeavour. "This country" he declared, "in this particular stage of its development, is in greater need of adopting the vocational trend, because the implementation and carrying out of projects require manpower, and that manpower should be drawn from the country's own sons."

Outstandingly, the largest educational institute is the Royal Institute of Riyadh whose long frontage of arches and massive pink dome are features of the Riyadh landscape. It was built at a cost of 25 million Riyals and at once became the best equipped technical institute in the Middle East. It provided elementary courses for skilled workers, which could then be followed by advanced courses, either for engineers or for teachers in technical schools. Already by 1970, over 4,000 students were receiving training in one branch or another of technical education. By the end of the decade, Saudi Arabia had already laid the foundations of its own class of skilled artisans and engineers. The country's commitment to a future of high technology and industry was reinforced by the readiness of students to enter the field of technical

education, in all parts of the country.

Those citizens, however, who were already too old to take advantage of the explosion of educational facilities resulting from the country's new wealth, were provided with their own opportunities to fill the gaps in their education by

*All skills connected with industrial metalwork are needed by Saudi Arabia which is committed to a massive programme of industrialization on the principle that economic and industrial self-sufficiency is the best long-term insurance policy.*

## The Eastern Province's University of Petroleum and Minerals

*Perhaps the most successful architectural achievement of recent years anywhere in the Middle East, the University of Petroleum and Minerals in Dhahran (pictured here) has been a focus of world attention since its launching in 1963. Sited on a dominating bluff above Aramco's headquarters, it*

*impresses the approaching visitor as a temple of learning. Its Texan architects provided it with a magnificent theatre/conference hall (top) and mosque; and enriched the natural stone of its water tower (right) with subtly tinted floodlighting. The original College began in 1963.*

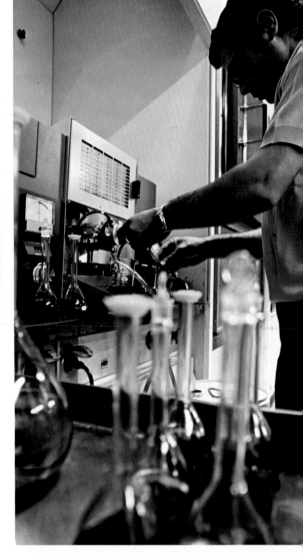

classes and courses for adults. The Ministry of Education developed programmes for vocational training for adults and for literacy among the more remote communities of Saudi Arabia's 900,000 square miles as a result of founding its Department of General Culture. At the same time, the Ministry of Public Health developed courses on health care and hygiene, to be carried out by members of its Health Unit, while the Ministry of the Interior organized literacy courses for serving police, and the

*Skills beyond the strictly academic, and a full social life bring a maturity to the young universities. While half the teachers came from abroad in the mid-1970s, and diversity of nationality is preserved, the number of Saudi lecturers and professors grows steadily.*

Ministry of Defence conducted similar courses for serving soldiers. The Ministry of Information, through its publications, and by television and radio, was in turn bringing many aspects of edu-

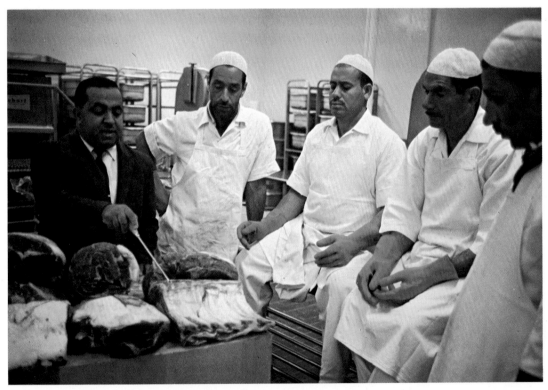

## *Literacy courses reach the remote villages.*

cation and general culture within reach of the adult population both in the cities and the outlying areas. The Ministry of Agriculture played its part by developing instruction in modern agricultural techniques.

Literacy programmes are largely carried out through evening classes, organized on the basis of a two-year course and spread over eight months of the year. They involve up to twelve hours of work per week for the first year and fifteen for the second. During the two years the adult is given an intensive course in reading, writing, arithmetic and religious instruction. Text books have been specially written and published for the benefit of adults taking such courses and are distributed free by the Ministry of Education. There is also a programme of follow-up courses to prevent backsliding into illiteracy which are enthusiastically attended.

The longer literacy courses are supplemented by summer courses given when teachers in ordinary schools are free. Literacy courses lasting three months are organized in villages and isolated areas. These are known as Summer Literacy Campaigns and are concentrated in those areas where normal schooling is still inadequate.

Besides founding the Department of Culture, the Ministry of Education cooperated with the Community Development and Social Services Centre in the campaign against illiteracy. Art teachers and instructors in manual work have been delegated by the Ministry to put into effect programmes based on practical work. Already by 1970 seventeen Community Development Centres were functioning, covering virtually all areas of the country.

# Sport

Relative newcomers to international sports competitions, young Saudis have been quick to learn jiu-jitsu (*above*) and basketball (*below*) now that the facilities are available.

THE traditional sports of the Arabian peninsula belong, as one might expect, to the desert and to the people that inhabit the desert – above all, the sports of hawking or falconry, hunting with saluki hounds, and the racing of camels and fine Arabian horses. These sports are alive, indeed flourishing, in Saudi Arabia today; but such are the exigencies of urbanized life, and the need to protect what game remains in the peninsula, that they can now only be for the few. The traditional game of the falconer – the large *hubara*, the stone curlew, and the hare – have all diminished as a result of widespread use of firearms, but by 1977 King Khalid had banned the use of the gun altogether in the interests of conservation; hawking or coursing are the only forms of hunting now permitted (*see* page 44). As for the traditional prey of hunting salukis, the gazelle and the oryx today must be regarded, alas, almost as animals of the past. Horse racing, on the other hand, is vigorously supported: Riyadh's fine race course is well attended. On occasions, camel races, which frequently occur among the desert communities, with the camels carrying the owner's colours, appear upon the race card.

Group sports, meanwhile, of an international variety, including athletics, are now coming increasingly within reach

*While young soldiers at Khamis Mushayt endure the rigours of army training* (left), *the football bug caught by youngsters in Jiddah* (above) *brings them spontaneous exercise and training on a piece of open ground. Some will perhaps qualify to play in one of the fine stadia in the country* (below and right).

of the general population, stimulated in particular by the Organization for Youth Welfare, which serves as fountainhead for many of the sporting enterprises in modern Saudi Arabia and protectively watches over the several youth and sporting federations. The Kingdom's relative isolation from the international community until recent generations has meant that it is without much experience in international sporting competition. The demanding standards of international sport were experienced by the small athletic team which Saudi Arabia was able to enter for the Olympic Games in Montreal in 1976.

The Organization for Youth Welfare has set about the construction of major new sporting facilities. The International Sports Stadium in Riyadh, to be completed during the next decade, is planned for a capacity of 80,000 spectators. Its cost is estimated at SR 1,280 millions. It will contain running tracks designed to Olympic standard around a football pitch, a restaurant for 2,000 people and accommodation for athletes.

*Horse racing (there is no betting) draws enthusiastic interest in Riyadh – but not at the expense of traditional camel racing, which has recently been brought under racecourse rules for racecourse fixtures; desert rules apply elsewhere.*

## *Glory on the soccer field is a common ambition*

In addition, youth welfare centres are now open in ten of the major cities, with indoor swimming pools and gymnasia in Riyadh, Jiddah and Dammam. Seven youth hostels and ten permanent youth camps were opened by 1978, while fourteen youth club recreation areas and eleven children's playgrounds located in various cities and towns were to be completed by 1980. It is hoped that students of outstanding merit in their chosen athletic fields will be able to enrol in a specialized institute which the Ministry of Education was to establish by 1978.

Tremendous enthusiasm, however, does prevail, and increasingly sporting fixtures in the regional international community are involving Saudi Arabian teams. An American sporting organization is contracted to organize instruction in athletics, swimming, and basketball – all increasingly popular outdoor activities. It is, however, above all the international sport of association football that attracts the enthusiasm of Saudi youth.

The challenge of bringing forward Saudi Arabia in international football was presented to the well-known British coach, Jimmy Hill, in 1976. With a substantial budget, his brief was to establish the playing of football on a national basis, by the setting up of small leagues at all age groups at district level, starting training sessions, organizing administrative staffs, including a national group of some two hundred officials centred upon a National Football Federation, and producing an effective national team.

Saudi Arabia's handicap is not only lack of experience. The climate itself makes training difficult; in the heat of the day, playing football is not possible, and the aridity makes the maintenance of grassed pitches a constant headache. But the new network of stadia and sports centres – some sixty-five communal centres are planned to be added to existing facilities – will be equipped with flood-lighting for training in the cool of the evening after sunset. There is no presumption that success in international sport, least of all in football, can simply be bought. Young Saudi Arabians are learning about the rigours of hard training and the need for discipline, for punctuality and for sustaining training programmes over long periods.

Football, therefore, is seen as the core of the Kingdom's new sporting endeavour. The inspirational focus is bound to be the national team. Success at the top end, it is reckoned, is an essential inspiration to emerging youth. For the first time, Saudi Arabia fielded a team for qualifying ties in the world cup, against its neighbours, Iran, Iraq and Syria, in 1976–77.

*Statistical sources:* Ministry of Labour & Social Affairs and Organization for Youth Welfare.

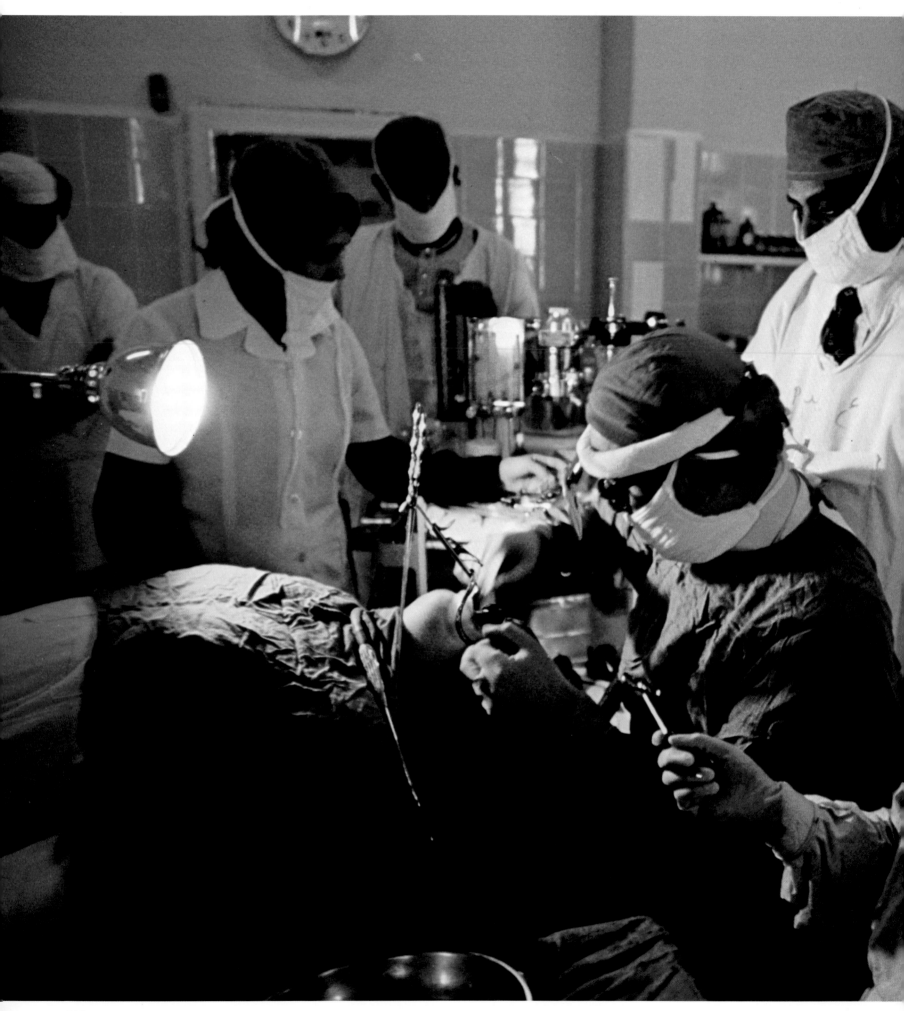

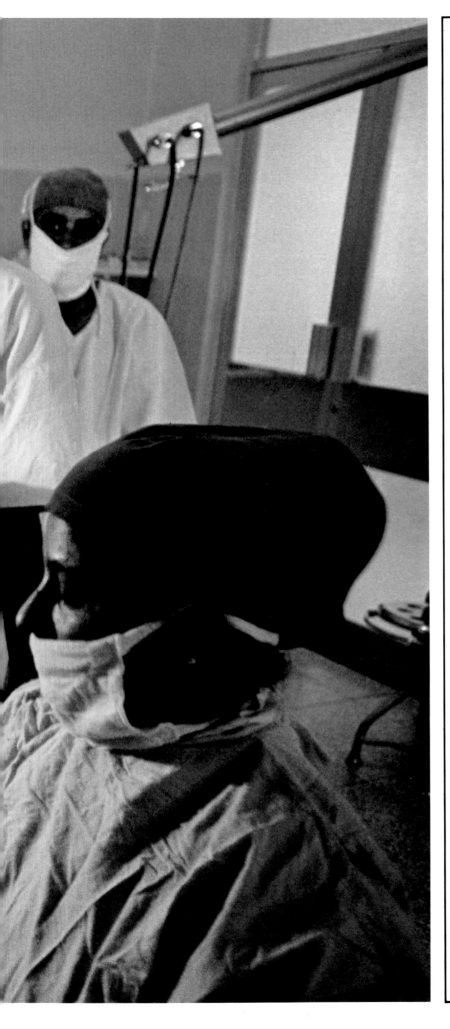

# 10 Social Development

*The Holy Qur'an repeatedly enjoins on man responsibility for his fellows. The Government is the prime dispenser of the nation's wealth. High standards are set in social insurance and welfare for the needy – as high in terms of quality as in thoroughness of coverage.*

*Medicine, and care of the sick generally, has played a major role in Saudi Arabia's internal allocation of its massive resources. Newly equipped with some of the finest medical technology in the world, it is seeking to establish the human infrastructure of doctors, specialists, nurses and patient aftercare services to make the country self-sufficient in medical terms.*

# Health

ONE of the greatest benefits flowing from Saudi Arabia's new wealth is the enormously improved system of health care which has been made possible. King Faisal decided that the State should provide free medical treatment for all its citizens, and for the pilgrims who visit the holy places of Islam.

By 1980, there were eighty-seven well-equipped modern hospitals with almost 14,000 beds belonging to the Ministry of Health and the private sector alone, including a 1,000-bed TB hospital and a 200-bed hospital for the treatment of leprosy. The Ministry of Health's five-hospital scheme was adding 2,275 beds in Jizan, al-Khubar, Hofuf, Jiddah and Medina. The Third Plan was to introduce thirty-six new hospitals and upgrade others to create over 5,000 more beds by 1985 with the same number again being added a few years later. In addition it called for over 300 new primary health care centres to provide both preventative and curative services.

Various other Government agencies and Ministries, notably the Ministry of Defence, the National Guard and the Ministry of Education developed their own health services. Altogether, in 1978, they had provided 1.9 beds per thousand of the population. And in 1980, there were 6.7 doctors per 10,000 of population, significantly ahead of the Second Plan target of five.

The Third Plan, however, called for a ninety-one per cent increase in total medical manpower in its emphasis on improving the quality and efficiency of the Kingdom's health services, especially with preventative measures based on new research into prevailing health conditions. A system of medical record for all citizens was to be introduced.

Doctors, nurses and technicians of many nationalities working in the Kingdom today will be supplemented and eventually succeeded by Saudis. Medical training centres at the Riyadh, King Abdul Aziz and King Faisal Universities were to be expanded. Two new health training institutes were to be opened in Medina and Abha as well as five nursing schools. In 1980 2,700 students were enrolled at the Saudi University colleges of Medicine, Pharmacy, Dentistry, Nursing and Medical Technology.

The health units at women's colleges in Jiddah and Riyadh have been enlarged. Only in 1975, however, did the first batch of thirty female medical students begin their course in Riyadh University's medical school. Since it was considered improper for them to be taught by men, much of their instruction had to be by closed circuit television.

Saudi Arabia's most spectacular achievement, so far, in developing new medical facilities was the opening, in 1975, of a huge hospital and research centre, built on the outskirts of Riyadh. It was a project about which King Faisal was particularly enthusiastic – an essential facet of his intention to place Saudi Arabia among the world's most advanced nations. He was assassinated just a few weeks before the project was completed. It became a memorial to him, and is known as King Faisal Medical City.

The 250 beds available when the hospital was opened were to be increased to 500. Its main function was to provide specialist services, to which cases could

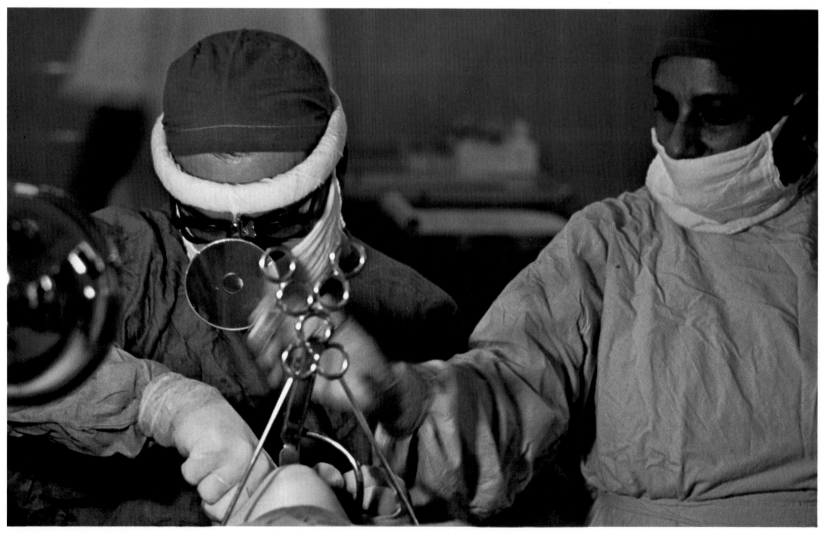

be referred from anywhere in the Kingdom. Patients who, until then, would have had to go abroad, would thenceforward be treated at the King Faisal hospital.

The complex includes villas and flats for many of the 1,200 staff who run this

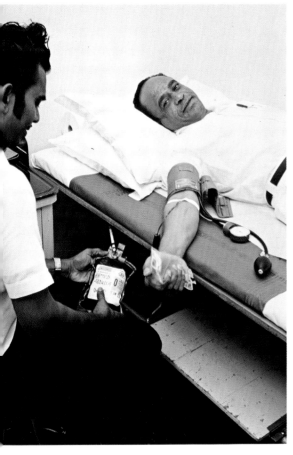

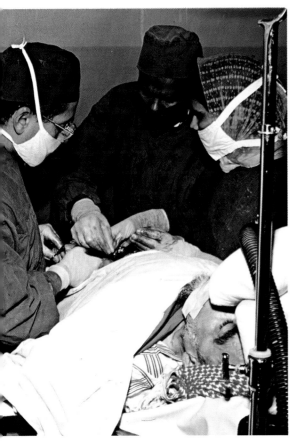

*While major operations take place in the hospitals of the large cities* (left), *preventive medicine and treatment for common ailments takes place at dispensaries, clinics and treatment centres scattered through the country.*

## Health Facilities & Personnel

| | MINISTRY OF HEALTH 1980 | PER CENT INCREASE FROM 1974 |
|---|---|---|
| HOSPITALS | 70 | 13 |
| HOSPITAL BEDS | 12,525 | 62 |
| DISPENSARIES | 506 | 135 |
| HEALTH CENTRES | 299 | |
| DOCTORS | 3,312 | 69 |
| HEALTH INSPECTORS & TECHNICIANS | 4,740 | 34 |
| NURSES | 6,081 | 44 |

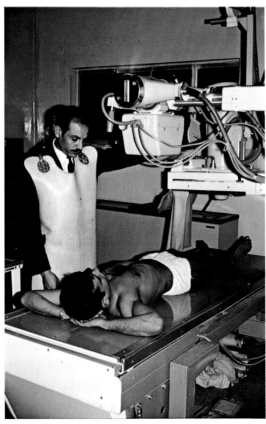

miniature city. Heating and lighting is generated by its own power station.

There are fourteen separate computer systems. The patient arrives in a reception area, rather like the reservation desk of an airline. His personal details are fed into the communications and computer network. Out-patients then go to a softly furnished consulting room where they are "interviewed" by

a machine, giving "yes" or "no" answers to questions about their medical record. This is not a substitute for diagnosis by a doctor, but a preliminary process to save time and ensure that nothing is overlooked.

Laboratory tests are made by an automatic analyser, which – again – saves time, and eliminates a great deal of human error. The patients are all accommodated in luxurious private rooms. Communication sets beside each bed are linked to a central console, from which the operator can speak directly to the patient or relay messages to the nurses and other staff. Drugs, diets and scheduled treatments, stock control, radiotherapy, the monitoring of patients under intensive care – all are regulated by different sections of the computer network. It has been calculated that the medical capacity available in the King Faisal hospital is equivalent to at least seven conventionally equipped hospitals and clinics.

An elaborate ambulance service was established for patients in need of intensive care, including air ambulances which land at the hospital's own heliport. Portable cardiac machines in the ambulances and aircraft can relay signals to the main hospital, so that a severely ill patient has, in effect, been admitted and is being treated before he even arrives.

The Saudi Red Crescent Society, which functions much like the Red Cross in Europe, is an important part of the country's system of medical care. It provides first-aid and emergency services, particularly on the roads and during the period of the *hajj*. From a General Centre in Riyadh, the Society operates three branch offices, eight health centres, twenty-seven first-aid centres which are open twenty-four hours a day, and 120 ambulances. Ambulances in the *hajj* areas are equipped with radios, and a First-Aid Training Institute has been established.

The annual *hajj* confronts the Kingdom with unique health challenges. Pilgrims from Africa, say, or Asia could so easily enter bringing with them communicable diseases like cholera. Special medical teams are briefed for such emergencies. Moreover, the main port of entry, Jiddah, is provided with a quarantine centre containing two isolation hospitals in an enormous site comprising a self-contained village of over 150 buildings.

## Riyadh's King Faisal Hospital

At a cost of over $300m the King Faisal hospital and medical centre in Riyadh constitutes the best equipped medical centre that money can buy. It includes, for example, the hyperbaric unit illustrated (*below right*). With technically trained people at a premium, the cutting down of routine paperwork, avoiding delays in finding patients' records, speeding the process of laboratory tests and reducing nursing chores have been paramount factors. An elaborate computer and communications system – one of fourteen such systems (*below centre*) – aims at fulfilling this function.

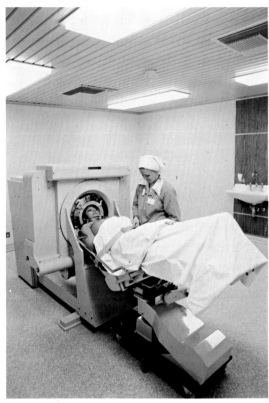

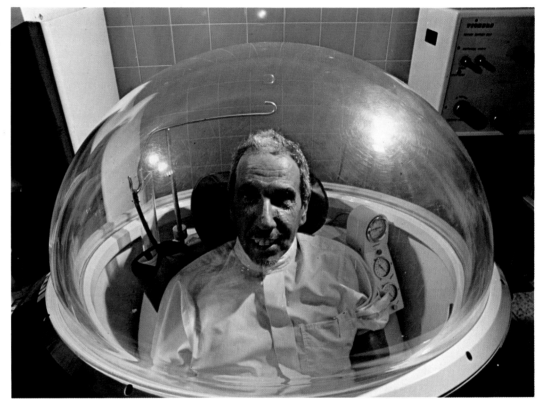

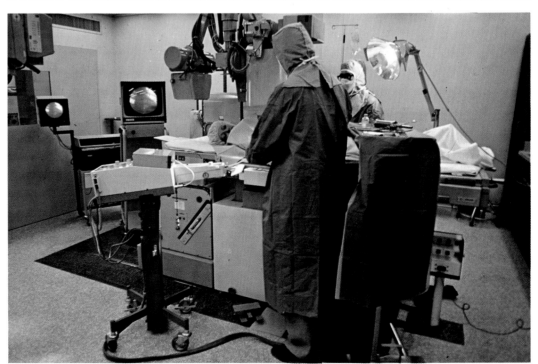

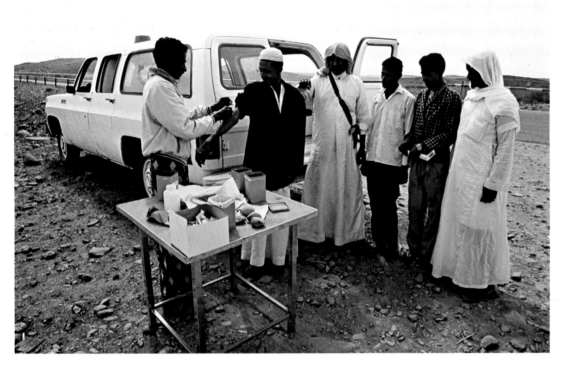

# Preventive Medicine

## *Clinics cut infant mortality.*

SAUDI ARABIA is, climatically, a healthy country. The arid atmosphere, the traditional hardihood of a desert people, sensible dietary customs and the rules of hygiene strictly observed by all good Muslims, combine to prevent the spread of sickness.

There is, for example, one of the lowest rates of heart disease *per capita* in the world. This is particularly true among those living the Beduin life.

Communal health hazards do exist, however, expecially in certain areas. In the south-western coastal regions bilharzia occurs; so does malaria – indeed, malaria is quite widespread, even where there is relatively little standing water. The trachoma virus, which attacks the eyes, is a common scourge, as in hot dry climates. And epidemics – of cholera, diphtheria and smallpox – are still a constant threat.

There is no settled community in Saudi Arabia beyond the reach of the network of medical care now provided. The urban areas are served by major general and specialist hospitals: elsewhere there are district dispensaries and health centres, and even the smallest and most remote desert community has access to mobile clinics and dispensaries, the "flying

doctor" and other emergency services.

At the same time, there is a continuous programme of vaccination, nutritional instruction, pre- and post-natal care for mothers, x-rays and dental care. Sources of carrier-bred disease, such as malaria and bilharzia, are systematically treated. Among the obstacles to be overcome is the over-readiness of unsophisticated people to accept disease as an inescapable fact of life.

One effect of the improvement in medical care has been a sharp upturn in life-expectancy. Infant mortality, which in some desert communities has been as high as twenty per cent, has fallen sharply. The linking up of road systems, especially in the northern and north-west parts of the country, should accelerate the process; so one of Saudi Arabia's chief obstacles to development – the lack of indigenous population – is being diminished in the most desirable way.

Meanwhile, Aramco and Harvard University have, for a long while, been engaged in joint trachoma research. In an effort to develop an effective vaccine, studies have been made of the natural immunity which occurs in some young people as they become adults. Other research units are planned, and there

will also be a network of mother and child care clinics; the immediate hope is to reduce the infant mortality rate to no more than one in a hundred births.

Health education is itself a form of preventive medicine, and widespread efforts are being made to increase the public's awareness of health problems, their causes and how best to deal with them.

# Mental Health

## *The Qur'an enjoins kindness.*

*Blood tests, quarantine and vaccination programmes all reach remote parts of the country.* Below, *the mentally sick – a relative rarity in Saudi Arabia – are cared for in a specially built hospital.*

THE mentally defective or retarded constitute a special category of handicapped people, and one for which Islam has traditionally been particularly solicitous.

By and large the Kingdom has escaped the widespread mental health problems that afflict Western countries. This is ascribed to the strength of family ties and the security that the extended family provides: it is rare indeed for an Arabian infant or child to be deprived of the continuity of love and care within the family. The other factor that brings to society balm and balance is the depth and ubiquity of religious conviction. But there are, inevitably, a number of citizens suffering from mental defectiveness or brain damage.

An institute for retarded children was opened in 1968, offering full boarding facilities for fifty boys and fifty girls; and there are other institutes to care for the mentally retarded of all ages. Attached to each institute are social workers, whose responsibility it is to make a special case-study of every pupil. They visit homes and parents, and try to establish a relationship of trust.

Everything is done, as far as possible, on an individual basis. At the institute for retarded children, the maximum number of students in any house or class is five. A clinic is available for psychotherapy. Monthly meetings are held, to which both parents and pupils come. The discussion may be led by a visiting psychologist or social worker.

# The Handicapped

*Respect for Qur'anic principles lies behind Saudi Arabia's particular concern for the handicapped, the blind and the crippled. Many institutions and schools give work and education to the blind, seen working a loom (left and top), and (above) reading Braille in Arabic. Opposite, right, a marvellous example of embroidery by blind patients in Jiddah shows a Saudi family tree.*

THE Saudi Arabian Government, in accordance with the principles of Islam, makes special provision for the care of handicapped people.

In 1958, the Ministry of Education was asked by Abdullah Al-Ghanem, who afterwards became Director of Special Education, to establish an evening institute for the blind. Within a year the institute had come into being. Based in an existing school in the suburbs of Riyadh, it provided classes for a hundred students. During the daytime they attended religious institutes; in the evening they came to this new Institute for the Blind, where they learned Braille and received vocational training.

When it was reorganized as a day school in 1960, the Ministry of Education accepted full responsibility for the academic and technical education of the students, whose number had now grown to 110.

Two years later, institutes for the blind were also established in Makkah and Unayzah. Their teaching staff had been trained, and had acquired experience, at the Riyadh Institute. In the same year, 1962, the Ministry created its own Department of Special Education.

During the next few years several similar, or related, establishments were founded – institutes for the blind at Hofuf, Medina and Qatif; two institutes for the deaf and mute at Riyadh (one for men, the other for women); and an institute at Riyadh to train women teachers of the handicapped.

The Department of Special Education provides everything necessary – buildings, audio-equipment, books in Braille and so on. The students are entitled to free transport from their homes to the institute; and they receive a small monthly grant throughout their training.

There are now several centres where teachers can learn how to care for, and work with, handicapped students; and the Department offers fellowships for advanced training abroad.

More institutes for the handicapped are being either built or planned and, in the light of experience, general policies have been evolved.

In the institutes for the blind, two courses – one academic, the other vocational – are normally provided. Pupils are admitted to the academic courses from the age of six to the age of eighteen, when they can sit the examination for a Secondary Education Certificate. Teaching methods are not dissimilar from those of ordinary schools, except for the use of Braille.

For pupils between the ages of six and twenty, vocational training courses are available in such subjects as basketwork, weaving and the manufacture of household equipment. These courses usually extend over six years, and culminate in the examination for a certificate in technology. Some general education is included as well, and all pupils are trained to read and write Braille. Amply equipped workshops are available. The items which the pupils make – chairs, beds, baskets, cane tables, brushes, cloth, carpets – are usually of good quality,

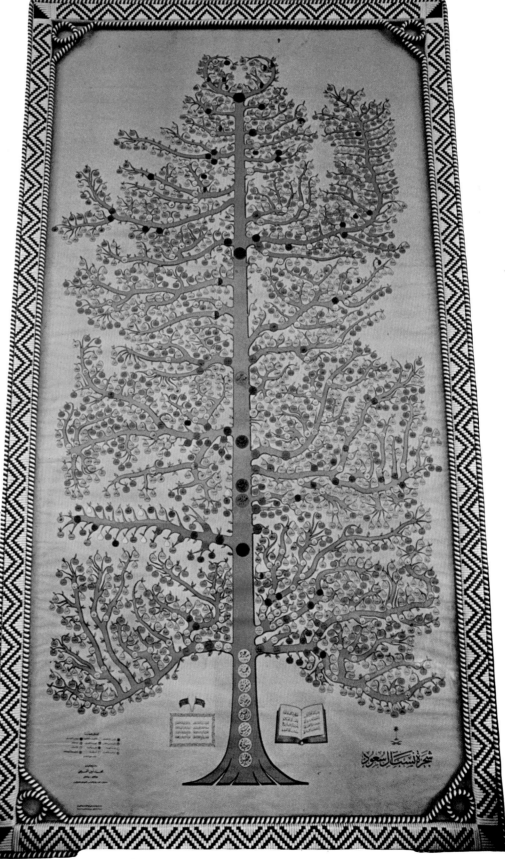

228

and sell quite readily on the open market.

The institutes for the deaf and dumb have to cope with even more difficult problems. A preparatory course is provided for young children aged four to six. Their exact degree of deafness has to be ascertained, and their ability tested. Deaf and dumb pupils are fed and clothed, as well as receiving their monthly grant and enjoying the medical and welfare services available to all handicapped people. They are taught in classes containing not more than ten, or fewer than five, pupils. For general supervision they are divided into houses of ten.

Every institute has social workers and a full-time nurse on the staff. The hope is that all students will acquire a trade, with the encouragement of the Labour Law's stipulations that companies employing more than fifty should give two per cent of their jobs to disabled workers. For the broader development of their personalities, and to give them satisfying lives, they are encouraged to take part in a full range of *extra-curricula* activities. It is wonderful to see them flower.

*Deaf and mute children are taught by skilled instructors with the assistance of electrical devices that produce perceptible vibrations* (left).
*Below: playgrounds and special facilities in institutions are helping to enrich the lives of children crippled at birth or by accident.*

# Social Insurance

NO major developing country has exceeded Saudi Arabia in its concern for its workers and their families.

Social Insurance is a system originally based on Islamic principles through which the State ensures the worker's safety and provides for a secure future in which he and his family can lead a decent stable life. The General Organization for Social Insurance (GOSI) began enforcement of the Social Insurance Law in 1393 AH (1973 CE). This Law lays down several types of protection for workers regardless of nationality or sex – disability, old age and death benefits (Annuities Branch), occupational injuries and occupational diseases (Occupational Hazards Branch), temporary disability due to sickness or maternity, and family grants in cases where the insured has several dependants. Unemployment compensations are made available and there is good protection for the self-employed.

The main parts to be applied so far have been the Annuities and Occupational Hazards provisions. By the end of 1399 AH (1978 CE) the bulk of the labour force, employed in more than 800 private and public organizations, were covered under the Annuities programme.

The Annuities Branch includes: old-age annuity, non-occupational disability, payment of lump sums to insured persons who do not qualify for pensions, funeral expenses grant, heirs' annuity, marriage grant to widows, daughters and sisters, and voluntary insurance for old age.

When the insured worker retires at the age of sixty or more, the General Organization for Social Insurance pays him a monthly annuity for the rest of his life. The amount of the annuity depends on the contributory period and the average of his wage during the last twenty-four months of insurance. It is calculated on the basis of two per cent of his average monthly wages during the previous twenty-four months, multiplied by the number of years of his contribution in insurance. Added to the annuity is a dependants' allowance – ten per cent of the annuity for the first dependant, five per cent for the second dependant, and five per cent for the third dependant.

Annuities are paid monthly for the rest of his life, and the annuitant's heirs, after his death, are also entitled to monthly payments.

If the insured sustains a non-occupational disability and is crippled before he reaches retirement age, he is entitled to receive from GOSI a disability annuity payable to him monthly for the duration of his life. The amount of this annuity is computed in the same way as the old age annuity, at two per cent of the average monthly wage for the twenty-four months preceding the occurrence of the disability, multiplied by the number of years of his participation in insurance or forty per cent of such an average, whichever is the higher figure. A total disability allowance of fifty per cent of such annuity is added if the disabled person needs the assistance of others in the performance of his everyday activities. Both the annuity and the allowance is paid to the annuitant as long as he is incapacitated. If he is still disabled at the age of sixty, the annuity is then payable for life. After his death, the dependent members of his family are entitled to heirs' annuities.

The insured who has reached the age of sixty and who for at least six months has been without a job subject to insurance, and likewise the insured who is afflicted with a non-occupational disability before he reaches sixty, receives from GOSI a lump sum equivalent to his total contributions (five per cent of his wages) paid throughout the insurance period, plus a grant of five per cent of the total of such contributions, provided that he has completed a mimimum of twelve insur-

ance months and does not qualify for an old age disability annuity. If he dies, GOSI pays the lump sum to the widow or to the children, to the father and mother or, in the absence of any other person, to the brothers and sisters.

A grant of SR 400 is paid to the person who undertakes to pay the funeral expenses of an insured worker who dies in service after completing at least six insurance months during the last year before his death. A similar grant is available on the death of an aged or crippled annuitant. Upon the death of an insured person who received a non-occupational disability annuity, his dependants are entitled to the same annuity which used to be paid to their supporter (minus the dependants' allowance or total disability allowance). The heirs are entitled to the annuity if the deceased was not an annuitant, on the basis of the disability annuity to which he would have been entitled had he sustained the disability on the date of his death. If a son or daughter has lost both parents, the annuity is doubled.

The widow is given one half of the husband's annuity, and each of his other dependants receives twenty per cent of such annuity, provided that the total monthly amount payable does not exceed the original annuity; if the annuities exceed one hundred per cent of the deceased worker's entitlement, all the annuities are reduced in proportion. The widow is entitled to the annuity provided that the marriage took place at least six months before the death of the insured if he was in service, or at least twelve months before his death if he was an old

*Typical of Saudi care for the unfortunate is this orphanage built in the Qasim area.*

age pensioner or crippled annuitant. She continues to receive it until she remarries, in which case she is given a marriage grant. Male orphans under twenty years of age are also eligible for the annuity. The age limit is extended until they are twenty-five, if they are pursuing their studies in an educational or vocational institute. If they are unable to work by reason of a chronic disease or an infirmity, the annuity is paid to them as long as they are thus afflicted. Female orphans are supported until they marry, provided that they were supported by the deceased at the time of his death. Brothers and sisters of the deceased are provided for, subject to the same conditions applicable to orphans. Parents of the deceased who were supported by him at the time of his death, provided that the father is over sixty years of age and unable to work, are also entitled to the annuity. If an old age or disability annuitant's widow, daughter or sister marries, she is given a marriage grant equal to eighteen times the annuity she used to receive, and payment of the annuity ceases at the end of the month during which the marriage takes place. The allocation of this grant terminates any right derived from the insurance.

A worker who has been subject to the annuity insurance branch for at least five years and no longer qualifies, for any reason, to be subject to this branch, may continue his affiliation provided he submits an application to the General Organization for Social Insurance within six months after the date on which he ceased to be subject to insurance, and

undertakes to pay the contributions required both of him and of the employer (five per cent of his wages paid by the insured and eight per cent by the employer).

The Hazards Branch provides for insurance against employment injuries and occupational diseases. The accumulation of benefits in kind and cash is not conditional upon any qualifying period of insurance. The rate of contribution is fixed at two per cent of the wages of the insured and the employer alone is responsible for its payment.

The Social Insurance scheme operates on a contributory basis, that is, GOSI revenues comprise contributions from both employees and employers, as well as investment revenues and government subsidy. GOSI's annual revenues in the late 1970s were estimated at well over SR 200 million.

GOSI is administered by a Board of Directors. The Directorate General in Riyadh supervises regional offices in Riyadh, Jiddah and Dammam, and a branch office in Abha. As with other government organizations, there is great difficulty in recruiting suitably qualified staff; only about sixty per cent of the positions were filled by the mid 1970s.

GOSI has therefore concentrated on improving its efficiency. Steps taken include better availability and utilization of statistics, improved training for administrative and other personnel, planning for improved computer utilization, analysis of work methods, improved co-ordination with other government agencies and assessment of new building requirements.

The primary objective is to provide a comprehensive range of insurance programmes for workers and their dependants, in accordance with the provisions of the Social Insurance Law. As the first priority, coverage of the Annuities programme will be completed for all workers in establishments employing five persons or more. Secondly, the Occupational Hazards programme will be extended to include all workers covered by the Annuities programme.

Insurance programmes will be developed to apply the remaining major provisions of the Social Insurance Law; temporary disability due to sickness or maternity, family grants for dependants of the insured, unemployment compensation and social insurance for the self-employed. The second major aim is to maintain GOSI on a financially self-sustaining basis without increasing the level of contributory payments. A high level of internal operating efficiency and a sound investment policy for GOSI's reserves will be adopted. Operations will be co-ordinated with those of other government agencies to avoid duplication of payments, data storage, and claims verification.

The Social Insurance Law is being expanded. By 1405 AH (1985 CE) the pension scheme is expected to have covered one and a quarter million employees, and the Occupational Hazards scheme, some 400,000. For the pension scheme was to expand to cover all establishments employing over five staff and the Hazards scheme those employing over five hundred. A Comprehensive report on GOSI's finances was to be made annually, and a new investment plan for its finances would serve a new professional pension fund management department.

New branch and regional offices are being opened throughout the Kingdom. The productivity of employees should be increased by a series of measures relating to training with promotional incentives. For example, ten scholarships are to be awarded each year to senior Saudi personnel for training overseas; five of these scholarships will be for academic courses and five for practical training.

*Statistical sources:* Ministry of Labour & Social Affairs and Ministry of Planning.

# Social Life

ALL over Saudi Arabia today traditional patterns of life are being affected both in their outward form and more intimately by swiftly rising levels of education, the dramatic impact of increased income, and the consequences of industrialization. Television, sound broadcasting, and the surge towards literacy are swiftly expanding the knowledge both of those living in cities and towns and of the peasantry and villagers. The new metalled roads and the internal airline system and railroad, linking rural areas with towns and cities, and the major centres with the outside world, have brought about an unprecedented flow of new ideas.

Simultaneously, the cities are attracting from the outlying areas, at an accelerating pace, people whose way of life in the desert has scarcely changed for centuries. They are brought into the towns and cities by the promise of work and are at once confronted by the complexities of modern urban life and the racket of a culture where technocracy rules. An industrial revolution which, in Europe, gathered pace over generations, is in Saudi Arabia being compressed into a matter of years. There is an advantage – to which those guiding the country have laid claim – that lessons can be learned from the experiences, both achievements and mistakes, of the already developed nations.

The strains and pressures within Saudi Arabian society today are recognized as inevitable. Yet the intent to preserve what is right and true in traditional values, while accepting the enlightenment of education and the challenge of so-called progress, wins the admiration of all who look at Saudi Arabia today closely.

The central point is that Saudi Arabians put first their role as guardians of the holy shrines of Islam and as the inheritors of the homeland of the Prophet. This role in their peninsula is their *raison d'être* as a people. They have standards to maintain on behalf of Islam. They grow up in the knowledge of this unique heritage. Whatever the temptations, they refuse to dispense with it.

The outsider is at once struck by the restraints which Saudi Arabians at all levels willingly accept. A devoutness, even an asceticism, prevails at all levels of society, even when luxury or great wealth is easily within reach. Young men and women who may have completed their education in the West will return to Saudi Arabian society and, with apparent effortlessness, shed those aspects of indulgence and licence which the West takes for granted. The Qur'anic prohibition against alcohol is taken seriously. Modesty is indeed expected of womenfolk, and the segregation of the sexes in open society – while it is being modified in certain aspects – is widely accepted.

One of the central strengths of the Kingdom is that this subtle balance between traditional values and the modern world is struck by the Royal Family. By its vast network of relationships, it permeates almost all areas of authority in the Kingdom. Yet it has a subtly and determinately liberal attitude which is evident in general attitudes towards women. Up to the early 1960s there was no formal education for girls.

*The central factor is the strength of the family. In a period of swift outward change, widely spread family links produce a complex of allegiances which ensure continuity and high standards of conduct.*

*Commerce (below, and opposite) brings social intercourse. But the home is where friends meet, and homes – though sometimes given eye-appeal from without (left) – are small fortresses of privacy.*

By the early 1970s, over 270,000 girls (probably one third of the girls in the country) were attending school, and the number and proportion were swiftly growing. The impulse for this remarkable development came directly from the top. By and large, this profound change has been achieved without ruction.

Similarly, for example, in the field of broadcasting and television the late King Faisal was alive to the educative potential of the medium. Some of his counsellors were not so persuaded. The King presented a closed circuit demonstration of readings from the Qur'an. The doubters soon became impressed. Today television plays a notable role in the religious life of the nation, indeed a role which reaches beyond that into general education and information, right into the home, where the women and children are to be found.

Traditionally in Saudi Arabia, the women's role centred exclusively on the home. Social contact with men outside the home was forbidden. While in the intimacy of the home a wife would play as full a part as her energy and intelligence and strength of character allowed her, the basic definition of a wife's role could be defined as that of serving her husband by obeying him, and serving her children by caring for them. If such a role has meant restrictions on the lives of women, it has nonetheless brought remarkable strength to the family unit in the country.

For womenfolk would meet womenfolk within the family, and family links have always been broad and often far-flung. Today the restrictions on the life and activity of women is often more apparent than real. The outsider can easily be deceived. In the streets women go veiled; in their homes, as in the schools and universities, they are unveiled. Indeed, they are unveiled when they enter the shops now selling expensive women's fashion in the major cities. The visitor from outside the country will not normally find himself in the company of women when taking a meal at the home of a Saudi friend. But this would not be so if he were a member of the extended family.

There is no woman in Saudi Arabia – of any nationality – to be seen behind the wheel of a car. On the other hand, Saudi women are taking university degrees in their own universities. The problem of listening to lectures given by male professors is overcome by the use of a closed circuit television. At the same time, more and more Saudi women are travelling abroad with their husbands, many of them executives in the modern structure of Saudi government or in Saudi-based international firms. Saudi women now carry their own passports, their unveiled faces appearing in their passport photographs.

It has been speculated that women may soon play their part in industry and government, and they are readily accepted as doctors, teachers, nurses and social workers. For several years they have been employed as radio and television announcers and commentators.

Furthermore cautious moves towards the participation of women – many of them quietly instigated following the accession of the late King Faisal, who was known to respect relatively progressive views of his wife Iffat, have included education, developing work opportunities and the opening of special bank branches for women under their Koranic right to engage in business as many do. There are a few Saudi women who would not vigorously defend the virtues of the paramountcy of the woman's classic role of wife and mother, and there are few who wish to rush headlong into the much vaunted but often unhappy emancipation of womanhood in the West. But a wider role in the Kingdom's economic life is slowly emerging for them. The law already states their right to work, and a senior ministerial council was in the early 1980s investigating the

way to introduce them more widely into the workforce. For women represented a major pool of precious Saudi labour which could help displace the growing numbers of foreign workers who, it was thought, threatened the delicate balance of traditional Saudi life.

However, despite these singular moves towards the participation of women, the system of marriages being arranged between families is universally honoured as its success has long been proved. Westerners often forget that it is a system that prevailed successfully in the West itself until a few centuries ago.

Traditionally, it is the girl's parents who negotiate her marriage and the dowry which the future husband is expected to provide. Such is the basic system prevailing today. But an element of choice by the young people themselves is creeping in, especially among those girls who are beginning to become wage earners and therefore have more influence in their families. But this is not to imply that marriages take place against parental wishes. And if marriages in Saudi Arabia are seen by both families clearly not to work, the way in which married partners are separated is far less fraught than in, say, Western societies. Because divorce may not be a complicated process, it does not mean that it is excessively frequent. Qur'anic law provides quite clearly for marriages which do not work. Divorces take place privately, without fuss.

Privacy is a virtue of Saudi Arabian life. As elsewhere in the Islamic world, homes are built around an open centre. They do not look outwards. They are self-contained. Their freedoms are internal freedoms. Indeed, the liberality and ease of relationships within a family are well known.

Beyond the towns and cities, among the Beduin – perhaps ten per cent of the population – it is the tribal allegiances that still strongly prevail. The influence of the ancient, disciplined and dignified way of life markedly pervades all levels of Saudi Arabian society. And although the force of tribal loyalties is certainly diminished in town life, the loyalties are not forgotten. Among those from the families who hold the leadership of tribes and who have come to live in cities and to make their fortunes there, there is a widespread tendency to maintain the tribal links. The Beduin "wing" of the family or tribe is visited at festival times throughout the year. Conversely,

## Beduin Life

In the desert, the social life of the Beduin – literally 'the desert people' – retains much of its time-honoured forms and styles. Life is centred on the family tent. The traditional black tent is woven by the women of goat hair (the most waterproof), sometimes mixed with sheep's wool and camel hair, in strips which are sewn together. Gaily coloured woven internal 'walls' divide the men's section from the general living quarters where the women do the cooking and the small children's leather cradles are slung between tent poles. Many of the desert artefacts are of camel leather or goat hide – belts and waterskins, bags (often decorated with beads and shells) and saddles and cradles and, in the past, shields.

In the self-sufficient desert life, crafts retain their importance. Each tribe will have its weavers, leatherworkers, coppersmiths and silversmiths and, until recently, gunsmiths. A bride's dowry is

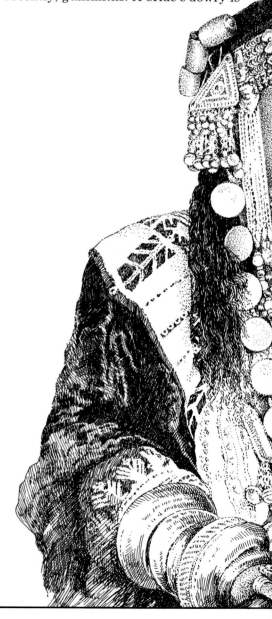

Pictures courtesy of Heather Colyer Ross,
*Bedouin Jewellery in Saudi Arabia.*

camels and the herds of goats and sheep are the prime responsibility of the men. Of late, pick-up vehicles have supplemented, but not supplanted, the camel as a means of transport in parts of the desert, just as bore-holes and pumps have supplemented wells. But the camel is irreplaceable in true desert travel, which the Beduin's search for grazing requires. An Arabian camel can survive in winter, when there is moisture in the pasturage, for several days without being watered, although in high summer only for two or three days. (A really thirsty camel – its suffering expressed by low groans and by tears rolling down its cheeks – may drink up to twenty-five gallons at a time.) She-camels are the most useful. They produce milk for up to six months after giving birth, and they possess greater stamina than the male. It is the mare camel that is used for riding by mankind: the male camel carries the baggage. It is the men who do the milking. White camels are widely admired in Arabia, although in the past the darker-hued well-camouflaged camel was sometimes preferred in the chivalrous activity of raiding, in which the tribes were often engaged.

By night, camels are often hobbled to keep them close to the tent, though the family herds (of an average number of forty or fifty beasts) always preserve the homing instinct. The branding mark, or *wasm*, distinguishes tribal or clan ownership.

Desert hospitality is invariably generous and leisurely, and attendance upon the guests involves distinct obligations. The visitor is welcomed by a rug spread on the ground. He will first be offered tea, and in due course the ceremony of coffee will begin. A few coffee beans are roasted on an iron skillet, then placed in a decorated pot to cool. Three times the coffee is brought to the boil, then poured into the character-istic sharp-snouted coffee pot containing ground cardamom seeds, from which it is served in tiny handle-less cups. Then, if the visitor is to stay, and is of significance, a young goat or sheep will be slaughtered, and at length served up on a great heap of steaming rice.

The meretricious attractions of the city can, of course, seduce the younger people of the desert. And with the spread of education and of the cultivation of the soil, there are strong inducements to adopt the settled life. Yet those that live the Beduin life in today's Arabia are convinced of the rightness, indeed of the superiority, of their way of life, because it is hard, uncluttered, unhurried, and brings a closeness to God.

largely comprised of her silver jewellery, and at her wedding she may be heavily caparisoned with headpieces and collars, necklaces, bracelets and bangles, and amulets and belts. The silverware, often studded with amber, coral, pearls, lapis lazuli, garnets, agate, carnelian or turquoise, is wrought anew for each bride, and as a rule is melted down at her death. Yet the designs (so widely admired today throughout the world) have remained extraordinarily constant for hundreds, indeed thousands, of years, as pre-Islamic grave relics demonstrate. The jewellery is both capital and a celebration of matrimony and the approach of motherhood. Although many desert marriages are between cousins – often the preferred union – young Beduin usually marry for love.

If the well-ordered tented home is the daily responsibility of the women, the tribesmen visiting cities or towns unfailingly find hospitality at the homes of relatives or tribal leaders who have taken up residence in the urban communities.

The Western visitor is frequently struck by the way in which drivers or servants may be ushered into the presence of the mighty along with distinguished visitors. The practice is exemplified by the accessibility of the Monarch himself, whom many subjects may visit at appropriate times and, in visiting, bend to kiss his cheek in welcome. Similarly – and in accordance with a Qur'anic principle – does the Saudi leadership eschew expressions of obeisance. All are equal in the sight of God; bowing and scraping do not take place in the Saudi court or in Saudi society.

In the desert, the life of the women is relatively less sequestered than in the cities. Veiling is largely unnecessary. There are no strangers in the group. Worship takes place within the group. In the Beduin encampment, there is no mosque – always a male preserve – to separate the sexes. Tasks of every kind must be performed jointly.

Despite the onslaught of technology, Saudi Arabians as a whole seem in no doubt as to where their values lie. Already a generation has passed and the structure of those values is largely intact. They are a people who have proved themselves unafraid of what technological progress can bring; at the same time they have proved themselves indifferent to the shallow carpings of those ignorant of the meaning of Saudi social traditions.

**Population Distribution and Growth**

Saudi Arabia's population is growing fast. Most estimates, extrapolated from the 1974 census, put the population at the end of the 1970s at well over seven million. In common with other fast developing countries the movement to the towns and cities has been marked since the 1950s. During the current phase of unprecedented development, the population is temporarily swollen by large numbers of foreigners, bringing manpower and skills. The largest contigents are from neighbouring Arab countries – Yemen, Egypt, South Yemen, Palestine, Jordan and Sudan – and also from Pakistan. Other significant temporary additions to the population are provided by Lebanon and Syria, and by non-Muslim countries engaged on con-

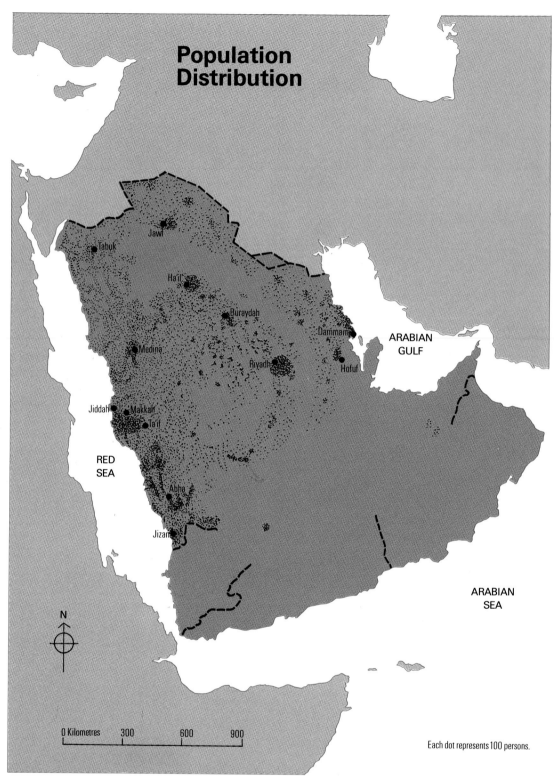

**Population Distribution**

Each dot represents 100 persons.

tracts, notably South Korea and Taiwan in the Far East; and by the U.S., Britain, France, West Germany and Italy in the West. Conversely, large numbers of Saudi Arabians were residing abroad, many of them engaged in study and research.

In the report issued in 1976 by the Central Statistics Department of the Ministry of Finance and National Economy, the administrative area with the largest population was that of Makkah, with 1,754,108 people. The administrative area of Riyadh contained 1,272,275 people, and the Eastern Province 769,648, Asir 681,648, Medina 519,694, Jizan 403,106, Qasim 316,640, Ha'il 259,929, Tabuk 193,764, al-Bahah 185,905, Najran 147,970, Northern Frontiers 128,745, Jawf 65,494 and Qurayyat 31,404. These figures were drawn from the 1974 census. Beduin residing in the border areas were numbered at 210,000 and Saudis residing abroad were listed as 73,000.

Extracted by kind permission from *Saudi Arabia: A Case Study in Development* by Dr. Fouad Al-Farsy.

236

# The Westerner in Saudi Arabia

*The Saudis are most decidedly masters of their own house. But in meeting its responsibility as a power in the world of today, and in its commitment to adopt for its people the benefits of modern technology and systems, Saudi Arabia has invited the help of many specialists from abroad. The appropriate relationship is, as Saudi Arabians see it, one of host and guest.*

FOR Western readers of this work, who may be visiting Saudi Arabia for the first time, the Publishers deferentially offer the following guidance on certain aspects of form in Arab society.

As providers of **hospitality**, Arabs are well renowned. There is a genuine delight in social interchange, and most Arabs take pride in the range and variety of their friendships.

The most familiar gesture of hospitality in Saudi Arabia, whether it is Arabians entertaining one another or foreign visitors, is the serving of coffee. The coffee is offered in small cups without handles, which are usually only half filled when offered. The coffee itself is strongly flavoured with cardamom, and sometimes with cloves and saffron. It is admirably refreshing in a hot climate. The server of coffee will refill the cup until the guest returns the cup to him giving it a little shake. To accept three such cups of such coffee is normal; more may be considered excessive. Sweet milkless tea often follows.

An invitation to dinner may prove to lead to the offering of a meal in the Western style. Alternatively, it may be a more grand affair in which Arab food is served in large dishes placed on a table-cloth on rugs on the floor, and the guests assemble seated on the floor, as round a table, to eat with the fingers of the right hand. The central dish could be a young camel, or a sheep – either boiled or roasted whole – served on a mound of steaming rice on large copper or brass trays. To eat with the left hand is not regarded as acceptable. Before and after such meals the right hand is washed.

Women do not mix with strangers in Arab society. Dinner engagements and more elaborate feasts are all-male affairs.

Westerners are often surprised at the ease of relationship between various **ranks in society**. This equality of men in the eyes of God derives from the teachings of the Holy Qur'an. Frequently,

drivers or others in relatively humble capacities will accompany those in whose service they are employed into the presence of those of standing and high rank. There is little rigidity in social stratification, so far as it exists at all. The *sayyids* and *sharifs*, or descendants of the Prophet Muhammad, are accorded, however, special esteem.

It is customary to shake hands on meeting and parting. Hearty behaviour seldom impresses, and to give a sense of haste can cause affront. Those seeking to discuss matters with people in high positions may find that when they are admitted there are several others present who have quite different business to discuss, or who are simply paying their respects. Conversations may thus overlap, and frequently be prolonged by interruptions. The reason is two-fold: Arab hosts strive to avoid abruptness and excessive briskness in social and business life; and those in authority like to be accessible.

It is customary for hosts to accompany visitors to the door of the house or of the office, or to an awaiting car. Such gestures should be reciprocated by Westerners receiving Arab guests; and a Western host should not be misled by the protests that his journey from desk to front door are hardly necessary.

As for **dress**, Saudi Arabians of virtually all ranks hold firmly to their traditional manner of dress in their own land, and may well prefer to keep the head covered indoors. To be less than well turned out is unacceptable.

Most Saudi Arabians rightly consider their own form of dress to be more appropriate to the climate of their country. Men wear the headcloth, *ghotra*, on the head, held in place by the *taqia* beneath, and the black woven circlet, *iqal*, above. The *ghotra* is usually of chequered red and white in the cooler months and of white in the hot months. The main body garment is the long white

shirt, *thaub*, above which may be worn the loose and flowing gown, *mishlah*, not infrequently of a brown colour. Women wear the *abaya*.

The ubiquity of English among educated classes can easily mislead the visitor into overlooking the pleasure a knowledge of Arabic can bring to the Arabs with whom he may be associated. Even to be able to greet and to reply to a greeting in Arabic is regarded as a mark of some deference towards the society which the visitor is entering. Frequently **Arabic salutations** are extended. Here are a few of them:

| Salutation | Response |
|---|---|
| *is-salaam 'alaykum*<br>Peace be upon you | *wa-'alaykum is-salaam* And upon you be peace |
| *sabaah il-khayr*<br>Good morning | *sabaah in-nuwr*<br>"Morning of light" |
| *masaa' il-khayr*<br>Good evening | *masaa' in-nuwr*<br>"Evening of light" |
| *kayf haalak?*<br>How are you? | *tayyib, il-hamdu lillaah!* Well, praise be to God! |
| *fiy amaan illaah*<br>Good-bye – "in the care of God" | *fiy amaan il-kariym*<br>"in the care of The Generous One" |

The usual term for *please* when requesting something or a service is *min fadlak*; and when offering something *tafaddal*. Use of the term *shukran* is perhaps most common for the English *thank-you*, but *mashkuwr* and *askhurak* may also be used.

## Estimated Financial Requirements of Five-year Plans IN SR MILLIONS

### SECOND PLAN 1975–1980

EXTERNAL ASSISTANCE, EMERGENCY FUNDS, FOOD SUBSIDIES & GENERAL RESERVE
**63,478** (12·7%)

DEFENCE
**78,156** (15·7%)

ADMINISTRATION
**38,179** (7·7%)

PHYSICAL INFRASTRUCTURE DEVELOPMENT
**112,944** (22·6%)

SOCIAL DEVELOPMENT
**33,212** (6·7%)

HUMAN RESOURCE DEVELOPMENT
**80,123** (16·1%)

ECONOMIC RESOURCE DEVELOPMENT
**92,135** (18·5%)

**TOTAL 498,230**

### THIRD PLAN 1980–1985

EMERGENCY RESERVES,
**49,600** (6·3%)

ADMINISTRATION
**31,400** (4·0%)

PHYSICAL INFRASTRUCTURE DEVELOPMENT
**249,100** (31·8%)

SOCIAL DEVELOPMENT
**61,200** (7·8%)

HUMAN RESOURCE DEVELOPMENT
**129,600** (16·6%)

ECONOMIC RESOURCE DEVELOPMENT
**261,800** (33·5%)

**TOTAL 782,700**

## The Structure of Planning

| | |
|---|---|
| PLAN APPROVAL | His Majesty in Council |
| PLAN POLICY DIRECTION | The Ministerial Planning Committee |
| PLAN CO-ORDINATION | The Central Planning Organization in Consultation with Ministries & Agencies |
| MINISTRY & AGENCY PLANNING | Ministries & Agencies in Consultation with The Central Planning Organization |
| PROGRAMME & PROJECT PLANNING | Ministries & Agencies with some inputs from The Central Planning Organization |
| DATA COLLECTION & ANALYSIS | |

# 11
# The Future

*Perhaps the first requirement is to have the resources. The next is to have the vision. But the resources and the vision are not in themselves enough for reality. The planning is the third require-ment – co-ordinated effort linking money, minds and hands, that month by month and year by year allows achievement to catch up with hope.*

*The Kingdom's communications' difficulties are overcome by the most modern technology, such as the microwave link* (opposite page).

*The first requirement: To maintain the values of Islam; the second: Assure the Kingdom's defence.*

# Planning the Future

S AUDI ARABIA is, in one conspicuous way, unique – and it is a way which touches everything in the Kingdom. The spectacular increase in the revenue from oil has provided the financial resources to implement a development plan far larger, not only than could have been contemplated a few years earlier, but than has ever been possible for any country of comparable population at an early stage in its development into a modern industrial society.

This fortunate circumstance offered the Kingdom an unprecedented opportunity to improve the prosperity, security, health, education and general well-being of both present and future generations of its people. It also offered a challenge to demonstrate that abundant financial resources could be successfully used to produce, in a very short time, a modern nation capable of sustaining a high standard of living for all its people through the development of its human skills and material assets, without destroying its traditional values. Inherent in this opportunity and challenge was the risk that achievement would fall short of expectation.

On 1 Rajab 1400 AH (15 May 1980 CE), the Third Five-Year Plan became operative, having been endorsed at a special session of the cabinet under the chairmanship of HM King Khalid ibn Abdul Aziz. Expenditure during this five year plan would run to SR 783 billion on social and economic development alone. Sheykh Hisham Nazer, Minister of Planning presented the plan to King Khalid, making it clear to the public that it would build on the considerable achievements of the Second Plan. It would concentrate no longer on building infrastructure, but instead on maintaining it as the base for new productive investment and in particular on human and social development.

It would consolidate and continue the drastic changes in the living standards of the Saudi people brought by the Second Plan, ensuring further prosperity and the highest levels of social security. It would focus on developing the nation's manpower, essential to a secure future, emphasizing compulsory school education, free academic and in particular

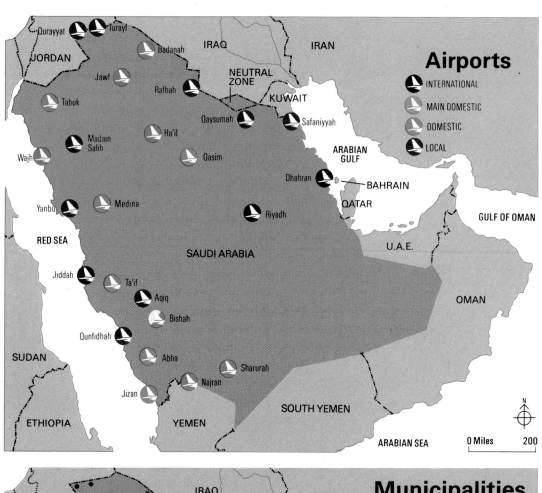

**Airports**

- INTERNATIONAL
- MAIN DOMESTIC
- DOMESTIC
- LOCAL

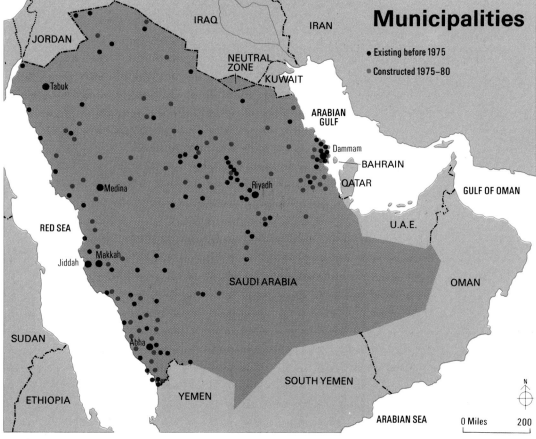

**Municipalities**

- Existing before 1975
- Constructed 1975–80

*Tree-lined boulevards grace Arabia's cities, among them al-Khubar* (above).

vocational training while encouraging Saudis to work in new jobs, in modern factories, offices and banks. The era of a Saudi work ethic had arrived.

Planning implies the efficient use of a country's resources in accordance with certain rationally determined priorities for the attainment of national goals. A country's development plan essentially reflects its fundamental values and principles. The development Plan 1400–1405 AH (1980–85 CE) provided for further advance towards social and economic goals, while maintaining the religious and moral values of Islam. The fundamental principles which guide Saudi Arabia's balanced development were set out in the plan:

To maintain the religious values of Islam by applying, propagating and fostering God's Sharia;

To assure the defense of the religion and the country, and maintain the internal security and social stability of the Kingdom;

To continue balanced economic growth by developing the country's resources, by increasing the income from oil over the long term and by conserving depletable resources, thereby improving the social well-being of all citizens and providing the economic strength to attain all the other fundamental goals of development;

To reduce dependence on the production of crude oil as the primary source of national income;

To develop human resources through education, training and the raising of health standards;

To complete the basic infrastructure which is required for the attainment of these other goals.

The plan especially aimed at diversifying the Kingdom's economic base, in order to lessen its dependence on oil, which constituted half of the gross national product and ninety nine per cent of exports. It was preparing the Kingdom for the days ahead when it could no longer live on exports of depleting supplies of oil but on the productive base its temporarily extraordinary wealth al-

lowed it to build. Saudis were to be encouraged to replace foreigners whose numbers were to be kept virtually constant after years of high growth in the successful building boom of the Second Plan.

The country's natural resources – hydro-carbon, mineral and agricultural – were to be fully exploited. At the same time modern industry would continue to be encouraged, both hydrocarbon-based and manufacturing. The basic strategy inevitably depends on the petroleum and natural gas of the Eastern Province, both as a ready supply of cheap energy for heavy industry and the raw material for a petrochemicals industry downstream allowing the Kingdom to secure more added value from its natural wealth.

The Second Plan witnessed the exciting beginning of two new industrial cities – Jubayl on the Gulf and Yanbu on the Red Sea – rising under the control of a Royal Commission from tiny fishing villages to become the mainstays of the Kingdom's industrial future. They are linked by pipelines traversing Arabia to carry oil and natural gas to Yanbu. Stra-

# Current Private Sector Recruitment by Region

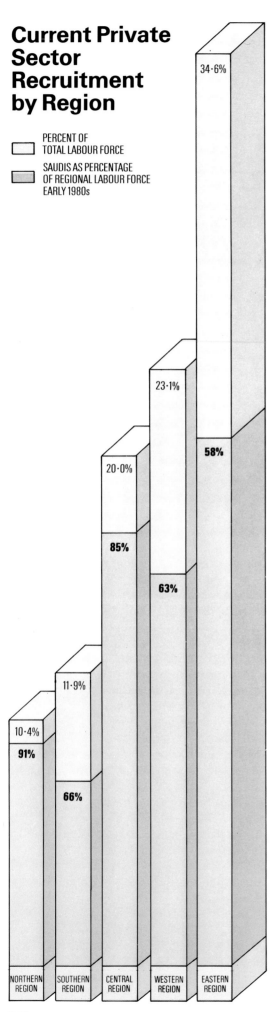

☐ PERCENT OF
TOTAL LABOUR FORCE

▨ SAUDIS AS PERCENTAGE
OF REGIONAL LABOUR FORCE
EARLY 1980s

| | | | | |
|---|---|---|---|---|
| 10·4% | 11·9% | 20·0% | 23·1% | 34·6% |
| 91% | 66% | 85% | 63% | 58% |
| NORTHERN REGION | SOUTHERN REGION | CENTRAL REGION | WESTERN REGION | EASTERN REGION |

**Planning Divisions**

JORDAN

IRAQ

NEUTRAL ZONE

KUWAIT

ARABIAN GULF

IRAN

Tabuk

NORTHERN

Dammam

BAHRAIN

QATAR

GULF OF OMAN

EASTERN (HASA)

CENTRAL (NAJD)

Riyadh

WESTERN (HIJAZ)

RED SEA

Jiddah

U.A.E.

OMAN

(RUB AL-KHALI)

SOUTH-WESTERN (ASIR)

SUDAN

Abha

ETHIOPIA

YEMEN

SOUTH YEMEN

ARABIAN SEA

0 Miles          200

*A watersports complex for Jiddah
on the Baghdadiya shore* (right).

tegically, the pipeline offers the Kingdom an alternative oil-exit to the potentially troubled tanker route through the Straights of Hormuz. Industrially, they were to provide the raw material and energy for Yanbu.

The Government-owned Saudi Arabian Basic Industries Corporation spearheaded negotiations with foreign corporate partners to found the Kingdom's heavy industry, shares of which would eventually be sold off to the public. In Jubayl, work began during the Second Plan on a gas-fuelled steel industry including an 850,000 tonnes per year direct reduction basic steel plant with an 800,000 tonnes per year steel rolling mill. In Jiddah, a 150,000 tonnes per year mill opened. As the Royal Commission's work at Jubayl and Yanbu continued to create cities of up to 370,000 and 150,000 people respectively under a twenty year plan, SABIC's petrochemical plans crystalized.

The Third Plan called for one ethylene complex in Yanbu and two in Jubayl. Polyethylene, methanol and urea plants were also allocated to Jubayl. Major oil

refineries to add to Petromin's domestic petrol and lubricated oil refining capacity were being built at Yanbu, Jubayl, and Rabigh on the Red Sea. Within a few years, Saudi Arabia was to become a new force in the international petrochemical markets, and an exporter of refined oil.

By the end of the Second Plan, the Kingdom already had large cement plants operating in Jiddah, Riyadh and the Eastern Province, and a new one was fast going up in the Southwest. Flour and animal feed complexes were operating in the three urban centres; smaller ones would be built in Khamis Mushayt and Jizan; grain storage facilities would be expanded kingdomwide for a basic six month reserve of wheat and flour.

Altogether, some SR 95 billion would be spent on industry in the Third Plan. While most would go to the large government organized complexes, at least a tenth was earmarked for soft loans to new private factories springing up on the cheap and well-serviced industrial estates existing or planned in most towns and cities. By 1980, the Government's Saudi Industrial Development Fund had lent some SR 12 billion in soft loans to nearly 600 projects, usually for half their start-up cost. Up to SR 10 billion more

would be disbursed by 1985. Emphasis was expected to continue moving away from the construction industry to modern plants, whether for consumer goods, plastics downstream further still from the petrochemical plants, car parts, or agricultural industry.

In the Agricultural sector, the Government would continue, though possibly reform, its extensive investment subsidies to encourage the growth of the large-scale modern farming that soared during the Second Plan particularly for crops, poultry farms and dairies. Wheat production was especially encouraged from the latter years of the Second Plan with high, centralized government purchase prices. Overall, however, the largely traditional agricultural sector grew inefficiently at a slower rate than the rest of the non-oil economy in the Second Plan. It was hoped that reorganization, research, training and government assistance together with the use of new land would help increase agricultural output to contribute to the Kingdom's food security. Vital water supplies would also be helped with improved flood control and aquifer recharging. Over forty new dams were to be built by the end of the Plan and hundreds of wells dug or deepened. Efficient modern irrigation methods would continue to spread, maximising the benefits of the Kingdom's precious water supplies.

Growing water needs for the population, industry and agriculture are met from a mixture of deep ground-water, renewable surface water, desalinated and recycled sources. Eighteen desalination plants were to be completed by the end of the Third Plan adding a further 1.4 billion cubic metres daily to national supplies. The building of five more was to begin during the Plan which was also to see the creation of a national water plan.

Fourteen of the desalination plants built by the Government's Saline Water Conversion Corporation (SWCC) would also be power stations, producing an additional 2,840 MW by the end of the Plan when a further 1,110 MW would be imminent from four dual purpose plants under construction. By 1399 AH (1979 CE), total installed generating capacity had risen to 5,207 KW reaching 4.2 million people. By the end of the Third Plan it would reach eighty per cent of the population and generating capacity would have grown by a further 7,568 MW, in addition to the capacity of SWCC's plants. Over 4,000 miles of transmission

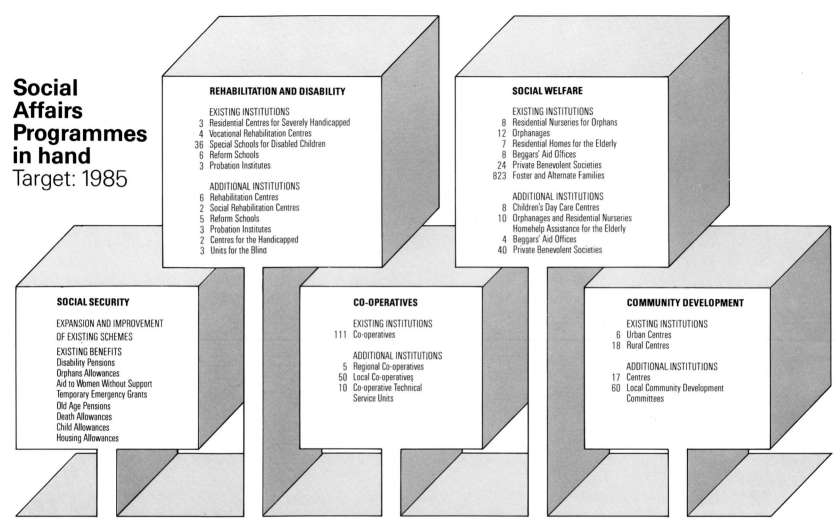

**Social Affairs Programmes in hand**
Target: 1985

**REHABILITATION AND DISABILITY**

EXISTING INSTITUTIONS
3 Residential Centres for Severely Handicapped
4 Vocational Rehabilitation Centres
36 Special Schools for Disabled Children
6 Reform Schools
3 Probation Institutes

ADDITIONAL INSTITUTIONS
6 Rehabilitation Centres
2 Social Rehabilitation Centres
5 Reform Schools
3 Probation Institutes
2 Centres for the Handicapped
3 Units for the Blind

**SOCIAL WELFARE**

EXISTING INSTITUTIONS
8 Residential Nurseries for Orphans
12 Orphanages
7 Residential Homes for the Elderly
8 Beggars' Aid Offices
24 Private Benevolent Societies
823 Foster and Alternate Families

ADDITIONAL INSTITUTIONS
8 Children's Day Care Centres
10 Orphanages and Residential Nurseries
Homehelp Assistance for the Elderly
4 Beggars' Aid Offices
40 Private Benevolent Societies

**SOCIAL SECURITY**

EXPANSION AND IMPROVEMENT
OF EXISTING SCHEMES

EXISTING BENEFITS
Disability Pensions
Orphans Allowances
Aid to Women Without Support
Temporary Emergency Grants
Old Age Pensions
Death Allowances
Child Allowances
Housing Allowances

**CO-OPERATIVES**

EXISTING INSTITUTIONS
111 Co-operatives

ADDITIONAL INSTITUTIONS
5 Regional Co-operatives
50 Local Co-operatives
10 Co-operative Technical
Service Units

**COMMUNITY DEVELOPMENT**

EXISTING INSTITUTIONS
6 Urban Centres
18 Rural Centres

ADDITIONAL INSTITUTIONS
17 Centres
60 Local Community Development
Committees

and sub-transmission lines were to be commissioned during the Plan which would see major regional load centres become connected to improve economies of scale and supply security as well as being the backbone of a national grid.

While basic geological mapping and research would continue on a uniquely intensive scale and over 700 mineral occurrences have been identified in the Kingdom, the early 1980s were expected to see the beginning of a modern mining era on the Arabian Shield. It would start with its most traditional mine, Ma'had Dhahab ("cradle of gold"), worked for gold in ancient times and briefly again in the 1950s. Exploration in the Red Sea suggested exciting deep sea mining opportunities, and possible iron mining was being further studied at Wadi Sawawin in the North where deposits could be of value to the new steel industry. Phosphate reserves at West Thanayat and copper at Nuqrah were among the more promising of dozens of prospects under strong Government encouragement in the new sector. Quarrying too was expected to continue increasing.

The Third Plan's emphasis on the pro-ductive sectors was unquestionably made possible by its predecessor's infra-structural work. This was to continue.

An additional 3,200 miles of road (1,100 underway in 1981) were to be built as well as extensions, road-widening, flyovers, bridges and mountain passes. Almost five thousand villages would also benefit from another 10,900 miles of new rural earth surface roads during the Plan which also called for a further 4,000 miles of urban and temporary – mainly feeder – roads.

Port expansion and improvement work would continue, principally at Jiddah, Dammam, Yanbu and Jizan. Quality improvements at the ports would include workshops, fire protection, and navigational aids. Construction also would improve the minor ports of al-Khubar, Qatif and Darin.

The mammoth new Jiddah international airport became operational in 1401 AH and Riyadh's new airport was expected to come on stream before 1405 AH. New airports were planned for Ta'if, Hofuf and Baha and four other domestic airports were to be upgraded to cater for wide-bodied jets. The Kingdom's air traffic control system was to be signifi-cantly improved with national flight information regions split between Jiddah and Riyadh. Major airports were to have improved engineering and maintenance capability. Saudia's domestic and international fleet was to continue expanding at an estimated annual growth of over eighteen per cent in seat capacity over the Plan. Maintenance and support facilities were to be correspondingly improved and expanded and the airline's operating efficiency increased.

Railroad traffic was also expected to increase by over eighteen per cent a year as new track was to be built linking Riyadh directly with Dammam and improving the link with Hofuf. Riyadh's freight terminal became operational and almost 300 miles of mostly new track was to be matched by new rolling stock – thirty-six locomotives, 1,300 freight cars and twenty passenger coaches. Feasibility studies on new lines would also continue, like that of the reopening of the Ottoman Hejaz line from Damascus to Medina which might be connected to Jiddah or even Riyadh.

An additional 480,000 telephone lines as well as 16,000 new mobile telephones would augment the Second Plan's sub-

*Desert rig* (above) *searches for oil beneath the sands of Arabia.*

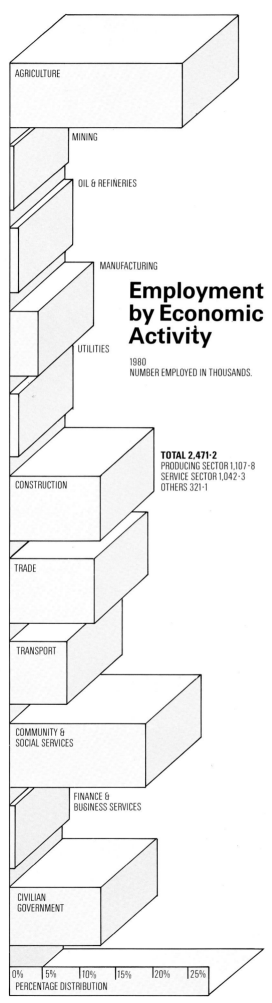

**Employment by Economic Activity**

1980
NUMBER EMPLOYED IN THOUSANDS.

AGRICULTURE
MINING
OIL & REFINERIES
MANUFACTURING
UTILITIES

**TOTAL 2,471·2**
PRODUCING SECTOR 1,107·8
SERVICE SECTOR 1,042·3
OTHERS 321·1

CONSTRUCTION
TRADE
TRANSPORT
COMMUNITY & SOCIAL SERVICES
FINANCE & BUSINESS SERVICES
CIVILIAN GOVERNMENT

0%  5%  10%  15%  20%  25%
PERCENTAGE DISTRIBUTION

stantial telecommunications work. Long distance microwave links were to be extended to the Gulf and other neighbouring countries while the domestic links would be improved. Another 15,000 telex lines during the Plan would bring the total to 30,286. More training facilities were planned and the Kingdom's telecommunications organization was to be studied for reform. The post would see a better regional service. New central offices were to be built and equipped in Medina, Burayda, Abha, Jizan and Sakaka. Postal efficiency was to be improved nationally. Franking machines were to be introduced.

Government housing would still be built, especially for the poor. Some 267,000 new housing units were expected to go up during the Third Plan. Almost seventy per cent were expected to be privately built and some 60,000 new dwellings would belong to government agencies and ministries, housing their employees. Some 10,000 new public dwellings would be built around the country, and by 1403 AH over 15,000 dwellings

started in the Second Plan's rush housing schemes were expected to be completed. Of these 6,000 housing units would be earmarked for the poor who would also receive some 14,800 plots of land in at least thirteen different locations. Interest free loans from the Government's Real Estate Development Fund were expected during the Third Plan to total SR 13.8 billion for new Saudi homes, and SR 800 million for investments. But the fund was to pay special attention to prompt repayment.

By 1405 AH, virtually all municipalities and villages in the Kingdom were expected to have water and sewage systems as well as paved roads. Three quarters of a million additional households would be connected to central water supplies, and 167 new reservoirs would be built. Half a million additional households would benefit from main sewerage systems. New equipment would treat up to 627,000 cubic metres of sewage a day. Some 100 miles of stormwater protection was to be built, most in the first half of the Third Plan. Over 900 new municipal buildings were planned including 184 markets, 155 for offices, 114 mortuaries, 55 warehouses and main-

245

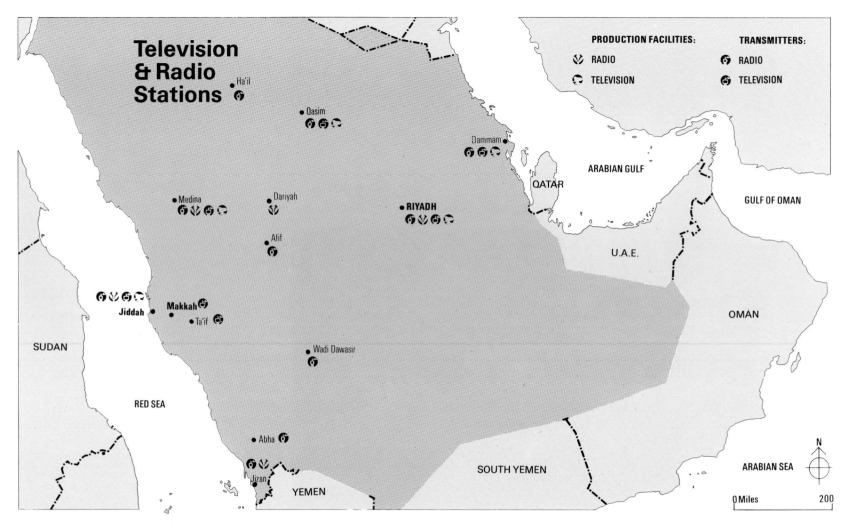

**Television & Radio Stations**

Ha'il

Qasim

Dammam

ARABIAN GULF

QATAR

Medina    Dariyah

RIYADH

GULF OF OMAN

Afif

U.A.E.

Jiddah    Makkah    OMAN
Ta'if

Wadi Dawasir

SUDAN

RED SEA

Abha

SOUTH YEMEN    ARABIAN SEA

N

Jizan

YEMEN

0 Miles    200

PRODUCTION FACILITIES:    TRANSMITTERS:
RADIO    RADIO
TELEVISION    TELEVISION

tenance depots, 49 slaughterhouses, 25 garages, 7 laboratories and 118 public toilets.

Saudi environmental protection and meteorological services were to be provided by a new agency attached to the Ministry of Defence. Air, water, and marine ecology and solid waste standards were to be developed and air pollution monitored. An oil spill emergency plan was to be forged. The Saudi Arabian National Centre for Science and Technology would continue its central supportive role.

Human development – the Saudi people themselves – however, has been the most important element in planning, especially for the Kingdom's Third Plan. By its end, 1.8 million – two-fifths of them women – were expected to be enrolled in its education and training system, from schools and universities to vocational training and adult literacy classes. Over the five years, the number of school graduates would grow by fifty-eight per cent from its beginning to 260,000 in its last year; 28,000 adult education graduates would represent a 126 per cent increase; 60,000 Saudis would be at domestic universities in its last year as

well as another 10,000 foreigners. During the Plan some 40,000 Saudis were expected to complete industrial induction and on-the-job training. New vocational training capacity built during the Plan would cater for another 10,600 students. Quality was to be stressed and improved throughout the system, and research would investigate employers needs to ensure its relevance. Training programmes were to be co-ordinated by an inter-ministerial committee on manpower. A similar committee was to identify the basis and areas of work for women without conflicting with the principles of Islam.

By 1405 AH (1985 CE) the civilian workforce was expected to reach 2,626,200, an increase of only 155,000 or an annual growth rate of 1.2 per cent, which is much lower than the rate of the Second Plan. All but 9,000 of these new workers were to be Saudis who together would number 1,557,400, including 120,000 women. The planners estimated that the low level of growth could still cater for some 310,000 new jobs as 85,000 would be lost from the construction industry, which saw its peak in the Second and only the early days of the

Third Plan, and another 70,000 leaving agriculture as it became more capital-intensive. Above all the planners were anticipating stunning effects from the modern facilities and technology being installed in the Kingdom's factories and offices – a productivity increase over the five years of twenty-seven per cent.

It had been felt that the growing influx of foreign workers – from North America and Europe, India and Pakistan, the Far East, and the Arab world – during the 1970s had threatened the Kingdom's traditional conservative values of Islam. Furthermore it was increasingly felt that Saudi Arabians should depend, where possible, on their own work. So the inflow of foreigners was restricted to conform with these intentions. But it was also realized that a critical shortage of labour could easily come about, and the situation was to be carefully monitored, for one immediate risk of such a shortage was the possibility of soaring inflation.

Control of inflation was to remain a major government desire. A maximum level of seven per cent was sought, though with some imported inflation inevitable, single figures were considered acceptable.

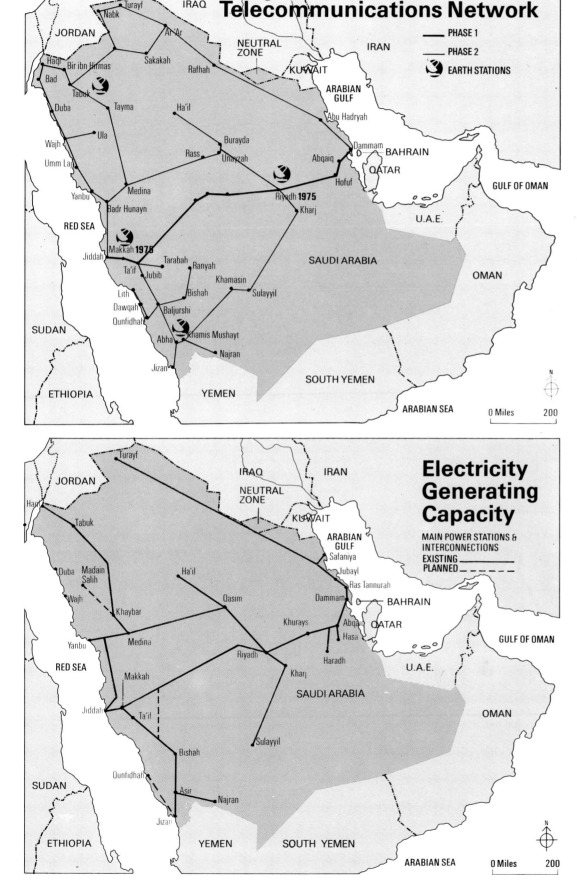

*See p. 246 for tv and radio stations. An additional eleven mobile stations placed over ninety per cent of the population in reach of television or radio by the early 1980s.*

*In the Third Plan, installed generating capacity would be expanded from 3,835 to 12,445 megawatts, and 4,000 miles of new transmission line would double the population served.*

The Kingdom's Gross Domestic Product was SR 247 billion in 1399 AH (1979 CE), about half of which was generated by oil. But whereas the non-oil economy grew at some fifteen per cent a year in the Second Plan, it was only expected to grow at 6.2 per cent in the Third largely because of the slowdown in the workforce's increase.

The 1980–1985 planned expenditure on civilian social and economic development was SR 782.7 billion. Administration would cost SR 31.4 billion, and emergency reserves and subsidies SR 49.6 billion. Of the remainder, SR 261.8 billion or 37.3 per cent was to be spent on economic resource development, well up on the equivalent 25.1 per cent of the Second Plan. Human resources were to receive SR 129.6 billion of 18.5 per cent, against 15.9 per cent in the second plan. Physical infrastructure, which accounted for 49.6 per cent of Second Plan development expenditure, was to receive only 35.5 per cent worth SR 249.1 billion. Finally social development was to take SR 61.2 billion or 8.7 per cent of total, just down on 9.4 per cent in the Second Plan.

Much of this was to be spent in the early years of the Plan, completing work launched in its predecessor, during which expenditure well exceeded original expectations. Planning must be a little flexible; the Kingdom was well aware of this in its Third Plan which spoke of a new type of roll-over planning, and specifically called for a major review of plan programmes and the Government itself in 1402 AH as well as close monitoring of performance throughout.

It was without doubt an ambitious call, in essence that the Saudi cab driver of the mid-1970s should become a lab technician or air-conditioning mechanic in the mid-1980s. But the 1975–80 Plan had without doubt proven that Saudi Arabia was a ready match for its ambitions.

His Majesty King Khalid told the nation: "It is a grace allotted to us by Allah the Third Five Year Development Plan should be sanctioned tonight. It shall be, Allah willing, a new blessed step towards bringing about prosperity and welfare for our people and nation. We supplicate Allah Almighty to bring our aims and aspirations to fruition, and to bestow upon our country permanent security, stability and progress, so that our nation may be in the forefront of developing and advanced nations."

# Bibliography

This selected bibliography includes books covering a wide range of aspects of Saudi Arabia, but does not attempt to be definitive.

**Abdel Wahab.** *Education in Saudi Arabia*, Macmillan, London, 1971

**Al-Farsy, Dr. Fouad.** *Saudi Arabia, a case study in development,* Stacey International, 1978

**Ali Abdullah Yusuf.** *The Holy Quran*, Lahore, 1938

**Aramco** *Handbook*, The Arabian American Oil Company (Dhahran), revised edition, 1968

**Armstrong, H. C.** *Lord of Arabia*, Khayyat, Beirut, 1954

**Asad Muhammad.** *The Road to Mecca*, Simon and Schuster, New York, 1954

**Assah, Ahmed.** *Miracle of the Desert Kingdom*, Johnson, London, 1969

**Azzam, Abdel Rahman.** *The Eternal Message of Muhammad*, Devin-Adair, New York, 1964

**Brémond, E.** *Yemen et Saoudia*, Paris, 1937

**Brockelmann, Carl.** *History of the Islamic Peoples*, Putnam's, New York, 1947

**Brown, W. R.** *The Horse of the Desert*, Macmillan, New York, 1948

**Bullard, Sir Reader.** *The Camels Must Go*, Faber and Faber, London, 1961

**Burckhardt, J. L.** *Travels in Arabia*, 1826

**Cheeseman, R. E.** *In Unknown Arabia*, Macmillan, London, 1926

**Collins, Robert O. (ed.).** *An Arabian Diary: Sir Gilbert Clayton*, California, 1969

**Cragg, Kenneth.** *The Call of the Minaret*, Oxford University Press, 1956

**De Gaury, Gerald.** *Arabia Phoenix*, Harrap, London, 1946

**De Gaury, Gerald.** *Arabian Journey and Other Desert Travels*, Harrap, London, 1950

**De Gaury, Gerald.** *Faisal, King of Saudi Arabia*, Arthur Barker, London, 1966

**Dickson, H. R. P.** *The Arab of the Desert*, Hodder and Stoughton, London, 1957

**Dimand, Maurice S.** *A Handbook of Muhammadan Art*, The Metropolitan Museum of Art, New York, 1958

**Doughty, C. M.** *Travels in Arabia Deserta*, Jonathan Cape, London, 1964

**Esin, Emel.** *Mecca the Blessed, Madinah the Radiant*, Elek, London, 1963

**Fisher, Sydney N.** *The Middle East, A History*, Knopf, New York, 1969

**Fisher, W. B.** *The Middle East: A Physical, Social and Regional Geography*, 6th revised edition, Methuen, London, 1971

**Gibb, Sir Hamilton A. R.** *Mohammedanism*, Oxford University Press, London and New York, 1953

**Glubb, Sir John Bagot.** *The Life and Times of Muhammad*, Hodder and Stoughton, London, 1963

**Graves, P.** *Life of Sir Percy Cox*, London, 1941

**Guillaume, A.** *Islam*, 2nd edition, Penguin Books, Harmondsworth, England, 1956

**Hartshorn, J. E.** *Oil Companies and Governments*, 2nd revised edition, Faber and Faber, London, 1967

**Hitti, P. K.** *History of the Arabs*, 7th edition, Macmillan, London, 1961

**Hogarth, D. G.** *The Penetration of Arabia*, F. A. Stokes, New York, 1904

**Hopwood, Derek (ed.).** *The Arabian Peninsula*, Allen and Unwin, London, 1972

**Howarth, David.** *The Desert King*, Collins, London, 1964

**Keiser, Hélène.** *Arabia*, Silva, Zurich, 1971

**Kiernan, R. H.** *The Unveiling of Arabia*, Harrap, London, 1937

**Lebkicker, Rentz and Steincke.** *The Arabia of Ibn Saud*, Russell and Moore, USA

**Le Bon, Gustave.** *The World of Islamic Civilization*, Minerva, Geneva, 1974

**Lenczowski, George.** *Oil and State in the Middle East*, Cornell University Press, New York, 1960

**Lenczowski, George.** *The Middle East in World Affairs*, Cornell University Press, New York, 1962

**Longrigg, S.** *Oil in the Middle East*, 3rd edition, Oxford University Press, 1968

**Meinertzhagen, Richard.** *The Birds of Arabia*, Oliver and Boyd, Edinburgh, 1954

**Meulen, D. van der.** *Faces in Shem*, John Murray, London, 1961

**Monroe, Elizabeth.** *Philby of Arabia*, Faber and Faber, London, 1973

**Musil, Alois.** *The Northern Hejaz*, American Geographical Society, New York, 1926

**Musil, Alois.** *Arabia Deserta*, American Geographical Society, New York, 1927

**Niebuhr, Carsten.** *Description of Arabia*, various editions, 1774

**Palgrave, William Gifford.** *Narrative of a year's journey through Central and Eastern Arabia 1862–63*, 2 volumes, new edition, Macmillan, London, 1868

**Pesce, Angelo.** *Colours of the Arab Fatherland*, Riyadh, 1972

**Pesce, Angelo.** *Jiddah – Portrait of an Arabian City*, Falcon Press, 1974

**Philby, H. St. John B.** *The Heart of Arabia*, Constable, London, 1922

**Philby, H. St. John B.** *The Empty Quarter*, Henry Holt, New York, 1933

**Philby, H. St. John B.** *Arabian Jubilee*, Robert Hale, London, 1952

**Philby, H. St. John B.** *Saudi Arabia*, Ernest Benn, London, 1955

**Philby, H. St. John B.** *Arabian Oil Ventures*, Middle East Institute, Washington, 1964

**Philips, C. H. (ed.).** *Handbook of Oriental History*, Royal Historical Society, London, 1963

**Pickthall, M.** *The Meaning of the Glorious Qur'an*, New American Library, New York, 1953

**Purdy, Anthony (ed.).** *The Business Man's Guide to Saudi Arabia*, Arlington Books, London, 1976

**Ross, Heather Colyer.** *Bedouin Jewellery in Saudi Arabia,* Stacey International, London, 1978

**Ryan, Sir A.** *The Last of the Dragomans*, London, 1951

**Sanger, Richard.** *The Arabian Peninsula*, Cornell University Press, New York, 1954

**Shroeder, Eric.** *Muhammad's People: A Tale by Anthology*, Bond Wheelwright, Portland, Maine, 1955

**Smith, Wilfred Cantwell.** *Islam in Modern History*, Princeton University Press, Princeton, 1957

**Thesiger, Wilfred.** *Arabian Sands*, Book Club Associates, London, 1959

**Thomas, Bertram.** *Arabia Felix*, Scribner's, New York, 1932

**Thomas, Bertram.** *The Arabs*, Butterworth, London, 1937

**Twitchell, K. S.** *Saudi Arabia*, 3rd edition, Princeton University Press, Princeton, 1958

**Vidal, F. S.** *The Oasis of Al-Hasa*, Arabian American Oil Company, 1955

**Vincett, Betty.** *The Flowers of Arabia*, 1977

**Wahba, Hafiz.** *Arabian Days*, Arthur Barker, London, 1964

**Wellsted, J. R.** *Travels in Arabia*, John Murray, London, 1838

**Winder, R. Bayly.** *Saudi Arabia in the Nineteenth Century*, St. Martin's Press, New York, 1965

**Yale, William.** *The Near East: A Modern History*, University of Michigan Press, Ann Arbor, Michigan, 1958

**Zirikli, Khair al Din.** *Arabia under King Abdul Aziz*, 4 volumes (in Arabic), Beirut, 1970

# Glossary

| | |
|---|---|
| *abal* | scarlet-fruited shrub; eglantine |
| *abaya(h)* | woollen outer cloak |
| *adabi* | arts stream at secondary school |
| *adat* | customs |
| *Ahadith* | *see Hadith* |
| *alim, pl. ulama* | Muslim scholar; scholar of Islamic law |
| *arfaj* | yellow-flowered shrub |
| *arikah* | half-baked dough covered with honey |
| *bayt Allah* | house of God |
| *dabb* | plant-eating lizard |
| *Dhu 'l-Hijja(h)* | the twelfth month in the Islamic calendar (in which the *Hajj* occurs) |
| *Diwan al-Mazalim* | Board of Complaints |
| *ghotra (ghutra)* | headcloth worn by Arab men |
| *hadh* | prickly saltbush |
| *Hadith, pl. Ahadith* | traditions giving the sayings or acts of the Prophet Muhammad |
| *Hajj* | pilgrimage to Makkah and other holy places obligatory for every Muslim |
| *hajj, hajji* | Muslim who has performed the *Hajj* |
| *hara* | quarter of a city |
| *Haram* | the holy *Ka'bah* sanctuary |
| *Haramayn* | the two holy cities of Makkah and Medina |
| *harrah* | extensive lava fields |
| *Hijra(h)* | the migration of the Prophet from Makkah to Medina |
| *hijrah* | encampment; agricultural settlement |
| *hubara* | MacQueen's bustard |
| *ibtida'i* | primary stage of education |
| *Ihram* | pilgrim's dress |
| *ijma* | consensus of non-specialist opinion on points of Islamic law |
| *Ikhwan* | "the Brethren"; specifically a religious movement founded by King Abdul Aziz |
| *ilmi* | scientific stream at secondary school |
| *iqal* | rope-like circlet holding *ghotra* in position |
| *jar Allah* | God's neighbour |
| *jihad* | holy war |
| *Ka'bah* | venerated square stone building in Makkah, the house of God |
| *kafa'ah* | examination taken at end of intermediate school stage |
| *Kiswah* | black cloth covering the *Ka'bah* |
| *kutab (kuttab)* | small group of children to whom private tuition is given |
| *majlis* | session for meetings and audiences |
| *malpolon* | (name first used in 1926) species of desert snake |
| *marsum* | royal decree |
| *mashrabiyya* | lattice window in the Egyptian style |
| *maslaha* | welfare |
| *Mataf* | parts of the pilgrimage area around the *Ka'bah* |
| *mihrab* | prayer niche in mosque (cf. qibla) |
| *mishlah* | loose outer cloak worn by Arab men |
| *muqallid* | lawyer who accepts as binding precedent in legal decisions |
| *mutawassit* | intermediate stage of education |
| *mutawwif* | guide for pilgrims performing the *Hajj* |
| *nizam* | regulation |
| *nomes* | (from Greek) provinces of ancient Egypt |
| *qadi* | judge; ruler |
| *qibla* | recess in a mosque indicating the direction of the *Ka'bah* in Makkah; prayer niche |
| *Qiran* | combined performance of *Hajj* and *Umrah* |
| *rababa(h)* | simple violin |
| *rajaz* | song with lines of four or six beats |
| *rawda(h)* | kindergarten school |
| *rimth* | saltbush |
| *sabkhah* | salt basins |
| *Sa'y* | the running from as-Safa to al-Marwa in the *Hajj* |
| *sayyid* | descendants of the Prophet |
| *Shari'ah* | Islamic law derived from the Qur'an |
| *sharif* | the Prophet's descendants and their families (a wider meaning than *sayyid*) |
| *Suahil* | (Arabic: Sawahil) coasts of East Africa |
| *Sunnah* | orthodox interpretation and commentary on the life of the Prophet Muhammad and on the Qur'an |
| *suq* | space in town where the market is held |
| *Talbiyah* | words of acceptance of the pilgrimage duties chanted by the *hajj* pilgrims |
| *Tamattu* | separate performance of *Hajj* and *Umrah* |
| *taqia (taqiyyah)* | cap worn under the *ghotra* |
| *Tawaf* | circumambulation of the *Ka'bah* |
| *tawjihiyyah* | the Saudi baccalaureat, taken at end of secondary education |
| *thanawi* | secondary stage of education |
| *thaub (thawb)* | inner gown worn by Arab men |
| *ulama* | *see alim* |
| *Umm Salim* | "Salim's mother", hoopoe lark |
| *Umrah* | short form of pilgrimage to Makkah only |
| *uruq* | crescent sand-dunes |
| *usul al-fiqh* | sources of Islamic legislation |
| *wadi* | former water course, now dry |
| *Wudu* | ablutions before prayers |
| *Wuquf* | final prayer of the *Hajj* made standing on Mount Arafat |
| *Zakah* | regular giving of fixed alms |
| *ziggurat* | (from Assyrian ziqquratu) Sumerian brick tower |

---

## Note on transliteration

The system of transliteration employed in this work reflects the influence of two main aims which, to some extent, are in conflict with one another.

First, it was deemed important that the general reader should be spared the complexities of the elaborate system developed for scholarly purposes, and that transliterated forms should be similar to those encountered in the British and American press.

Second, it is clearly desirable that transliterated forms should represent the original as accurately as possible.

Where names have been in use in English and have achieved an accepted and established form, the latter is employed even where this results in some inconsistency with the rest of the system, e.g. Medina rather than Madinah.

In accordance with the first-mentioned aim, the Arabic consonants *hamza* (glottal stop) and *'ayn* have been represented (as ' and ' respectively) only where their omission would have produced an unacceptable distortion of the original.

Arabic and vernacular words have been italicized except where words may be regarded as in common usage among non-Muslim people throughout the world – e.g. *ijma*, and *taqia*; but Qur'an, and sheikh.

## Quotations from the Holy Qur'an

Unless otherwise indicated, the quotations from the Holy Qur'an have been taken from the rendering of Mohammed Marmaduke Pickthall The rendering by Arthur J. Arberry has been preferred where the requirement has been to indicate the tonal flavour of the original Arabic.

In deference to Muslim readers, the usage CE (Christian Era) has often been used in place of AD (Anno Domini), more familiar in Christendom.

# Index

*Mainly for reasons of regional variations in sound values, no generally accepted transliteration of Arabic nomenclature into Roman lettering has been established, nor indeed of Arabic usages in this volume (see note on transliteration on page 249). The difference in accepted usages in various contexts (e.g. historical, religious, commercial) is sometimes unavoidable.*